CHALK STREAM FLY FISHING
A 21ST CENTURY ANTHOLOGY

EDITED BY GRAHAM CHALMERS

OUTDOOR MEDIA LIMITED

Published by Outdoor Media Limited
Hollister Cottage
Coombe Lane
Shere
Surrey
United Kingdom
GU5 9TD

ISBN 978 0957381 704

British Library Cataloguing in Publication Data.
A catalogue record for this book is available from the British Library.

Typeset by Troubador Publishing Ltd, Leicester, UK

THIS BOOK IS DEDICATED TO

THE SALISBURY & DISTRICT ANGLING CLUB

An association of men and women from all walks of life whose differences are transcended by a shared passion for angling and whose diversity combines into a force to be reckoned with.

Contents

Editor's Introduction – Graham Chalmers vii

Chapter One – The Ecology of a Chalk Stream – Malcolm Anderson 1

Chapter Two – How to Approach a Chalk Stream – Gordon Mackie 15

Chapter Three – The Entomology of Chalk Streams – Dr. Cyril Bennett 25

Chapter Four – Artificial Flies for Chalk Stream Fishing – Dennis Shaw 53

Chapter Five – The Madness of the Mayfly – Peter McLeod 80

Chapter Six – Seasonal Tactics – John Stoddart 92

Chapter Seven – Presenting the Upstream Dry Fly – Ian May 102

Chapter Eight – Chalk Stream Nymph Fishing – Alwyn Lindsey 119

Chapter Nine – Expeditions after Grayling – Jan Szakowski 127

Chapter Ten – Chalk Stream Fly Fishing for Coarse Fish – Dominic Longley 141

Chapter Eleven – River Management – Andreas Topintzis 172

Chapter Twelve – The Future – Theo Pike 184

Acknowledgements 201

Index 203

EDITOR'S INTRODUCTION

Many people have asked me what motivated the creation of this anthology. On the one hand, it was the observation that nothing comprehensive had been written about chalk stream fly fishing for several decades; and on the other it was the discovery of a vast reservoir of experience and expertise amongst the members of the Salisbury and District Angling Club, of which I am a member. The club is both a venerable institution and a dynamic modern organisation that has been procuring affordable chalk stream fishing for its members for seventy-one years. Although this book is not a 'club' publication in any way, it could not have come into existence without the help and guidance of the club's management and members.

Eleven of the twelve contributors are long-standing members of the club and the twelfth is a new member. Although each author has some special expertise or experience that abundantly and independently qualifies him to write the chapter in question, all of them could dip into the knowledge reservoir constituted by the club's membership as the need arose and with over two thousand members, there is always somebody who knows the answer. Having said that, each chapter is the distillation of the individual contributor's views on the subject discussed and does not necessarily represent the views of other contributors, the publisher, the club or me. Ultimately, each contribution is an essay by an expert, standing alone upon the platform of his chapter and so the book is designed to be consumed one chapter at a time, like a packet of biscuits rather than a bowl of trifle. (As an aside, I must mention that virtually all the contributors to this book will hotly deny that they are experts in the subject matter about which they have so competently and comprehensively written. All they will concede is that they know a little bit about it. What can I say? They're English. On the other hand, I am a hairy colonial recently returned to the homeland of my ancestors, so I can tell you how absolutely expert they all are with some prospect of being forgiven.)

Unavoidably, there is some duplication where different authors cover similar ground on issues that are relevant to more than one chapter topic, but these tend to be crucial matters that bear repetition from different perspectives. Taken as a whole, the book covers extensive ground and whilst not completely exhaustive of the endless subject of chalk stream fly fishing, is a fair summary of the current state of play in the chalk stream world. If you are a newcomer to chalk stream fly fishing, it will lay bare many of the things that seem so mysterious when you start out. If you are experienced, then I hope you enjoy the company of these experts and find common cause with what they say, or at least find meaty matters for healthy disputation.

Personally, I did not see a chalk stream until my forty-third year. They do not occur in Southern Africa, where I come from. But I had heard of them. It is not really possible to be a trout fisherman, anywhere in the world, and not hear of chalk streams. Chalk streams are fundamentally entwined into the lore and history of fly fishing. Primarily, this is because the great fly fishing authors of the early twentieth century were almost all chalk stream men. The prose of these famous English writers completely dominated the world of fly fishing literature until the Second World War and the intricacies of their fly fishing practices on chalk streams created an ethos that came to inform the theory and practice of fly fishing everywhere. Of course, the literary baton was passed to the talented legions of American writers who have overwhelmed angling literature ever since, but they were building on a base and that base inextricably involved chalk streams.

A chalk stream in good condition is exquisite. Honestly, the beauty of it all is almost painful, even if you are not an angler. If you are an angler it is close to overwhelming. Crystalline water glides silently over glades of waving green and ripples down runs of clean, pale gravel. Pepper-speckled brown trout hold position here and there amongst the streaming fronds, lifting to the drift of the little sail-boat flies to dimple the smooth surface with gentle rises. The pink-fringed, silver grayling lie deeper than the trout and slip from side to side, endlessly grazing on herds of invisible nymphs – perfect art-deco fish; feminine and serene until tempted beyond restraint into a mad launch to the surface after one or other fluttering delicacy. In the shallows, amongst the reed roots and sunshine, the dace scatter like drops of mercury, ever fearful of the brindled, slashing strike of the jack-pike, wolf of the stream. In the slow, shadowy depths big chub sedately patrol like medieval knights; tough, with armoured scales, but no defence against the bear-trap jaws of the massive and lurking hen-pike, teeth like shattered glass and power beyond all others save the last few remaining salmon ghosting upstream in an echo of more abundant times. These extraordinary streams are set like bright ribbons wandering through the verdant gentleness of the English countryside. It is a perfect environment in which to enjoy the most aesthetically pleasing of all the angling arts.

Chalk streams are also famous because they can be almost ideal habitats for desirable fish that take flies. This being so, it comes as a surprise to learn that chalk streams are essentially man-made. But however they came into existence, they have the huge advantage of enjoying a continuous flow of pure, cool water from natural underground aquifers. The whys and wherefores of this, and a discussion of the historical impact of man on the streams, are the subject of Malcolm Anderson's chapter on the ecology of chalk streams in this anthology. Malcolm is an Environmental Practices Adviser with the National Trust and is an avid, deeply experienced angler who has spent an enormous amount of time around chalk streams. His visceral affection and concern for the environment shines through in his writing. It is gripping stuff.

The consistency of the water in chalk streams, in purity, acidity, temperature and (hopefully) quantity, is very nice for the fish, but its principal importance is to the insects and other small creatures upon which the fish feed. All other things being equal (which, unfortunately, in the modern world they usually are not), chalk streams generate fabulous forests of underwater plants and are capable of truly prodigious yields of fish food when compared to most free-stone or spate-fed rivers in the British Isles, or anywhere else for that matter. This is a crucial foundation from an angling perspective – good plant growth equals many insects and other bugs and results in many happy, healthy, relatively large fish that can grow up from egg to lunker entirely naturally and without any help from the hatchery or the fish pellet. Of course, in the days before heavy angling pressure and stocked fish, all fish in chalk streams were wild and what set chalk streams apart was that they had abundant fish of a size that was fun to catch and worthwhile to eat. But, it is the insects that are the basis of it all. In his chapter, Dr. Cyril Bennett guides us through the important chalk stream flies with the aid of his stunning photographic plates illustrating both the adult and nymphal/pupal stages of these insects. Cyril is a renowned entomologist and author. In recent years he has devoted much of his time to projects aimed at the re-introduction of fly species to streams that have seen dramatic reductions in fly life. We face a real problem on chalk streams which Cyril explains. In short, the flies aren't what they used to be, either in diversity of species or in population numbers and things continue to deteriorate. If we don't address this, then we are going to lose one of the crucial distinguishing features of chalk stream fly fishing, which is being obliged to cast an imitative fly to fish that are feeding selectively on the naturals. If you want to catch a fish, that is. Fish become selective only in conditions of abundant fly life. Take away the abundance and you can generally catch them on any old fly, which is not as much fun. Cyril, being a man of action and not just words, has suggestions about what can be done about this right now.

While on the question of flies, I like to tie my own artificials, as do many other anglers. However, I am a rank amateur (after thirty years) when compared to someone like Dennis Shaw. Dennis, one of the country's finest fly dressers, has contributed a chapter that firstly sketches the fascinating history of artificial flies that have influenced the design of flies used on chalk streams, then concentrates on six patterns that he recommends as being sufficient for any situation at any time during the season and concludes with a review of recent developments and trends in fly tying that are likely to impact on the chalk stream flies of the future. If you are a beginner, this chapter will save you a great deal of time and money and will get you out on the stream with a small selection of artificial flies that will definitely work, if you can present them properly. If you are an old hand the topic is just extremely interesting, but I am under no illusion that it will reform your normal practice of going fishing armed with seven thousand of your favourite patterns.

To return for a moment to the ethos that attaches to chalk stream fly fishing, there is a recognised way that a chalk stream fly fisherman should go about fishing a chalk stream. There are traditional and very specific rules of conduct that vary somewhat between fisheries and which are discussed a bit later, but it is really about a fundamental attitude that is quite subtle. To guide us through this in a practical sense, Gordon Mackie, popular angling author and esteemed elder of the chalk stream world, has contributed a chapter on how to approach a chalk stream. Gordon is by far the most experienced writer amongst the contributors to this book and his delightful, anecdotal style captures the spirit and the joy of this intricate, yet gentle, sport.

When I first designed the content of this anthology, I thought to include a detailed chapter on the history of chalk stream fly fishing to serve as a foundation for understanding the ethos so ably expressed by Gordon Mackie. In the end, I decided against it. The topic has received vast treatment in earlier angling literature, in countless magazine articles and most recently in Andrew Herd's comprehensive history of fly fishing *The Fly* (reproduced as a new edition in 2011 entitled *The History of Fly Fishing*). There is one aspect of the history that I must deal with though because it is alluded to by a number of the contributors and that is the perpetually controversial "upstream dry fly only" rule. Nothing causes more heated debate and general trouble amongst chalk stream anglers than this rule and it has done so for about a hundred years. It is in fact two rules, one regulating casting direction and the other regulating what type of fly may be used. These rules are enforced on some chalk stream fisheries, either continuously or at least during the early part of the season. Many fisheries relax the rule specifying 'dry fly only' and permit the use of sub-surface nymph patterns from about the 1st July onwards, after the notional end of the mayfly hatch, but you are still required to cast upstream. As far as I know, these rules are only found on English chalk streams and on no other fisheries anywhere in the world and they are somewhat mystifying to other fly fishermen. They simply cannot be understood in a historical vacuum.

To leap nimbly over several thousand years of fly fishing history to arrive at a convenient starting point, let me just say this: before the modern era, fly fishing was done differently to how we do it now. A long, heavy, solid rod was used; a fixed length of line, usually made of braided horsehair and roughly the same length as the rod, was attached to the rod tip; a fly, consisting of a hook with a body of some or other natural material and feather wings, was attached to the end of the line; the angler cast as best he could, usually downstream and with a careful eye to the wind, to fish that were very close by modern standards (probably ten yards or less); the fly fished on the surface or just beneath it; a fly was a fly and there was no concept of 'a dry fly' or 'a wet fly' – a fly was both, as the circumstances allowed and the fish took it without much regard for whether it was 'on' or 'in' the water. Casting upstream had particular problems because the only way the line could be shortened as the fly came downstream towards the angler was to raise the rod. This made striking a fish difficult and the method was not popular. This angling technique, or something very like it, persisted from time immemorial until the 19th century, when several remarkable technological innovations took place, the most important of which were the invention of the tapered silk fly line and the split-cane fly rod. The fly line could now be cast exactly as we do it today and once anglers had figured out how to make the fly line float, modern fly fishing had arrived, along with a differentiation between flies that were specifically designed to float (modern dry flies) and those that were not. It was against this backdrop of a very short history of modern fly fishing that Frederick Halford strode onto the scene in the late 19th century.

It is not possible to do justice to Halford's contribution to fly fishing in a single paragraph because that contribution was mighty indeed. For our purposes though, his contribution can be distilled into two material elements. Firstly, although he neither invented modern dry flies nor invented the upstream method of their presentation, he designed a series of small imitative dry flies that could be used effectively all season long in contrast with earlier dry fly patterns which, through their bulky construction, were only suitable for use during hatches of large insects like the mayfly. Secondly, he proposed that the most effective and pleasing way of catching trout on a fly in a chalk stream was to find a rising fish, observe what natural flies were hatching, select a dry fly that matched the natural precisely and then present it to an unsuspecting quarry by means of an upstream cast delivered in such a way as to ensure the fly drifted back over the fish in the most natural manner possible. He presented these views in his writing as a set of prescriptive rules designed to define fly fishing on chalk streams, which was audacious at a time when a wide range of methods were in common use. Others took it even further by devising a distinction between the 'purist' and 'ultra-purist' dry fly schools. Halford, at least initially, happily contemplated casting a dry fly to non-rising fish if the occasion arose, but 'ultra-purists' limited themselves to rising fish only and must have often found themselves sitting idle on the river bank enthralled by the intransigence of their own narrow minds. Halford's influence as a writer was enormous and had truly global reach. His name became synonymous with chalk streams and adherence to his views gained great momentum, until those who counted themselves as members of the purist dry fly school had the premium trout waters in a complete stranglehold. It is here that the trouble started in earnest because the purist school began to legislate for their method only and outlawed all other methods. Their reasons for doing so have been the subject of fierce debate ever since and the situation has been exacerbated by a particularly infuriating bit of spin indulged in by members of the purist school from time to time and that is to suggest that fishing the upstream dry fly, a method that is relatively easy and is devastatingly effective on rising fish, is in fact more 'sporting' and therefore, by implication, more difficult or more noble than other methods.

It is important at this point to distinguish between the upper and lower reaches of the chalk streams. Brown trout, historically the principal target of the chalk stream fly fisherman, predominate in the upper reaches along with grayling. The lower reaches are a more diverse habitat and are occupied by a wide range of fish species, including trout. It was the premium trout waters of the upper reaches that the purist dry fly school set about capturing as the exclusive preserve of the upstream dry fly method. They were not interested in the lower reaches which, to this day, entertain anglers from all freshwater angling disciplines in relative harmony. By stipulating upstream dry fly only on the upper reaches, the purist school necessarily excluded all forms of angling that are designated as 'coarse', meaning anything that is not fly fishing. Nobody has a problem with this, not even the coarse anglers. The upper reaches are exceptionally suitable for fly fishing and it is generally considered appropriate that they be exclusively reserved for this type of angling. The problem was rather within the ranks of the fly fishing fraternity itself because the upstream dry fly only rule also swept away the time honoured and popular downstream wet fly technique, a method that involves moving steadily downstream repeatedly casting so as to cover the water with a wet fly (or team of wet flies) swung across the current. The principal argument advanced by the purist school in support of banning downstream wet fly fishing was that the method is very disruptive of the water. In the context of a chalk stream with its smooth flows and clear water, this is undoubtedly correct and the method would irredeemably prejudice the prospects of any other angler who might follow the wet fly fisherman. It is important to note though that the disruption is caused by the act of repeated casting and possibly also by the sweeping of the fly line and flies across the current and not by the simple fact that the flies are wet flies as opposed to dry flies.

The elimination of the classic wet fly method (and with it classic wet fly patterns, no matter how they were fished) from premium chalk stream fisheries eventually achieved more or less universal acceptance. That would have been that, had it not been for the intervention of G .E. M. Skues in the early 20th century. Skues, who achieved great fame as an angling writer, solved a problem that much puzzled chalk stream fly fisherman of the day. That problem was the phenomenon of 'bulging' fish – a rise form caused by a fish taking a nymph just beneath the surface and creating a hump-like disturbance in the process. Dry fly fishermen quickly learnt that bulging fish could seldom be taken on a dry fly and as the classic wet fly method had been banned for being too disruptive, the purist school strangely leapt to the conclusion that such fish were uncatchable. It just simply didn't occur to them that there might be some other method of fly fishing outside of the conventional dry fly and wet fly methods that might succeed. But it did occur to Skues, who proceeded to more or less invent modern upstream nymph fishing and then wrote a book about it. There was instant controversy because Skues' new nymphing method contravened the upstream dry fly only rule then universally and continuously in force on most premium fisheries. The stage was set for an extraordinarily bitter and protracted dispute that has still not been fully resolved.

The new nymphing school argued that, self evidently, the criticisms levelled at downstream wet fly fishing could not logically be applied to fishing sub-surface nymph patterns with an upstream cast in exactly the same way that a dry fly is fished, with the only difference being that the fly sank rather than floated. But the dry fly purists set their minds against this compelling proposition with a stubborn refusal to accept the distinction between nymphs and traditional wet flies and a mistaken conclusion that it is unsporting or even harmful to fish sunken flies on a chalk stream in any circumstances. Although the debate ebbed and flowed over the decades, the purists were eventually overcome, their hegemony of the chalk streams was broken and upstream nymph fishing became an accepted chalk stream method. However, the purists retreated with extremely bad grace and so slowly that today there are still fisheries that insist upon upstream dry fly only for some or all of the season, although these days this is more likely to be motivated by a desire to alleviate fishing pressure on hard-fished waters coupled to an apprehensive conservativism, rather than by quasi-religious ethical convictions.

I know it is difficult to walk away from a fight when logic is offended and passions have been unreasonably inflamed, but to my mind continuing this debate in the 21st century overlooks an important point. With the passage of time, these quaintly anachronistic rules have become a distinctive tradition that partly defines what chalk stream fly fishing is and how it is distinguished from other types of fly fishing. Nobody else, anywhere in the world, could credibly introduce rules like this today without them seeming to be an affectation. Chalk stream fly fishermen should thus revel in the distinction conferred upon them by an iconic history and in honouring that history, should happily observe the traditional rules where these are still in force. It is just the way this very English game is played – like bowling with a straight arm in cricket or wearing white at Wimbledon. Believe me, everybody else is jealous as hell and it is great fun teasing other types of fly fishermen by adopting a posture of implied superiority and spouting irritating aphorisms like 'it's not how many, but how, that counts'.

The one time that everybody is entirely happy to be restricted to the use of an upstream dry fly is during the annual mayfly hatch. Vast numbers of hatching mayfly create a festival atmosphere amongst both the anglers and the fish. For many anglers this is the highlight of the year and for some it is actually the only time they fish on chalk streams. It is a special time and so it gets an entire chapter devoted to it, written by Peter McLeod. Peter is a professional fishing guide and runs a company that organises fly fishing trips around the world. Although he rushes about stalking bonefish and wrestling six foot long tarpon to the ground, he was born and raised around chalk streams and can still be found there now and then, guiding clients or fishing himself. Fly fishing is basically his entire life, so it is very worthwhile listening to what he has to say about the specialised techniques effective during the mayfly hatch.

Mayfly time is not the beginning and end of chalk stream fly fishing by any means. It is just a highlight in a seasonal progression of different conditions, different hatches of flies and different fish behaviour. John Stoddart is one of those very fortunate anglers who is retired and lives in a house that overlooks a chalk stream smack in the middle of chalk stream country. Every day sees him out on some chalk stream somewhere, fishing or working on one or other fishery improvement project. He lives through the seasonal changes on a continuous basis and is thus ideally placed to contribute a chapter on seasonal tactics for chalk stream fishing. This chapter will be very useful to those many anglers who fish on chalk streams but do not live anywhere near them. Although close observation of conditions on the stream before actually starting to fish is extremely important, it helps to know what is supposed to be going on and to have some idea of what to do if it is.

Rules or no rules, fishing the upstream dry fly is often the most effective way of catching fish on a chalk stream. It is also almost everybody's favourite way of fly fishing. There is just something inexpressibly thrilling about drifting a dry fly over a fish and watching it rise up and take the fly. You never get tired of it, no matter how often you do it. But there is skill in executing the upstream cast effectively and that skill revolves mainly around the elimination or reduction of drag on the fly. To put it simply, except in certain very limited situations, fish will not take a dragging dry fly. Most fly fishermen know this in a theoretical sense because it has often been written about, but surprisingly few consciously employ drag reduction techniques while fishing and fewer still actually practice to become proficient in those techniques. Learning to avoid drag will dramatically improve your performance on a chalk stream and how to do that, amongst other things pertaining to presenting the upstream dry fly, is the subject of Ian May's chapter. Ian is a casting instructor and I first met him one balmy afternoon in late spring on a stretch of the Nadder. We chatted a while and then split up to do a little fishing. Some time later I came upon a large brown trout in an impossible lie, tucked in near the bank under a wide canopy of trees, with branches extending low over the river from both banks. I thought about it for a while and just as I concluded that there was no way at all to get a fly over that fish, along came Ian. I pointed out the fish and expressed the view that here was a fish that was invulnerable. Ian smiled and then retreated a long, long way downstream, well below the canopy of trees. Squelching out to a precarious position in the middle of a reed bed, he then stripped out virtually all of the fly line from his reel and proceeded to cast most of it out onto the water in front of him in a series of roll casts. When he was ready, he lifted this huge amount of line into the air above the reed bed and cast diagonally upstream across the river as close to the overhanging trees as possible. In what was almost a continuous movement, he then roll cast the line forward, changing direction and shooting more line into the cast so that the fly shot into the tunnel under the trees. It took a few goes, but eventually the fly drifted down over the fish in what seemed to both of us to be a perfect presentation. That cast really deserved to catch the fish, but nobody told the fish that, so he didn't rise and we didn't catch him. It didn't matter because the casting challenge had been extremely entertaining and demonstrated the important point that properly presenting the fly is an engrossing amusement in its own right.

With all the fuss about upstream nymph fishing over the years, you would think that chalk stream fly fishermen would leap at the chance to practice this method whenever and wherever it was allowed. Not so, I am afraid. Perhaps only 30% of chalk stream fly fishermen attempt the method with any regularity and less than 10% become truly proficient at it. This is because it is a more difficult method than dry fly fishing and requires the development of special skills that take time and practice to perfect. The difficulty arises from the introduction of depth as a third dimension into the angling process and by the extremely subtle visual indications that a fish has taken the fly. This requires a much higher level of concentration than dry fly fishing and the development of an almost instinctive capacity to lift the rod quickly in response to tiny visual clues. Timing of the strike is a pressing issue because the speed with which a fish can take and reject an artificial nymph is extraordinary. Many anglers, perhaps lacking in opportunities to spend much time on the water, find it just too taxing and challenging of rusty reflexes to persevere with the method and stick to the dry fly. This is a pity because once the skills have been acquired, the method is deadly and gives the angler an excellent chance when fish are feeding exclusively on sub-surface prey, which is often. Alwyn Lindsey is an angler who has developed nymph fishing skills to a very high degree and he has contributed a chapter that explains precisely how to go about it. Alwyn's chapter is probably the clearest explanation of nymph fishing techniques that I have ever read. He has not surrounded the principles with fluffy mystique and just tells it like it is. You come away from the chapter thinking: 'Yes! I can do that.' And you should.

To this point you might have detected a slight bias towards trout in this anthology, with grayling receiving only tangential mention. In fact, today grayling enjoy an equal status with trout in premium chalk stream fisheries and in my view they are the equal of trout in every way, irrespective of the fact that trout are capable of growing bigger. I find it inexplicable that in times past these lovely, sporting fish were regarded as vermin and serious attempts were made to exterminate them to make room for more 'noble' trout. Thankfully, these misguided efforts met with little success and a predominantly wild population of grayling still graces many chalk streams. Jan Szakowski is another lucky retired person who goes fishing more in a month than you or I do in a year and he has a thing for grayling. His chapter on grayling is quite different to the other chapters in this book because after explaining the basics about this species, he takes us fishing with him on some of his favourite streams. This is a pleasure if you are an experienced angler because you are instantly right there with him, water pressing past your waders, eyes scanning the riverbed for the ghostly shape of your next target. If you are a beginner it is invaluable because it captures the rhythm of a session on a chalk stream and explains in detail how an expert overcomes (or sometimes fails to overcome) the continuous series of challenges involved in a day on the stream.

The resurrection of grayling from persecuted vermin to esteemed game fish is the first fully realised consequence of a fundamental shift in the philosophy of chalk stream fly fishing in recent years. This shift is away from the rigid and narrow precepts that surrounded it in the past towards a more expansive fly fishing ideology in tune with the concept of balanced and naturally sustainable river ecology. Other noticeable consequences of this shift, as yet not fully realised, are the increasing popularity of catch and release and an ever growing enthusiasm for truly wild fish. The days of big bags of dead fish to impress your friends and family are gone and today the ego is placated by a quick snapshot taken with a smartphone before releasing the prize back into the river to continue a happy and hopefully long life. Smartphones must have saved literally millions of fish and the practice of instantly emailing the photo to everyone you know often elicits sardonic replies before you even have a chance to cast again. Of course, releasing fish has a very direct bearing on the effects of fishing pressure. Instead of no fish, you have plenty of fish that are just harder to catch because they get educated. If there are plenty of fish, you don't need to stock and probably should not stock if fish population balance is to be maintained. Not stocking creates the prospect of an essentially wild, self-sustaining population and that is the dream of the wild fish aficionados, so the one feeds into the other. I suspect that catch and release and enthusiasm for wild fish are just the beginning. There is a growing interest in fly fishing for 'coarse' fish in chalk streams and so it is possible that other species may find themselves elevated to 'game' status along with trout and grayling in the future. Fly fishing for coarse species will be quite a radical notion to the many chalk stream fly fishermen who limit themselves to trout and grayling and Dominic Longley's chapter on this topic is an exciting and mind expanding tour through the possibilities. Dom is a fisheries scientist with the Environment Agency who spends time actually in the rivers observing the fish through his diving mask and his insights into the behaviour of the various species and into when, where, why and how they can be persuaded to take a fly, are fascinating. There is so much more available to the chalk stream fly fisherman than I had ever imagined.

Only one fish that can be taken on fly in a chalk stream has been left out of this anthology and that is salmon. Salmon fishing is an arcane and specialised art about which much has been written and there are no material differences between the approach taken on a chalk stream and that taken on any other type of river. I thus felt that the topic fell outside the ambit of what is generally considered to be chalk stream fly fishing. The same applies to fly fishing for sea trout, the sea-run version of the brown trout.

Increased interest in targeting coarse species could have interesting implications, particularly for the premium trout and grayling fisheries of the upper reaches. Many fisheries that are designated as 'premium' include stretches that are really intermediate in nature and naturally contain a fair proportion of coarse species along with trout and grayling. On most of these fisheries the approach is to try and rig conditions in favour of higher populations of trout (usually stocked) by removing coarse species through electro-fishing in a never-ending uphill battle against the natural propensities of the river. Such an approach is obviously founded on current angler demand, but if anglers come to prefer catching a 6lb wild chub to a 1lb stocked trout, then both management practices and fishery rules will change. The lower reaches will also be affected as chalk stream fly fishermen expand their horizons downstream towards the sea. On the front line of these changes will be the long-suffering fishery managers and their teams of river keepers.

I fear that anglers do not fully appreciate the complexities of river management that underpin the quality of fly fishing on chalk streams. Increasing the general understanding of what is involved is the purpose of the chapter contributed by Andreas Topintzis, General Manager of the Salisbury and District Angling Club. Andreas is a talented and resolute character from the business world, which is just as well because he has his work cut out for him managing two thousand anglers and more than twenty miles of water. Chalk stream fisheries are subject to intense pressures from many quarters and almost everything involves striking a balance between conflicting interests and concerns. The fishery manager navigates a sea of perpetual compromise and learns the truth of the dictum that a good compromise leaves everybody feeling unhappy. A well-managed chalk stream provides one of the world's great angling experiences. A poorly managed stream does not provide good angling for long and in a worse case scenario, may cease to offer anything that even remotely approximates the challenges of proper chalk stream fly fishing.

It is difficult to know whether overall demand for chalk stream fly fishing is set to increase or decrease in the future. Historically, there have always been more fishermen than opportunities to fish on chalk streams. Current prices are high and waiting lists are long. But it is very noticeably a branch of angling dominated by mature anglers who are not in any way being pressed by an advancing horde of youngsters. Perhaps this is because older anglers have more time and more money, but I suspect it also owes a great deal to the Xbox, the i-Phone and social networking websites. Opportunities for affordable chalk stream fly fishing offered to teenagers do not meet with an overwhelming response. I have little doubt that demand will continue to be strong for the next decade or so as the baby-boomer generation retire and go fishing, but beyond that I can foresee a possible problem. Perhaps a future reduction in fishing pressure on chalk streams would in fact be a blessing. The streams are under very severe pressure from all sorts of problems and the truth is that they are deteriorating under the strain. Theo Pike is a professional writer and is well known for his efforts in the restoration of the Wandle, a stream just south of London that was more or less dead, but which has been brought back to life through the efforts of people like Theo. In the final chapter of this book, Theo explores the future prospects of the chalk streams and what can be done politically, legally, economically and socially to ensure that if the younger generations ever wake up to the sublime pleasures of chalk stream fly fishing, there will still be chalk streams for them to fish.

Fly fishing in general and chalk stream fly fishing in particular is such a fascinating and absorbing activity that it is quite easy to become carried away by it all and succumb to passionate irrationalities in advancing or defending a particular point of view. To assist in maintaining a proper perspective, I leave you with the words of the late Harold Blaisdell, a great angling philosopher:

There is an altogether splendid sense of escape and freedom which results from making a fool of yourself, and the man who can fish a dry fly with both deadly seriousness and the knowledge that his seriousness is ridiculously misplaced enjoys the full blessing of this relief. Accordingly, he comes to love dry fly fishing for what it is: an absurdity upon which he can focus his full powers of concentration with only superficial concern for the outcome. Whether a man raises a trout to his fly matters as much as it matters little, and as little as it matters much. It is because dry fly fishing proffers this comfortable option that it is both a field of battle and a blessed haven of peace. The Philosophical Fisherman *(1969)*

Graham Chalmers

March 2012

Chapter One

The Ecology of a Chalk Stream

Malcolm Anderson

When I was first approached about writing a chapter on ecology I had immediate doubts about whether I was the right man for the job. My botany is pretty weak; I don't know the Latin names for all those plants that give off whiffs of glorious perfume as I push through them on still June mornings searching for my fishy quarry. To me it's "the one with the purple leaves that smells of mint" or it's "the spiny one that really tangles fly line". Indeed, I've been known to give such sage advice to my fishing companions as; "a fish just rose on the far bank, there, right where the green bush falls into the water – no, no, the other green bush". My entomology goes about as far as 'small and brown' or 'big and yellow', although I can recognise enough to match hatches reasonably well and I understand the signs that reveal whether a fish is taking nymphs, duns, spinners or emergers.

No. I'm definitely a fisherman, not an ecologist.

But as I mulled over the predicament of being asked to write this chapter, I thought a good place to start would be to go and look for a definition of ecology. There are dozens of definitions of the word littered across the internet, but all have a certain core meaning which amounts to:

The science concerned with the interactions of living organisms between each other and with their environment.

I began to realise that despite my not thinking of myself as an ecologist and despite my inability to accurately describe for you, dear reader, the intimate details of the mating habits of the blue-winged olive, there is one aspect of my beloved rivers that I do know well. I have, over the years through my angling and my work, developed an understanding of the bigger picture, the top-down view, the macro level – call it what you will. I like to think that I grasp the links between geology, climate, land use, botany and so on; the systems that make these rivers not only special, but also so fragile.

This entire book focuses on fishing chalk streams, yet we are often guilty of glossing over what a chalk stream actually is. It is taken for granted that we just know. The dictionary definition of a chalk stream is quite unhelpful. They are classified as:

All watercourses originating from chalk hills, including winterbournes, streams and rivers.

That really doesn't give us much to go on apart from the fact that they flow off chalk hills. So, what is a chalk stream? I started by asking people for their own definitions, their personal perceptions. I talked to people in the Environment Agency, wildlife trusts, fishing clubs, Natural England and various luminaries from the angling world. Thanks to the always-on-connected-to-the-web nature of today's world, it didn't take long for answers to start dribbling into my inbox and in less than a week my poor old computer had been subjected to a virtual flood. Although there were a multitude of responses they were littered with similar phrases:

Constant flow. Crystal clear. Cold. Wafting crowfoot. Rising trout. Copious insect life. Pollarded willows. Grazing cows. Mayfly. Peaceful. Rural idyll. Quintessentially British. Summertime. Bygone era. Clean gravels. Mill pools. Exclusive. Limited access. Private. Aquarium. Aquifers. Spring fed. Delicate. Manicured riverside.

A couple of people touched on the words *man-made, artificial* and *contrived,* but these were the exception rather than the rule. There would seem to be quite a clear perception in many people's minds of what a chalk stream is, but I'm going to step away from perceptions here for a second and go back to the science bit.

Ninety million years ago (give or take) during the late Cretaceous Period there was a warm tropical sea covering the area now considered to be Southern England. The upper levels of this sea contained large numbers of plankton species. When these microscopic creatures died, their bodies drifted down to the sea floor where they slowly accumulated into a thick layer of ooze, along with the remains of bottom dwelling ostracods, bivalves and foraminifera. Over an immense period of time, this layer built in thickness, compressed under its own weight and consolidated into the soft, (mostly) white, pure limestone composed of Calcium Carbonate ($CaCO_3$) we know today as chalk.

At around the same time as the Alps were being formed this warm sea retreated and the consolidated layer of chalk was thrust upwards. Like an uneasy sleeper under a duvet, it buckled and creased to its own geological dance, forming the chalk hills, or 'downs' as they're known without any sense of irony, that reach across the South of England and into Northern France.

Warm moist air blowing from the south-west across the English Channel hits the chalk hills and cools as it rises upwards. The air unburdens itself of its heavy moisture load, which falls as rain. More precisely and because scientists love fancy names, we label this as orographic rainfall. The drops fall onto the thin soil cover of the chalk hills and disappear quickly into the porous rock. Chalk is generally highly permeable and water rapidly penetrates the fissures, being stored in a number of perched aquifers as well as in the main aquifers in the chalk marls. However, the chalk can only hold a finite amount of water and as the water hits the underlying impermeable clays, it is squeezed like garlic through a press and migrates laterally along the marl and flint layers, taking the path of least resistance through dips and synclines, until at last it escapes from the earth's clutches. The water emerges burbling and chattering, joining with water from other springs, tumbling together, forming rivulets, streams and rivers, collectively known as chalk streams, before finally falling off the edge of the known world and into the sea.

This process of being squeezed through the porous alkaline rock produces water with very little sediment content and a pretty constant temperature, even in winter. This clear, cool, abundant water, rich in minerals and low in sediment, supports an amazing array of life as it giggles its way downhill to the sea. This abundance of plant, insect, mammal, bird and fish life is one thing that sets chalk streams apart from other river types. The other thing is the influence of humans.

From the Welsh freestone rivers and Somerset Levels through to the Eastern Fens and majestic Scottish spate rivers, the effects of man's intervention are obvious, but in the case of the chalk streams the impact of man has been so subtle and yet so significant that we actually often fail to see the hand of man at all. This is interesting in an age where angling is moving towards an often mantra-like obsession with wild rivers, wild fish and wild fishing and it is apparent that many in positions of power to influence the direction taken in the management of these rivers do not actually understand the systems that they play with. People's perceptions of a chalk stream are intertwined with man's activity; with crystal clear waters running in defined channels through a pastoral countryside dotted with grazing cows, few riverside trees, thatched cottages and church spires in the distance. The truth is that if we really want to see a wild chalk stream, we need to travel back in time. Forget about Skues and Halford. Forget even about Izaak Walton. We need to go back to a point in time before the chalk valleys were tamed, before clearance and drainage. Back to a period before our ancestors worked out how to use the rivers as a tool to be manipulated at will. We arrive back at an environment that is completely at odds with our modern perceptions, at a time in British history when our ancestors traversed the ancient routes that criss-crossed the high, dry ground of the chalk downs; perfect farming land, perfect land for settlement, perfect land for long-distance travel. Peering through the mists of time we can only imagine how things were.

~Cue mists of time~

I'm travelling the ancient roadway along the top of a chalk ridge, heading towards the burgeoning settlement that one day will be considered the ancient capital of Wessex. It has been raining all day, but at least the paths are relatively clear up here. To both my right and left I can see the ancient wildwood lying like a green fog across the valley floor; a quagmire consisting of hundreds of ever-changing little channels of clear water choked with alders and willows. It is hard travelling in the valleys and people only go there for water and to hunt. The biting insects alone are enough to drive a man mad. However, for the brave or foolhardy, the rewards are good. Deer and birds thrive in the tangled, mossy shade.

Every once in a while one of the scraggly, green-furred trees that abound in the quagmire is toppled by an autumn storm or simply splits with age as they are wont to do, suffering the effects of time that come upon us all sooner or later. In place of the tree a patch of light appears and where roots have been ripped from their hold in the marshy soil, a deep hole exposes clean gravel. Water from a small channel fills the hole, creating a pool shimmering in the dappled light. With sunlight and abundant cool water, life flourishes in these pools. Waterborne plants take advantage of the sudden influx of light and explode into growth. With the cover provided by the plants, other life begins to colonize the pool. Along the margins, small fish shoal in and out of the shade, darting from cover to food source, trying desperately to bulk-up on the bountiful insect feast now sheltering in the watery green forests. Speckled trout and icy flanked grayling vie for food in the fast water at the head of the pool as it tumbles over the fallen timber, ever aware of the lurking presence of the dark menacing pike, hovering in the slack water behind. A gang of striped, spiky perch swagger around the middle of the pool, all front and attitude.

Now I've succumbed to an imaginative flight of fancy here, but it is grounded in reality. Small patches of wild chalk stream do exist. There's a patch of the Beer Stream, upstream of Beer Regis, where you can get a feeling of how things might have been, but even here you can see that the bank is artificial and has been straightened at some point. The closest I've come to what I would term a true wild chalk stream is a small area, no more than 100m x 50m on the river Bourne. The Bourne is heavily managed along most of its length from its source in the hills above Burbage until it tumbles unceremoniously into the Avon behind B&Q in Salisbury, but here I stumbled across a little piece of something altogether more feral. In a forgotten bit of the winterbournes, the river, just for a millisecond in its never-ending journey to the sea, becomes once more choked with crack willow and alder. The crystal clear waters flow effortlessly over and under tree roots through a mangrove swamp-like woodland of gnarled, green-clad trees that haven't been touched for at least 70 years. Donning my waders I've scrabbled through, Bear Grylls-style, and seen first hand the patch of light created by the fallen tree. I've seen the fish holding confidently in their seclusion and felt the eerie pull of the past whilst sitting on a moss-covered trunk. It would be considered completely useless from a fisheries point of view, but stands out for me as a glowing example of a river's ability to revert to a natural state if left well alone and given enough time.

This wildwood-choked swampland with its multitude of braided channels is not what the majority of people would consider to be a chalk stream. For better or worse, the rivers are not likely to ever revert to this state; at least, not while humans survive as a species.

Therefore the chalk streams that we know and love today are in fact the embodiment of a point in time, forever enshrined in fishing history and documented for us by a succession of bearded men who proudly stare out at us from sepia photographs, defiant in their tweed suits and wool ties. To understand the creation of the modern chalk streams and why their ecology is so unique, is to understand, in part, the history of land use. In particular, the history of land use in the southern counties of England and why this led to the evolution of the chalk streams into the rivers we know today.

At some point in history and with details having faded into obscurity, the river valleys of Southern England were cleared by our ancestors to increase grazing lands. Scythes existed in Roman Britain and would have been used to cut grass. Indeed, literary references exist as early as 679 AD which refer to meadow and pasture land being actively managed. Whether the valleys were cleared deliberately for the creation of irrigated water meadows or existing meadows were converted is of little importance at this point because either way, the practice of flooding pasture land via a series of ditches made its way to England from Italy and the Alps where it had been used since ancient times. The earliest written records in Britain that allude to managed water meadows date from around the early 1500s and by the mid-1600s it was a common practice on the rivers of Southern England. Chalk streams in particular, with their constant flows in both summer and winter were particularly suitable for the practice.

Engineered with military precision, often to tolerances of millimetres, water would be diverted from the main course of the river through ditches known as 'carriers' with flow being managed through the use of 'hatches' (sluices). To brazenly oversimplify what is an enormously complicated feat of historic engineering, the diverted water would be allowed to flow out of the carriers into channels through the use of a number of 'stops' (small earth or wooden dams) and onto the pasture where it would then drain away via a network of 'drawns' and back into the main river channel. The operation is often called 'flooding' or 'drowning', but the term is something of a misnomer because the point was not to have standing water on the land, but for it to be kept continuously damp.

The creation of the flooded water meadow is arguably one of the most important advances to take place in the history of agriculture in Britain. Flooding during the winter months provided protection from frost and allowed early grazing; repeated wetting stimulated extra hay crops and grazing throughout the summer months. This gave the southern landowners a distinct advantage. From anecdotal reports, one could reckon on a four-fold increase of hay from a well managed system. The flooded meadow systems required costly professional upkeep from extremely skilled craftsmen known as 'drowners'. Despite this expense, the advantages must have outweighed the cost as evidenced by records from 1632, showing groups of commoners in the Wiltshire village of Wylye collectively paying the fees for John Knight of Stockton to 'float the meadows'.

Along with the well-documented positive benefits for grazing and hay-making, the implementation of the water meadow systems had other unplanned benefits of more interest to us as anglers than the reasons why the Wiltshire sheep barons became so powerful. The water meadow systems took water away from the main river and out over the meadows, allowing nutrients and suspended silts in the water to drop out, fertilizing the land and inadvertently reducing euthrophication of the water course. Euthrophication occurs as a result of the addition of artificial or natural substances, such as nitrates and phosphates, through fertilizers or sewage and increased trophic levels in a water body can lead to a number of environmental problems including hypoxia (a depletion of oxygen levels), causing reductions in specific fish and other animal populations. This nutrient removal as a way of fertilizing land was such an important part of the function of water meadows that records show that the most successful places to site water meadow systems was downstream of a town or large cattle farm. J. Fitzherbert's *The Boke of Surveying and Improvements* from 1523 actually makes reference to establishing water meadows downstream of middens and dunghills. It seems these would '*make the meadowes moost rankest*' and rank meadows equated, of course, to cleaner river water.

The increased levels of sunlight reaching the river as trees were coppiced or removed to increase grazing area, coupled to a healthy, constant flow of water low in silt and organic matter, provided an excellent habitat for the growth of aquatic plants. The water, sunlight and weed cover provided a home and food source for invertebrates, which in turn became a food source for larger insects, fish and bird life. Yin followed Yang; insect followed plant, otter followed fish. Populations of the insects, plants, fish, birds and mammals most suited to the new habitat exploded in number and thrived in their various ecological niches.

Thus the creation of the flooded water meadows system forever changed the ecology of the chalk streams. Gone were the tree-choked marshes; gone were the wild woods and dark, mysterious valley floors. The expansion of the water meadow systems created a basic form of chalk stream that would be recognised by anyone from Walton, through Halford and Skues and all the way to Anderson (I know, I know, I've placed myself in a sentence alongside Halford – I'll be struck by lightning in the morning).

So, these rivers, these crystalline veins through which the gin clear blood of England flows, are a *naturalised* environment not a *natural* one. A fine distinction to be sure, but one that needs to be recognized if we are to understand the simple fact that, for the most part, a chalk stream is the product of the hand of man and, from an angling point of view, is the result of accident rather than design. Not that this is necessarily negative of course, but the hand of man has never been known for letting things alone; it's in our nature to tinker, meddle and otherwise bugger about with things that would have been absolutely fine if left alone.

Over the last two hundred years the ecological niches formed by the constant flow of cool, clear water which resulted in such a fantastic abundance of life have seen a slow but steady decline. Today there is markedly less abundance and diversity of species than there was even one hundred years ago and alarmingly, the rate of decline appears to be accelerating. In order to identify what's causing the internationally important ecological potential of the chalk streams to dwindle, we need to understand some of the factors that are causing it. Like an overrun on a multiplier reel, the reasons are many and intertwined. As a general rule, humans as a species are not good at dealing with the threat of a problem. If it 'may' happen in the future, the chances are we will prevaricate and 'um and ah' about what needs to be done, but carry on as normal. Give us a crisis and we will respond decisively. Unfortunately for the health of our chalk streams there is no single issue, no immediate crisis, threatening catastrophic failure; instead we appear to be suffering death by a thousand cuts. As I'm writing this from an angler's perspective, I'm going to break down the potential causes of the decline of our chalk streams into two parts; those that are a direct result of the way that we manage our rivers for fishing, and those that exist outside of our sphere of activity – internal and external influences if you will.

Fishing on the chalk streams evolved over the years from a way to feed your family into a sport (if indeed 'sport' is the right word to use in this context, 'game' might be more appropriate). As the sport developed and burgeoned in popularity, the ethos of the chalk stream fisherman began to shift accordingly. In a terribly British way, our ancestors began to fiddle with the rivers as they found them by both attempting to tame and shape nature into a romantic vision of pastoral countryside and by managing them in a way that facilitated easier fishing. As fly fishing became more popular and access to rivers improved, a different type of angler started to appear on the bank. The old obsessive angler, patiently watching a solitary fish for days on end before casting became the exception rather than the rule and a more 'casual' angler appeared. Not casual in a fashion sense, deary me no, sartorially they were (and are) often beyond reproach, but casual in the sense of someone who could only fish once or twice a year and didn't quite get round to developing casting, line control, fly selection or concealment skills fully. I'm stereotyping horrendously here, but there has been a seismic shift in the last one hundred years in the type of fly fisherman seen on the chalk streams and in the sort of access to the river that someone with a limited skills set needs in order to have a chance of catching a fish or two. To put it succinctly: we've witnessed the rise of the 'duffer'. Given the increasingly commercial nature of fisheries as businesses run for profit, it was inevitable that fisheries management would evolve to accommodate the change. Trees and snags were removed, banks were cut and paths created. Trout were stocked to increase populations, fish were fed pellets over winter to keep them growing and stop them spreading up and downstream. Coarse fish were removed by whatever means necessary and areas that were not naturally suitable habitat for trout were artificially stuffed with fish. The natural balance which had evolved to fit an ecological opportunity historically created by human hands was fundamentally impacted by more recent human hands. What the human hand creates, the human hand can also take away.

The mowing of paths and river fringe to ankle or knee height may make casting and line management easier, but it's a well proven fact that insect life is negatively affected by the reduction, particularly by the loss of emergent vegetation and the herbaceous fringe plants. If you look back at photos of Halford's Oakley Beat at the time of his tenure, they show clearly how the fringes are high and consist of a wonderful mix of species. The National Trust took over managing this exact stretch of river some five years ago, allowing the fringe to revert to a semi-natural state after many years of suffering at the hands of river keeping more suited to golf course management. Anecdotal evidence suggests that fly life has increased dramatically in that short space of time.

Arguments abound about the issue of introducing stocked trout into a river system and the genetic effect that this stocking has on native populations of trout. Things can get very complicated, discussing X's and Y's and the tracing of sub-species to individual catchments and even reaches of a river. The basics of it are that inter-breeding of stocked fish and native fish over the last hundred years or so may have led to a genetically inferior trout existing in our rivers. Over thousands of years trout genetically evolved into many, sometimes tiny, separate populations, each specifically adapted to a particular watercourse or even to a short stretch of a particular watercourse. Dumping stocked trout of a different genetic provenance into a watercourse is thought by some to be dangerous because if they inter-breed with the local strain the specific adaptations could be watered down. The result could be future generations of trout that are less suited to the particular water and which are more susceptible to population crashes through disease and habitat change. Even worse, over time the original wild strain might be lost forever and would be replaced by the mixed strain. Doubtless, evolution will once more take care of things, but that is a process spanning millennia.

Stocking trout into rivers with existing populations can also have other, more immediate, effects. Personally, I believe that although some low levels of stocking can be appropriate to bolster populations in heavily fished areas, in most situations it is pointless at best and damaging at worst. Fish introduced into an area will, once settled, look for food. It is simple population science to figure out that if the local food supply is not big enough to support the levels of fish introduced, they either wither and die or move on. Now if those stocked fish are 3lb lumps (and in some cases on the Avon I've seen fish of up to 9lb being introduced by commercial fisheries), even if they are triploids and cannot inter-breed with native populations, they will out-predate the existing wild populations and will also often eat their eggs and young.

A phenomenon linked to the stocking of trout is the obsession on the part of fishery managers over the years with the removal of 'pest' fish. It's not many years since grayling were viewed as vermin and were removed by the bucket load. These days pike and chub are still unwelcome guests and are removed, most often by electro-fishing. Scientific evidence suggests that electro-fishing for purposes of routine coarse fish removal is somewhat pointless because the river is in effect a large, long wildlife corridor. Unless you can guarantee the removal of every pike from the river, you can be sure that any you remove will be replaced in a pretty short space of time. If you remove a grand old dame, say over 15lb, she is likely to be replaced by more than one smaller fish. Smaller fish eat more food pound for pound than large fish because they are in their growing phase. So removing pike is not only a thankless task, like painting the Forth Bridge, but could actually be causing greater loss of other species than if you'd left the pike alone. Electro-fishing has also been scientifically linked to vertebrae damage in smaller fish, particularly when not done by fully trained professionals. There's still uncertainty around the impact of the electro-fishing process, but the evidence appears to show a reasonable doubt about its safety, especially in areas with good populations of small wild trout. Is the removal of those pesky roach really worth the risk?

It's unclear to me from my discussions with people whether the practice of cutting river weed developed for water level management reasons or to make fishing easier. Either way, the impact of weed cutting on invertebrate populations must be acknowledged. In a time when declining fly hatches are of major concern to anglers it must be appropriate to question the act of cutting and removing ranunculus from the rivers and allowing it to rot on the river bank. Next time you're wading near some wafting water crowfoot, pick up a handful and take a look. Amongst the network of moist, thread-like leaves will be hundreds and thousands of nymphs, larvae, shrimp and all manner of 'creepy crawlies' as David Bellamy would say. The fact is that by stripping out tonnes and tonnes of cut weed throughout a river catchment, we must be removing billions of invertebrates and their eggs and with declining populations, this simply must give us serious pause for thought.

After such a chunk of bad news I feel I need to inject a note of positivity here before we proceed any further. The good news is that the fisheries management profession and angling clubs and associations have at least begun the process of changing course. It may be taking longer to turn some of the old dinosaurs around than it would to stop an oil supertanker at sea, but the process has begun. We have sterling habitat improvement work being done by the Environment Agency, Natural England, fishing clubs, wildlife trusts and some extremely able river restoration companies right across our chalk stream catchments. We have the amazing work on invertebrates being done by Dr Cyril Bennett and others and the Wilton Fly Fishing Club is currently running a trial where they've stopped electro-fishing and the removal of pike from their waters. In fact, right across the UK, I am aware of examples of all of the issues above being looked at with a view to finding workable solutions. One of our problems is that even with the creation of the Angling Trust and with bodies such as the

Institute of Fisheries Management, Salmon & Trout Association and Wild Trout Trust working at a national level, we still don't really have a clear picture of what everybody is up to. There is no register of what has and what hasn't worked, it's all locked up in individuals' heads. Sure there's some communication between groups, but we are in danger of preaching only to the converted. We all need to be communicating to a much wider audience, particularly outside of fishing and fisheries. We also need to be a little less risk averse and more open to trying new things, regardless of tradition and the suggestion that we have seen it all before. Just relying on the reply that 'we tried that in 1859 and it didn't work' is far too complacent. Life moves on, maybe it's time to try again.

There is just one more thing I have to raise before we're done with the problems caused by internal, river management related issues. Chalk streams are unique. They are a habitat that has not just been shaped by the hand of man, but that has been cultivated, developed and managed by man as a tool. You can't just copy and paste the same restoration approaches used on other types of river onto a chalk stream. Sure the belt may contain the same tools, but there are differences in how you use them. The Strategic Restoration Framework for the river Avon catchment, for example, focuses heavily on the removal of impoundments and structures in the river channel. No-one questions the negative impact that structures and impoundments can have, to both upstream and downstream reaches, but I would argue that the beneficial nature of many of the structures is not being taken into account on chalk streams. As a naturalised environment, it's not a simple case of turning them back into being wild. As we have seen, wild in the context of a chalk stream means little channels running through a dense willow bog covering the entire valley floor and nobody wants that or could achieve it. Instead, what we are attempting to do with chalk streams is turn the clock back, but only as far as a time when mills were working and water meadows flooded and chalk stream ecology was at its most abundant. That abundance required functioning structures in the streams. The structures play a vital role in keeping water levels maintained and come the hot summer months the presence of deep, well-oxygenated hatch pools to retreat to has saved many a fish. Although it's not directly related to ecology, I also worry that this approach of removing hatches and culverts detracts from the perception of what makes a chalk stream a chalk stream in an environmental and historical sense. I worry about the unchecked removal of our agricultural archaeology. Most of the structures are unlisted and appear worthless, but when you look closely they are fantastic pieces of our history. Walking in the meadows along the Nadder near Burcombe you can see countless abandoned examples of brick built bridges and culverts and these are a heritage that is rapidly disappearing into the fields that they helped shape. We protect our historic buildings and many important landscapes, we even list 1960s concrete tower blocks, but this agricultural heritage is seen as worthless.

In fact, now that I've rambled onto this subject it will serve as a good introduction to the issues that exist outside of fisheries management that are impacting negatively on our chalk stream ecology. One of the first is that we have lost the link between the chalk streams and the land. The water meadow systems are the reason that our chalk streams evolved in the way they did and over the last hundred years we have seen a massive shift in land use away from operating the meadows. Hatches have fallen into disrepair and drawns and stops have disappeared. Without being able to flood the meadows, we lose the ability to deposit sediments and nutrients on the land. It is frustrating that at a time when government agencies spend millions of pounds on hard engineered flood defences around towns, we don't take the opportunity to simply re-engineer and operate water meadows as a form of flood management. At the time that the Environment Agency was spending huge sums of money to protect Harnham from the flooding of the river Nadder, just upstream a large area of former water meadow was up for sale. No-one seems to have examined the potential for simply buying the meadows and running them as a flood defence mechanism and at the same time providing an ecologically much needed nutrient and silt dump for the river.

This divorcing of the river from the land becomes even more important when we begin considering the changes in land use that have taken place in the last 25 years, let alone in the past one hundred. In his book *The Hampshire Avon*, published in 1950, Brian Vesey-Fitzgerald talks about how worried he is about the changes he is witnessing on Salisbury Plain. He mentions the shift away from sheep farming into cattle and the changes that this is bringing to the wildlife and vegetation. How horrified he would be today to see the development of wide scale pig farming on Salisbury plain. Not only do the farms look abysmal, reminiscent as they are of some semi-permanent Battle of the Somme, but the pigs completely churn over the top metre of soil, destroy any sort of vegetation and thus eliminate the habitat of a wide variety of mammals, insects, butterflies and birds. This may not directly impact on the rivers, but I can't help but feel that the plains are so intrinsically linked to the rivers that any loss of habitat on this scale cannot bode well. The other major problem is that by churning up the topsoil and removing all vestiges of plant life, they substantially increase the risk of soil erosion when the area receives heavy rain. Whereas in the past rain falling on the plains would soak slowly into the soil and the chalk would work its magic, it is now increasingly common to see soil-rich run-off heading for the ditches and gutters and that means ultimately the rivers. Of course, the increased silt load in our chalk streams is not solely the fault of pig farmers trying to make the best of a population demanding cheap British bacon. The increase in road drainage, building roofs and gutters as well as the significant increase in the ploughing of hillsides for planting crops have all massively changed the balance between the various sources of the water in our beloved streams. An ecology that formed around crystal clear water bubbling from springs is being hammered by ever increasing levels of nutrient-rich surface run-off.

The increase in run-off is also affected by another looming monster, climate change.

You'll notice I don't call it global warming. That's a deliberate distinction because there are so many uncertainties around exactly what will happen on a local level as a consequence of a rapidly changing climate that to mention the word 'warming' is counter-productive, conjuring images of vineyards and summer holidays. One thing that is certain though is that rapid global climate change is happening and the rate of change is accelerating. That isn't some obscure scientific theory, it's universally accepted science backed by the world's mainstream scientific community. Whatever the claims of certain interest groups or the spurious headlines in daily tabloids might be, these should not detract from the simple truth. After all, as the saying goes, change is inevitable, except from a vending machine.

Working as I do for the National Trust, I'm seeing the impacts of climate change first hand. It's affecting our buildings and our land in all manner of ways, from increased shrinkage and cracking due to drought, through to increased flash flooding from storm events. We're seeing diseases and plant and animal species arriving from other countries as changing climatic conditions allow them to expand their territories. What this means for the rivers locally is, in all likelihood, again a matter of where the water flowing in our rivers comes from. Uncertainties over exact effects aside, we can expect to see rainfall coming in different patterns compared to two hundred years ago, with increased storms and droughts. This will reduce the water that sinks into aquifers and recharges our springs, whilst at the same time causing more surface runoff from ploughed hillsides, roof spaces, car parks and roads.

Linked to this is the fact that our towns and villages have expanded at an alarming rate over the last two hundred years. In 1801 the population of Wiltshire stood at around 185,000. By 2001 this had increased more than threefold to a figure of over 600,000. At the same time some of our individual towns and villages have witnessed an unprecedented rate of growth. In 1801 Amesbury had a grand total of 721 residents. By 2001 this had increased to over 9000 – a mind-boggling twelve-and-a-half-fold increase. These figures don't even include the creation of the sizeable new residential estate of Archer's Gate where in the last few years hundreds of new homes have been built with very little thought to where their water is going to come from. Planners just leave that stuff to the water companies. Now this is a large amount of roof space, road drainage and associated runoff to add to the Avon as it wends its way south. More significantly however, at an average rate of about 150 litres per person per day, this is 1,350,000 litres being taken out of the Avon catchment each day, just for the population of one town. Multiply this by the population of Winchester, Salisbury, Andover and on and on and the water consumption numbers become hard to comprehend. This is just the tip of the iceberg however because we then need to take account of agricultural and commercial abstraction and then whatever the Ministry of Defence takes for its various uses. But, as anyone with a basic knowledge of physical geography will say, what's the problem? After all, the water cycle of evaporation and rainfall is well understood. Most water either passes back into the system via drains and sewers or evaporates into the atmosphere to fall as rain again on another day. So we take water from the rivers and aquifers, use it and then return it back into the river, right? Well, that's how it should work. Unfortunately for our chalk streams, the very thing that has allowed such a fabulous environment to develop, namely the crystal clear, clean water, looks like it will ultimately be its downfall. To a water company this clean water is irresistible. It is far, far cheaper to pipe this clear water out of its catchment and all the way to far-flung towns such as Yeovil and Bath, than it is to clean and use the dirtier water available there. Our precious, clean chalk stream water is mixed with water from local sources and then ends up being flushed down a toilet and into entirely different river catchments. There is no more insidious threat to the ecology of our chalk streams than the exploitation of their principal raw resource either for commercial profit or to maintain inappropriately low water charges, especially when that raw resource is removed entirely from the river catchments.

So without the basic natural resource, what hope for the ecology of our rivers? What can we, as individual anglers, do about it?

Given the man-made nature of the chalk streams, I can't help but feel that we could all gain from being a little less sensitive to change. If we are forced to accept the fact that the water isn't coming back and get used to the current levels of abstraction we have to deal with, then perhaps we need to think a bit more drastically about the shape of our rivers. One of the main problems is that there just isn't enough water to fill the old river channels which were formed for the water levels of bygone centuries. Perhaps, instead of just pinning in a bit of wooden debris, or pinching-in small sections, maybe we should narrow entire stretches? It's by no means a perfect answer, it's a solution borne of particularly dire circumstances, but perhaps we just have to put the JCBs to work, push the banks in on over-wide reaches and then just deal with the mess and loss of angling for a year while the river banks repair themselves. It would definitely be unpopular with this year's anglers, but next year's, and the years' after that would reap the benefits. It is this more flexible approach that is going to be needed as we move further into uncertainty and the health of our chalk streams and rivers becomes almost wholly the responsibility of anglers and angling clubs. There is some interest and buy-in by individual riparian owners, wildlife trusts, NGOs and the like, but lets face it, it's the angling community that has the biggest stake, but also has the biggest hand to play, in our rivers' futures.

As individuals we should open our eyes and understand the rivers better. Take some personal responsibility and acquire at least a passing knowledge of entomology and habitat. It doesn't take a lifetime to get a basic level of understanding; it's reading a bit, listening to others and thinking for yourself. By understanding the rivers more, not only will you be a better angler, but also you will begin to notice the things that aren't quite right. You'll be more aware of the plight of our rivers and more conscious of the things that can be done to help.

It sounds awfully trite but a more aware angler, whether coarse or game, is one of the biggest changes we can achieve in the short term. We can bore our friends and fellow anglers into submission over a pint, pressure angling clubs to change management practices and lobby locally to increase awareness of the plight of our rivers and streams. These are all things that we, as individuals, can do. There are, after all, over three million anglers in the UK and that's a powerful voice, whether used collectively or in multitudes of singular efforts. Don't be afraid to stand up for your rivers, even if sometimes feels like you're a lone voice in the wilderness.

Chapter Two

How to Approach a Chalk Stream

Gordon Mackie

Dame Fortune can sometimes save the day, but the chalk stream fly fisherman makes his own luck more often than not. Consistent success requires studied observation, an ability to interpret nature's signals and the stealth of the natural predator. That distinct regional fly fishing techniques have developed across the United Kingdom is due to the hugely diverse geological formations that exist, broadly categorised as limestones, granite, clays, sandstones and chalk. These specialised methods have evolved for common sense reasons; seldom, as is sometimes suggested, through fashion, narrow parochialism or blind conformity. Chalk streams are unique in character, since sustained summer flows depend upon spring water issuing from underground aquifers, yet for practical purposes these rivers may be likened to some of the clear limestone and sandstone streams, the main difference being that the latter generally receive more frequent run-off or 'freshes' which serves to prevent their drying up as chalk streams are increasingly apt to do in heavily abstracted catchments. Under natural conditions however, the chalk's amazingly efficient capture/storage/filtration system ensures absolute water purity at source, alkalinity values of around pH8 in most cases and constant water temperatures of 10° – 11°C throughout the year. The springs 'break' in January or early February each season, bringing a surge of pristine water which invigorates currents, cleanses the stream bed and stimulates early plant growths. This sets off a chain reaction, since ranunculus and some other 'weeds' which thrive in brisk flows are home to countless invertebrates and act as a springboard for those insects that cause trout to seek much of their food in the mid-upper layers. Thereafter, spring function continues to deliver adequate flows during the summer, even at times of drought, although the upper headwaters and winterbournes have always become dry when their springs lie at higher altitude than the receding water table. Another major advantage which spring-fed rivers have over most others is stability, for the absence of sudden spates and consequent shifts in temperature and turbidity is good news for insect regeneration. Although fewer species are normally present here compared with moorland streams, those ephemerids which appear do so at largely predictable seasons and times of day or evening and often in remarkably high numbers.

It is important at this point that younger anglers should receive an indication, a yardstick if you like, by which to compare insect fertility in the recent past with that of today. Only this way will a vision be carried forward to which future generations may aspire. One day on the Itchen, in September 1976, a hatch was building to such intensity that I decided to start counting. It was composed of half a dozen small up-winged species, with 20-25 duns to the square foot of water stretching right across the river, which was some 15 yards wide and flowing at a rate of around 2 feet per second. I watched for 30 minutes, counting only those on the surface and ignoring airborne insects. Allowing a substantial margin for error, a conservative estimate of the number of flies that floated past me in half an hour would be in excess of three million. Such a multitude is exceptional, yet counts of 10-plus duns per square foot were relatively common until the early to mid 1980s, while an aerial procession of spinners one June evening on the Wylye was not untypical. A swarm of blue-winged olives (sherry spinners) was flying upriver towards their egg-laying site on broken water and this activity – as sometimes happens – encouraged female mayfly spinners to join the throng. Standing on a footbridge I counted some 25 mays passing overhead every 10 seconds, along with the sherries which outnumbered them by about 15:1. A rough calculation suggests at least 15,000 mayflies and 220,000 blue-winged olives flew by in the space of just 10 minutes.

But I repeat the words under natural conditions, for small up-winged flies have declined significantly over the years, a situation which it is hoped will soon be reversed by addressing the root of the problem – borehole abstraction – which causes or exacerbates those factors contributing to the on-going deterioration of breeding habitats. Among the harmful effects of lower and slower flows are; a build-up of silt deposits, which often contain noxious substances; reduced dilution of water-borne impurities; declining oxygen levels; danger to spawning beds; and the loss of healthy weed growths. Fisheries strive ceaselessly to halt what has been described as 'the chalk stream malaise', sometimes aided by government-funded bodies, yet the outcome can be little more than cosmetic while the aquifers continue to be over-exploited. Addressing side issues may suggest that large-scale improvements are under way, certainly the proactive image portrayed would give that impression; but politically, crucial questions concerning the destruction of aquatic ecosystems are still met with prevarication or denial. We look to our representative organisations to lobby robustly for the implementation of a fail-safe water distribution network across English counties in which abstraction from source will be reduced to within naturally sustainable limits. We see real commitment at local level, particularly from bodies such as the Wiltshire Fisheries Association, but these jewels are a national treasure, our link with the eternal forces of nature, and must at all costs be preserved for future generations.

This preamble, though deviating a little from my theme, may serve to illustrate the uniquely fertile yet vulnerable nature of chalk rivers. It sets the scene for those fortunate folk the bulk of whose fishing days lie ahead, rather than in dog-eared diaries. The sport is more demanding today than when I first came to the Box Brook near Bath in 1963, and joined chalk stream clubs on the Kennet and Wylye in 1967–8. Prior to that, in addition to the occasional day permit on the Avon and Test, I had also explored rain-fed rivers in the West Country, Shropshire and South Wales, having caught my first trout on a fly from the Devonshire Erme some three years after the bombing raids on Plymouth had ended. My earliest memory however, is of a 6lb salmon speared with a pointed stake on the Tavy while at school near Tavistock. Rod or no rod, the hunter-gatherer gene runs deep! These were magical, uninhibited days, and the camping trips were sheer delight. I could fish upstream or down, wet or dry, or a team working the current in tandem. I inched out to my wader tops, casting into every stickle, glide and tumbling pocket among the boulders. No matter which patterns I offered, the little trout kept coming, even those under the rod tip, despite the disturbance I created. My greatest challenge lay in hooking them, but with a 7-inch size limit there were usually a few for the pan.

Chalk stream fishing came as something of a culture shock. The rivers ran sedately over a relatively even bed. No rocks were to be seen other than those placed there during the construction of the water-meadow systems three to four hundred years ago. The only areas of turbulent water were below the remaining hatch structures built at that time. Reading the water was no simple matter, but familiarity teaches us to focus on any kind of obstruction or distortion of the natural flow. Above, below and alongside ranunculus beds are prime hot-spots, firstly because they provide camouflage and immediate access to cover and importantly (as mentioned earlier) because they host a large proportion of the river's insect life. Bridges also attract many up-winged flies, some of which crawl down under water to lay their eggs on wooden or concrete supports. Trout seek both shade and security, which are generally available in abundance beneath the arches where fish are frequently found cruising along the brickwork as they pick off the hapless spinners. It pays to approach from below with extreme caution since unseen trout often lie out downstream, while those immediately upstream of buttresses may be almost uncatchable unless you can cast across river, without drag, from directly above the bridge. For the same reasons, i.e. security and food supply, we commonly find trout lined up along firm or undercut banks. Others may be spotted lying close to relatively small stones, posts, branches and assorted debris on the riverbed. Hatch pools, always attractive to anglers due to their seemingly endless possibilities, often prove less productive than we would wish. They hold plenty of trout and grayling as a rule, but seldom in the main current, although at mayfly time the former will occasionally rise porpoise-fashion, showing the head and back. For the most part however, they tend to conserve energy by occupying backwaters at either side of the race where they too may browse slowly to and fro along the walls. But the difficulty comes in seeing them do so, or indeed spotting a rise at the surface, since in popply water glinting with reflected light the tell-tale indications are rarely detected. Certainly in my case, the majority of trout taken from hatch pools have been stationed in the shallow glide at the very tail, just before it breaks into the run below. Here, especially at last light on a summer's evening, I've encountered several fish of above average weight poised side by side along the sill.

That first year or two represented a steep learning curve. I heard there are 'unwritten rules', codes of behaviour which are hinted at but seldom spelled out in print, that doubtless still create uncertainty in the minds of newcomers and beginners alike. It was assumed, perhaps as some echo from the days when candidates were introduced by existing members, that they would already be familiar with the way fishermen were expected to conduct themselves. Adhering to certain standards of courtesy and sportsmanship was considered paramount in order to maintain the quality of fishing and foster a harmonious spirit within the club. My indiscretions were pointed out early on. Although the rules on the Wylye allowed 'wading', for example, it was unclear what the word actually meant. What was meant, though not explained, was that entering the stream unobtrusively at the margin to cover an awkward lie was permissible, yet working your way up mid-river in chest waders was thought undesirable since it can disturb an entire stretch and subsequently render trout more difficult to approach. The same may be said of persistent 'flogging' and of needlessly hooking and returning large numbers of fish. I also learned that trampling the gravel bed can seriously affect spawning yields, particularly when grayling fishing during the trout close season.

Some clubs merely stipulate 'dry fly and upstream nymph', which might infer that fishing the former downstream is acceptable and that no restrictions apply as to size, weight or dressings in the case of the latter. The promotion of attractor patterns and lure fishing techniques at the time of the stillwater boom in the 1970s and 1980s led all-round anglers, including 'celebrities', to try their luck on the nearby rivers. Recently introduced stocked fish proved relatively easy to catch this way, but such methods threatened to change the face of chalk stream fishing as we knew it. A number of fisheries have tightened up their regulations to some extent, yet my own observations suggest that these are often misinterpreted today. Other clubs still skirt around the subject of ethics, possibly for fear of being seen as overly stuffy, 'draconian' or 'elitist'! My aim here is to illustrate how embracing these and similar principles can help to protect the stock, uphold the best traditions and preserve top quality sport for all concerned. And what better way than to take a couple of days fishing?

After jostling with the traffic we arrive at our destination, hurriedly assemble our gear and head for the river. It's still quite early, the three beats are unoccupied, so we choose the popular upper length flowing down from a set of hatches. We can hardly wait to begin and are tempted to have a few chucks on the vacant beats in passing. On reflection, however, this will almost certainly unsettle fish which the next chap rightfully expects to have been rested. Let's carry on to our beat, keeping well back from the margin. By now the urge to get casting is intense and a few fish are rising on the open shallow. Undue haste and over-enthusiasm can lead to bad fishing however, so we decide to sit on a log, dig out the thermos and consider our plan of action. Those are small grayling anyway; the trout have yet to put in an appearance. But where are they lying? Perhaps we can catch one on a nymph? The water is low and clear, with the occasional patch of weed here and there, but visibility is rather poor in these overcast conditions. Dry fly would likely be the better option and if rain sets in, the duns may start hatching. We do not wish to sit here indefinitely, but another fifteen minutes might provide a clue as to the wisest course of action. Without raising the head, we creep towards the bank, straining our eyes in an attempt to spot one. Noting the set of the current, we identify a promising feed lane by tracing the path of fallen leaves and blossoms on the surface, and that slightly rippled water nearby could denote a raised silt bank or gravel bed where the resulting 'cushion' may offer a comfortable lie. No fish are to be seen as yet, so should we try pitching our fly on the off chance? Chalk stream anglers frequently face this dilemma. But then the sun breaks though. Suddenly we see trout poised in mid-water, several within easy casting distance. So our question has been answered. If we had fished on spec those fish would very probably have scattered. We would have remained unaware of their presence and ruined a golden opportunity. Perhaps more tea breaks would improve our success rate!

As it is, we now have the chance to test our sight fishing skills. The trout range in size roughly between 8 and 16 inches. The smaller fish is the closest and the larger one is the third upstream of our position. We need to exercise extreme caution for the first two look undersized and should therefore be left alone, but our approach could cause them to sound alarm bells by dashing upriver. Our aim is to crawl very slowly along the left bank to get ahead of them, hoping they will simply drift away downstream. This manoeuvre brings us to within 5 yards of our target fish, a bit close for comfort perhaps, but needs must. There is no bank-side fringe here, but keeping low we can crouch among the taller tussock grasses. A hat is sometimes the number one fish-scarer in these situations, so we leave the cream-coloured Stetson on the ground behind us – or better still in a muddy puddle! With little cover, raising the head above tussock height is asking for trouble, but provided our quarry remains clearly visible through the foliage and shows no signs of unease, the odds will be in our favour. He is hovering some 18 inches beneath the surface, moving unhurriedly a foot or so to either side, presumably intercepting Baetis nymphs which commonly swim to and fro among the weed fronds and into open water. Shrimps are generally taken at greater depth and tend to provoke a more purposeful 'chomp'. We choose a lightly weighted pattern on a size 14 hook; dull, fawn coloured, more suggestive of the naturals than some concoctions displayed in the glossy pages which seem designed to drive fish into the next county.

Holding the rod horizontally we make a couple of false casts overland to our rear and shoot the line out to settle gently a yard or more from the trout's near flank. Arresting the line on its forward travel puts a curve in the leader, causing the nymph to land 4 feet ahead of his lie. If we've judged it right, the fly will sink to the fish's level and a little to his left, so the strike is more likely to set the hook firmly than if he were facing towards us. The trout moves across, we tighten smartly just before he turns back and play him as hard as we dare on a tight line, quickly slackening off on the two occasions he thrashes at the surface and once when he leaps into the air. What a prize, and a good deal larger than we thought at 17 inches and 2 lb 4 oz, but then trout usually appear smaller when viewed from this angle, quite the reverse of those we look down upon from a bridge. We weigh and measure this fish only because it is 'booked' for an elderly couple down the road; otherwise he would be unhooked while still underwater. Of the fish we originally spotted, four have gone to cover and the upper one at 12 oz will fit nicely into your frying pan – or mine! Either way, after such a tense session we feel we might call it a day. We have covered only a tiny proportion of the length available to us, but there is immense satisfaction to be gained from the knowledge that we have fished well, sparingly, leaving the great majority of the trout undisturbed. Some fisheries nowadays require anglers to cease fishing when they have secured a brace or so, whether or not the fish have been returned. This is to discourage what has been termed the 'numbers game', in which anglers sometimes place quantity above quality and the degree of challenge involved. The former can be arranged simply by tipping in more hand-reared stockies, but hunting truly wild trout possessing all their natural instincts for survival is, as Harry Plunket-Greene might have said, 'a poem of fair play and the chase'. One unwritten rule which is commonly ignored today is that we should, where possible, refrain from addressing undersized trout, either knowingly or by fishing the water at random. On returning to our car we find a note on the screen, politely reminding us that the tight parking spot will accommodate three vehicles. In our rush we had parked cross-ways! A seemingly minor crime perhaps, but humbly we vow that in future we'll always consider the needs of fellow members.

The following day it's back to typical English weather. A low pressure area has moved in and periods of heavy rain make us think twice about venturing out. But some optimist recently told us that such conditions can produce the kind of dry-fly fishing we dream about, so we'll give it a go. This time we delay our start until noon, for if it clears up later we may stay out for the evening rise. The length of river here is relatively deep, flowing smoothly at a steady pace except near the top where the inflow from a small tributary creates a lively 100-yd stickle. Fortunately, we have a modest fishing hut at the junction with the beat above where we can take shelter. There is a fair rise in progress, though somewhat intermittent and seldom in the same place twice. A few medium olives, pale wateries and blue-winged olives are hatching. So we select a suitable artificial with a CDC feather wound hackle fashion at the head, rather than a single tuft, knowing its buoyancy will be renewed after a drenching with just a couple of quick false casts. Since we cannot precisely pinpoint the trouts' positions we must take our cue from the last rise form, but apart from the occasional lunge and miss our efforts go unrewarded. After two and a half hours we're losing patience, fishing badly and end up thrashing water in all directions. Another thermos break is called for, after which we walk out in the meadow and back to the lower boundary.

What a difference. Here the fish are in rhythmic rising mode, each making rings in its chosen lie. Two or three species of dun are on the water, and by adopting a more controlled approach we are able to judge the whereabouts of the heavier fish, addressing them in turn. Big trout usually command a larger area of water and station themselves close to a convenient bolt hole. Also, in smooth water they often announce their presence by making a faint but audible 'sip', though the surface break may be so small we might assume they are dace. Two beauties come to net in this half-hour spell, weighing 1¼ and 2¾ lb, but sadly the rise then peters out. We have regained our equanimity however, so can rationally analyse our three-hour stint. The painful truth is that in our desire to 'get at 'em', we failed to read nature's signposts. In this case, beginning on the upper part of our beat was very understandable. Nevertheless, we should have twigged the situation earlier rather than waste over two hours of prime dry fly sport. Flies eclode more rapidly from broken, well-oxygenated water, but on slower or impounded stretches they have greater difficulty in freeing themselves from the nymphal shuck due to the clinging nature of the surface film.

Starting at the bottom of the beat offers the advantage that we can study the reach for some distance ahead, marking down risers as we go and approaching them unseen, whereas at the top we are inclined to keep looking back over the shoulder. We hear or see a rise behind us, then another, and before we know it we are working our way downriver, spooking fish. We may also be tempted to cast across and down. Well, there's nobody watching. But my old rough river tactics, though producing the odd tiddler perhaps, are wholly inappropriate in most chalk stream situations and may result in comments such as 'no fish in the river', 'trout not feeding' or 'about time they stocked' appearing in fishery record books!

We return to base for a wash and a change and enjoy a hearty supper. There's time enough, as the evening rise proper won't start until around 8.30 to 9 pm. We drive to a one-mile length which flows swiftly and is fairly shallow, with weed beds dividing the current into a series of streamy runs. This location is renowned for its blue-winged olive hatches and spinner falls. There are no beats here; we call it leapfrog water. Two other rods are out, one on the top stretch and the other 400 yards below him. The upper end is said to provide the cream of the fishing, so we walk upstream and ask the nearer angler whether we might begin by the bush 150 yards ahead. He agrees, generous sportsman that he is, but should we even have considered such a move? Perhaps he has previously marked down some sizeable trout and plans to revisit these in turn; or maybe he simply seeks solitude. Thank goodness we have second thoughts, wish him tight lines and retrace our steps. In the event we find a very attractive bit of water below and are rewarded with a hard fighting pounder on the BWO dun at sundown. Then in near darkness, having crossed the stream in order to look directly into the afterglow, two further bouncers come to the Sherry Spinner. Of course a number are missed or lost too, as ever in evening fishing, but we pick up valuable pointers along the way. First, it is important to know our fly's exact position among the naturals. A well-hackled pattern will help and often induces a vigorous take. The angle of vision can be crucial at last light; both the fly and the rise may be spotted more easily when stooping low with our eyes close to surface level. Our initial reaction to a take must involve decisive split second timing. The strike should be positive and hard enough to set the barb securely home. At late evening we may get away with using heavier nylon and with care can approach to within a rod's length of our quarry. Where weed beds flourish, trout are inches from safety, so when hooked must be instantly put off balance by applying immediate side strain. The fish seeks an alternative sanctuary, but we have gained the upper hand and need to keep firm control of his every movement. However, if he should plunge into thick vegetation it pays to work the net low among the roots and lift, rather than try going in from above. As for hand-lining, I've suffered more broken leaders this way than I care to remember. Such lessons come the hard way, but once learned are never forgotten, while each joyous outing adds a snippet or two to our little store of experiences.

We encountered little wind on this trip. "Good job too" you may say, yet many opportunities arise as the result of it. Much depends on the strength and direction, but we can usually 'engineer' situations in which even a gale becomes our ally. Terrestrial insects may be blown onto the glass edge near the bank, while aquatic flies are frequently concentrated along the windward margin. Certain bends and bays therefore become hot-spots, and by positioning ourselves for a gentle waft, roll or dap in which the line and fly are carried towards our target we could be in for some very exciting sport. By this means we can generally avoid pitching directly into the blast, while ruffled water disguises our presence to a degree. Trout are accustomed to swaying reeds and branches, so may take little notice of the rod waving nearby. We can also cheat the wind by employing a side cast at water level in the lee of the bank or any vegetation. Some feel there are occasions when an across and down delivery would seem perfectly sensible, especially on slower reaches where drag is unlikely to occur. We are normally prevented from doing this by the 'upstream only' rule, but perhaps there is scope for revision in certain cases? The main problem about relaxing any regulation, however, is that it may be the thin end of a very thick wedge and in this respect we anglers are sometimes our own worst enemies. If bending the rules is tolerated, what unbridled excesses might follow! Fishing clubs and societies hold regular meetings at which such subjects may be aired and votes taken following due discussion. This enables anyone seeking an amendment to attend, perhaps having canvassed the opinion of others, or alternatively send a written request to the Secretary that their proposal be considered.

Chalk stream fishermen come from far-flung regions, different walks of life and hold widely varying opinions. Lively debate ensues, controversy abounds, yet the common bond and mutual respect which exists enables us to discuss rationally those issues that might otherwise create an unbridgeable divide. A number of these have been touched upon in this chapter, yet others remain, some of which are the product of our increasingly urban lifestyles and the resulting disconnect between modern perceptions and the realities of life in the wild. My generation has been fortunate in this respect. Natural history was a part of our curriculum, 'red in tooth and claw'. It dealt with fundamental truths, whereas more recently – if the subject is broached at all – many children have been presented with a sanitised, sometimes wholly inaccurate, version which they can retain into adulthood. Media outlets often reinforce the 'cuddly' image, which in turn feeds into the general wildlife movement and may seriously affect the judgement of parents, teachers and decision-makers. Just last year, surrounded by acres of bluebells, I met a group of youngsters who informed me they were 'not allowed' to pick a bunch for Mothers' Day; and a fly fisherman who confessed he felt guilty after taking a couple of fish from a small Avon tributary so full of native trout that a degree of culling is clearly desirable. Such is the illogical thinking that can pervade a politically correct society!

That such a head of wild fish exists may come as a surprise to those who believe that regular top-ups are the norm on chalk streams. In fact, although introductions are certainly required on rivers where natural yields are poor, we now realise that the widespread stocking with sizeable trout carried out in the past was often counter-productive. The bulk of the resident trout may be displaced by stew-pond reared fish, which themselves are either caught or move downriver. Thus a void is created, sometimes lasting for weeks, between scheduled deliveries. Trickle stocking is the better option, although a majority of today's fly fishers appear to prefer waters to be managed for wild trout alone, possibly supplemented with locally bred fry or yearlings. It is heartening to hear that most clubs which have cut stocking levels on potentially fertile streams, or who have succeeded in breaking the self-perpetuating cycle altogether, have seen a corresponding increase both in the numbers and average weights of native fish. In either case, however, the wisdom of imposing blanket catch-and-release is questionable, not least because it may strengthen the case of the anti-fishing brigade who insist that we inflict pain or distress on living creatures simply for our amusement. My personal view, whether or not we wish to return our catch, is that trout fishermen should retain the option of taking up to whatever limit the club agrees is sustainable. Fishing has been called 'the blameless sport', the purest form of hunting, whose very essence on chalk streams is to stalk trout in one-to-one combat and enjoy the fruits in moderation.

Words like compassion and fairness cannot be applied to the natural world. It is dog-eat-dog out there. It has been estimated that on most chalk streams fewer than one percent of trout reach maturity, though we must remember here that nature over-produces to compensate for a huge wastage. Of the 99 percent which perish, the great majority fall victim to predators. Birds and mammals account for many, but the heaviest inroads are made by their piscine neighbours, notably pike and perch. We used to remove large numbers of coarse fish each autumn by electro-fishing, while keepers were also paid per head for those killed as part of their routine duties (and that included herons). Today, were it thought necessary, the Wildlife Trusts and similar groups whose mission is to protect native creatures – and who now exercise greater influence over keepering methods – would strenuously oppose any such move. Nonetheless, the fact remains that these practices significantly reduced predation levels in what are essentially 'mixed' rivers, while the removal of grayling (or their mass exodus, as in the droughts of 1975 and 1976) allowed the trout more space and freedom to feed unhindered. The grayling came back in force when flows returned the following autumn, but my diaries record that in their absence during the 1977 season on the Wylye, the trout were in finer condition and rose more consistently in open water than I'd known since I began there ten years earlier.

For all our pub talk and fishing hut chat, however, moral questions must remain a matter for each individual. Few would advocate a return to the tight controls of yesteryear, yet the knowledge we've gained over the last four decades helps us to develop new ideas and formulate new policies which, though compromise is inevitable, will ensure that our chalk streams continue to offer some of the best trout, grayling and coarse fishing in the world. Improved access enables more anglers to participate than ever before, while our growing understanding of nature's wondrous yet complex workings brings a fresh sense of optimism to beginners and old stagers alike.

Chapter Three

The Entomology of Chalk Streams

Dr. Cyril Bennett

It was over fifty years ago that I cast my first dry fly; fascinated by a method of fishing that demanded the right choice of fly to match the natural, I spent many years trying to perfect this art and where better to do it than on the rivers where it was first developed.

The English chalk streams possess some of the richest and most diverse communities of aquatic insect life to be found in the British Isles, supporting and enhancing the spectacular wildlife that we have always associated with these delightful rivers and streams. The aquifers deep within the chalk provide a constant flow of cool, clear and slightly alkaline water to give a unique and stable environment for the optimum growth of both plants and aquatic insects; and how fortunate we are to have them because, apart from those across the channel in Normandy, they are found nowhere else on Earth.

We therefore have a responsibility to preserve these very special habitats and not least because only with a rich and diverse aquatic insect life can we enjoy the genuinely challenging dry fly fishing for which our chalk streams have always been world renowned. For a feeding trout to become preoccupied with a particular fly, that species needs to be there in vast numbers and this is when our entomology skills are needed to select a good match for that blue-winged olive or iron blue drifting down on the current.

"*There is more to fishing than catching fish*", first quoted by Dame Juliana Berner, the First Lady of Fly Fishing, over five hundred years ago, is as true today as it was then. Chalk stream fly fishing is about matching your artificial to the natural fly, otherwise it just descends into catching fish; and you can do that with a worm! Over the years and with careful observations the great giants of chalk streams fishing: Halford, Skues, Lunn, Marryat, Goddard, Kite, and Sawyer all developed various imitations to match the natural chalk stream flies, many of which are known throughout the world. However, over the past twenty years, the fly life on some of our chalk streams has declined to such an extent that the challenge of dry fly fishing has diminished; finding even one consistently rising fish can often be difficult. Some species of fly that were commonly found in huge numbers are now just a shadow of what they once were and others may no longer be present at all. Not only do we need to identify where these losses have occurred, we also need to bring back these species to their former glory and that is to a level far above that accepted by the statutory bodies as a basic 'Good Ecological Status'.

Fortunately the Wiltshire Avon and its tributaries still have good populations of river flies (up-winged flies [mayflies], caddis flies and stoneflies), all of which are of enormous importance to the fly fisherman. But we must not be complacent because with increasing pressures on our chalk streams we could so easily lose these as well.

Insects Found on the Chalk Streams

Life cycle of freshwater insects

The life cycle of freshwater insects consists of two main types: those that pass through a complete metamorphosis, with a pupa stage, and those groups with an incomplete metamorphosis and no pupa stage. The former group includes the caddis flies (Trichoptera), midges (Chironomidae) and reed smuts (Simuliidae), and those in the latter group consist of the more primitive mayflies (Ephemeroptera), stoneflies (Plecoptera) and dragonflies (Odonata).

The Mayflies or Up-winged Flies (Ephemeroptera)

As the large *Ephemera danica* mainly emerge in May, English anglers have understandably given it the common name of 'mayfly' with the term 'up-winged flies' used to refer to the whole of the Ephemeroptera. This has led to a certain amount of confusion because apart from anglers in the UK, both entomologists and anglers throughout the world all use the general term 'mayfly' to describe all the Ephemeroptera. As I am both an angler and an entomologist, I tend to use both terms interchangeably, but for clarity in this chapter I will keep my English fly-fishing hat on and refer to them as 'up-winged flies'.

Upwinged Life Cycle (Incomplete life cycle)

The up-winged flies are an extremely primitive order and the oldest of the winged insects to appear on the planet. There is no pupa stage in the life cycle and they pass directly from the larval (nymph) stage to the adult. They are also totally unique in having two adult (winged) stages, the sub-imago (dun) and the imago (spinner). There have been a number of theories as to why the second adult moult is necessary and it could be that they are beginning to evolve out of it because the sub-imago stage of the *Caenis* species lasts just a few minutes.

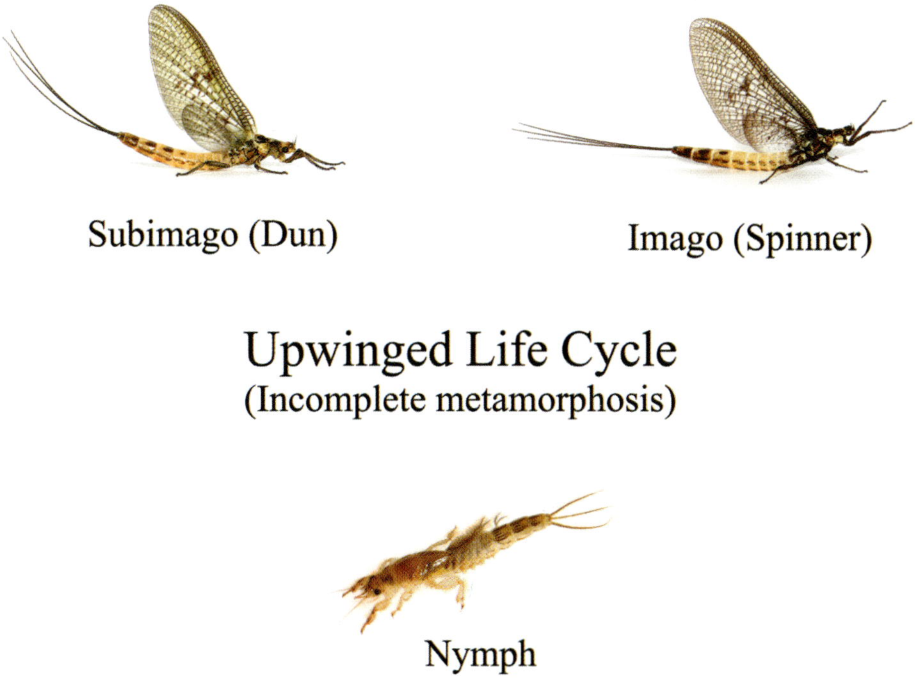

© C.J. Bennett

The adult stage is purely for reproduction and as they cannot feed, they have to rely on the energy reserves built up during the larval stage; this severely reduces the time available to find a mate and lay the eggs. The bodies of females are packed full of eggs, with the internal organs pushed to one side as they are no longer needed. As the eggs need to 'stick' to a substratum (weeds, stones etc.), they have various forms of attachment structures which are activated on contact with the water; in many cases the shape of these structures are specific to a species and can be used for identification. The adhesive qualities of the eggs exist for a relatively short period (about twelve hours) and if the eggs have not attached during this period, they never will. There is also evidence that deterioration in water quality can undermine these adhesive qualities causing the eggs to become detached from the substratum.

Attachment structures of Caenis eggs

The Mayfly (*Ephemera danica*)

I don't think anyone can be in any doubt about 'the' mayfly (*Ephemera danica*) and although there are two similar species with which it could be confused, neither occurs on the chalk streams. The mayfly is far larger than any of the other up-winged flies and the enormous hatches during the main emergent period in May are a common sight on most of our chalk streams. Whilst other up-winged flies have declined, mayfly populations have generally remained intact and on some waters may even have increased.

It is generally recorded as having a two-year life cycle, but increasing water temperatures on some rivers have pushed the mayfly towards a one year cycle. This results in smaller females producing fewer eggs and there is also a danger that with a long, wet and windy spring (the main emergent period) most, if not all, of a population could be lost. However, on the generally cooler waters of the chalk streams, a mainly two year life cycle still seems to be operating.

Females produce up to 6000 eggs (depending on body length) and, depending on water temperatures, these will hatch in about 24 days; large numbers of tiny nymphs can then be seen amongst the larger second year nymphs in September and October. The nymphs are 'burrowers' and with the aid of their modified mandibles, they excavate and live in 'U'-shaped tubes. Their long feathery gills create a current of water through the tube bringing not only oxygenated water, but also small particles of rotting vegetation (detritus), on which they feed. Therefore large numbers of nymphs can be found in the sediments beneath weed beds, where they have a constant supply of food.

There are a great many imitations that can be used to match the mayfly and everyone usually has their favourite; Lunn produced three and Goddards's Poly May Dun (for the sub-imago) and Poly May Spinner (for the imago) are probably as good as any. Whilst there are also imitations for the nymph, these are not normally allowed on the chalk streams at this time of the year and why would we want to anyway when fishing the dry probably gives us some of the most exciting fishing of the season? The mayfly is one of the relatively few up-winged flies to retain three tails in the adult; most lose the middle tail during the moult to adult.

The Olives (various *Baëtis* species)

Commonly known to anglers just as 'olives' in reference to their basic body colour and with a qualification relating to size and/or shade of colour to distinguish one from another, these consist of the large dark olive (*B. rhodani*), medium olive (*B. vernus*) and the small dark olive (*B. scambus*); there are also two other species that are not so commonly known, the dark olive (*B. atrebatinus*) and the scarce olive (*B. buceratus*). The olives can be found throughout the season although the large dark olive is most evident (and usually much larger) in the early spring when it is often the only fly on the water. The medium olive is a common fly on the chalk streams usually peaking in May and June, whilst the small dark olive tends to be more common in July and August. The adults tend to be smaller and paler as the season progresses, which is probably due to higher water temperatures.

The imagoes (spinners) are commonly known as the 'large red spinner' (large dark olive), 'red spinner' (medium olive) and the 'small red spinner' (small dark olive). The females go under the water to lay their eggs after which most are swept away on the current. All three species produce a number of generations a year, but whilst the large dark olive overwinter as nymphs, the other two overwinter in the egg stage. The adults of all of the *Baëtis* species have two tails.

The nymphs of all three species look very similar and belong to a group commonly known as 'agile darters' due to their rapid movements as they swim between weed-beds etc. They feed on algae which they scrape from the surface of plants and stones and large dark olive nymphs are often crammed full of the spring flush of diatoms which can often give them a yellow appearance.

As all of the adults are also very similar in appearance, they can be represented with the same pattern of fly but in varying sizes and there is a whole range to choose from including the Olive Quill or Greenwell's Glory for the dun and Lunn's Particular or Pheasant Tail for the spinner.

The Iron Blue Dun (*B. muticus*, *B. niger*)

The iron blue consists of two species, although there is a third which is much rarer and probably not found on the chalk streams. Although this is one of the smaller up-winged flies, iron blue adults are easily recognised due to their dark colouration. They are of great importance to the fly fisherman because when iron blues are on the water, the trout will generally feed on it to the exclusion of all else.

Although now much reduced, enormous hatches of iron blue duns were once common on the chalk streams. Suddenly these small 'inky blue' flies would cover the entire surface of the river, with trout seemingly trying to take every one of them for as far down river as you could see and then, just as quickly, the hatch would be over with not a rise in sight. This could happen at any time of the day, even in the early morning, and if the angler didn't have a good imitation, presented well, the hatch could be over without a single offer. Sadly, those large hatches now seem to be a thing of the past and in fact the southern iron blue (*B. niger*) is now listed as a rarity, although a few can still be found on the Wiltshire Avon.

The nymphs can be distinguished from the olives by their much narrower bodies and the southern iron blue has a pale stripe running down the whole length of its back and black bars in the tails. They are found amongst the in-stream vegetation and gravel in the riffle areas of the river. They feed by scraping algae from the surface of plants and stones and by collecting fine particulate organic detritus matter from the sediments.

Both species produce two generations a year, a slow-growing winter generation and a much faster growing summer generation with adults on the water between May and October. There are numerous suitable imitations of the adults, all called 'Iron Blue Dun', and Lunn's Houghton Ruby is a good imitation of the spinner.

The Pale Watery (*B. fuscatus*).

The pale watery is quite a small fly and as the name suggests, they tend to be much paler than the olives. Adults can be found on the water during most of the summer months and it is generally recorded as having one generation a year with overwintering eggs. However, with the large emergence of adults now being seen late in the year (after the season has ended), it is likely there is an additional late summer generation.

Apart from their generally paler colour, the females cannot be distinguished from other *Baëtis* species, but males can easily be identified by their bright yellow eyes. Whilst it is generally thought that the females crawl down below the water to lay their eggs (as with the other *Baëtis* species), some authorities think they are released at the surface. A good imitation for the dun is the Little Marryat and a Lunn's Yellow Boy for the spinner.

The nymphs belong to the 'agile darter' group and are chiefly found in the weed and gravel beds in the riffles of the river. They feed on algae scraped from the aquatic plants and fine organic detritus collected from the sediments.

The Small Spurwing (*Centroptilum luteolum*)

This is a very common fly found on most of the chalk streams. As it is a small and generally very pale fly, it is often confused with the pale watery; in fact at one time it was known as the little sky-blue pale watery. However, on close examination it can easily be identified by the presence of the small 'spur-shaped' hind-wings. Also, in contrast to the bright yellow eyes of pale watery males, small spurwing males have bright orange/red eyes. From an angling point of view they are so similar to the pale watery that the same pattern of fly can be used.

There are two generations a year, a slow growing overwintering population, which emerges in the spring and a faster growing population that emerges during the summer; they can therefore be seen on the water for most of the season. Emergence takes place during the day at the surface and male spinners can be seen swarming just above the surface. Once mated the female flies onto the water to release in the region of 2500 eggs and then falls 'spent' onto the water.

Nymphs are normally found in the more sluggish areas of the river, swimming in short darting bursts and climbing amongst the vegetation where they feed on algae and plant detritus.

The Large Spurwing (*Procloeon pennulatum*)

Although never found in large numbers, the large spurwing used to be a common sight on the chalk streams but is now seldom seen and may no longer be present. Both of the spurwings have two tails, but the large spurwing is the only up-winged fly that sits with its wings separated at rest. It is generally thought that there is just one generation a year with overwintering eggs.

The Pale Evening Dun (*Procloeon bifidum*)

The pale evening dun is a really lovely fly and the palest of all of the up-winged flies. It has a light straw-coloured body and pale grey wings; the male is one of the few flies with yellow eyes although not as bright as the pale watery. As the name suggests, adults tend to emerge during the evening and look very similar to the pale watery and small spurwing, but have a greenish tinge to the leading edge of the forewings. Whilst a pale watery artificial can be used effectively, Major Oliver Kite perfected an excellent pattern which he simply called the Pale Evening Dun. This is one of only two up-winged flies that have no hind-wings, the other being the much darker pond olive.

Very little is known about this species except that adults have been seen during most of the summer months but never in large numbers and this is another species that may have disappeared from many of our chalk streams; I have not seen one for many years. It is thought to have more than one generation a year, with overwintering eggs. The nymphs are chiefly found in the slower flowing sections of the river.

The Pond Olive (*Cloeon dipterum*)

As the name suggests, this very common fly is mainly found in still waters but is included here because with reducing flows it is increasingly being found on the chalk streams. This is clearly not a good sign. It is a medium-sized fly and apart from the eyes, which have red lines across the centre, they look very much like the other olives and for imitation purposes, can be treated as such. The adults have no hind-wings and this is the only up-winged fly that gives birth to live young (ovoviviparous); when the eggs are released on the surface of the water they immediately hatch and swim away.

The Yellow May Dun (*Heptagenia sulphurea*)

A medium sized and very distinctive yellow fly, a few of which can often be seen emerging amongst the large mayfly hatches in the spring; there is also a slower growing cohort that emerges in August and September. It is a fly that is far more common on upland rivers, where Peter Lapsley's Yellow May Dun is a useful pattern.

The nymphs are very distinctive, having large eyes on the top of their heads and flattened bodies, which gives them the general name of 'stone clingers'. This enables them to keep low and cling to the rocks out in the faster riffles of the river, where they feed on algae and organic detritus. The nymphs are generally dark in appearance but turn yellow as they mature; they occasionally swim with a rather laboured 'jerking' movement.

There are only two other yellow up-winged flies; the scarce yellow may dun (*Heptagenia longicauda*), which is so scarce that it is now probably extinct in the UK; and the yellow mayfly (*Potamanthus luteus*) which is now only found on the lower reaches of the Welsh Wye, although a single adult was found a few years ago on the Test at Wherwell, so there is a possibility that it could still be found on the chalk streams. It can be distinguished from the yellow may dun because it is much larger and has 'three' tails, whilst all of the *Heptageniidae* family only have two. The nymphs are burrowers and similar in appearance to mayfly nymphs except the gills stick straight out from the side of the body. The spinner is a lovely apricot colour.

The Autumn Dun (*Ecdyonurus dispar*)

The nymph of the autumn dun is another of the 'stone clingers' found in the riffle areas of the river clinging to submerged plants and rocks. The adults are slightly larger than the yellow may dun and as the name suggests, they appear later in the season (from July onwards) but never in large numbers. It has one generation a year with overwintering nymphs.

The Large Green Dun (*Ecdyonurus insignis*)

I wouldn't normally have included this fly because it is usually only found on upland rivers, but having travelled to Cornwall to photograph it a few years ago (without success), I found a small population on the river Nadder. It is therefore possible that it is present at other sites in the Wiltshire Avon catchment. The adult is relatively large and, as the name suggests, slightly green; both the nymph and the adult have distinct markings (lines and dots) on the abdomen. It has one generation a year with overwintering nymphs which are similar to the two previous species described, but larger.

The Olive Upright (*Rhithrogena semicolorata*)

Usually a fly of the upland rivers, but quite a large population can be found in the upper reaches of the chalk streams. Adults look very similar to the olives although they have much larger hind-wings. Both the nymph and the adult have distinctive spots on the legs which are unique to this genus. Its big brother, the March brown (*Rhithrogena germanica*) is not found on the chalk streams.

The Angler's Curse (*Caënis species*)

This family consists of nine species, all of which are rather small (5-6mm) and difficult to separate, therefore, for angling purposes, all are known by the common name of 'angler's curse' or just *Caenis*; the Last Hope is usually the artificial pattern used. The dun (sub-imago) stage of these species is extremely brief, usually lasting just a few minutes. The adults have three tails.

The Blue-winged Olive (*Serratella ignita*)

This is one of the most important flies for the chalk stream angler, providing good sport on summer evenings when duns emerge and female spinners (sherry spinners) return to the water to lay their eggs in huge numbers. Females also return to the water in the early morning although there are seldom any anglers there to take advantage of it. Unfortunately, this fly has suffered great losses on the chalk streams in recent years.

It is a small to medium-sized fly with three tails and wings that appear to be slightly larger and out of proportion to the body; the duns have a slight orange tinge; hence the Latin name '*ignita*'. The colour of the spinners can vary from a light brown to brick red, depending on age and they have a unique way of depositing the eggs which are attached to the rear part of the abdomen (as an egg ball) and dropped into the riffle areas of the river. This fly is usually recorded as having one generation a year with mainly overwintering eggs, but recent research on the Wiltshire Avon has shown two and maybe even multiple generations a year. There are numerous patterns used to imitate this fly including Lunn's Blue-winged Olive Variant and Orange Quill Variant for the dun and Lunn's Early Evening and Late Evening Sherry Spinner for the spinner.

The Turkey Brown (*Paraleptophlebia submarginata*)

Whilst never seen in large numbers, the turkey brown, with its dark mottled wings and three tails, is often seen on the chalk streams. There are two other closely related species, but both are somewhat rare; the purple dun (*P. cincta*) which can easily be mistaken for an iron blue, except that it has three tails not two; and the scarce purple dun (*P. werneri*) which is restricted to the parts of the Winterbournes that dry up, such as the upper reaches of the river Till and whilst this fly is of little interest to the fly fisherman, it is an extremely rare fly found at only two other locations in the British Isles and with reducing flow rates, its habitat is under considerable threat.

The nymphs have long 'strap-like' gills and long tails which are characteristic of this family. They are poor swimmers and therefore chiefly restricted to the pools and margins of the river where they feed on fine organic detritus collected from the sediments.

The Caddis Flies (*Trichoptera*)

The caddis flies (or sedge flies) resemble moths in their general appearance and are in fact related to moths. They are a large group with nearly two hundred British species, many of which have no common names. Although this is an important group of flies, apart from a few notable exceptions, most are so similar in appearance that it is quite unnecessary for the angler to identify each species. Therefore only those of most importance to the angler, those which he is likely to come into contact with, will be described here and relatively few artificial patterns, based on size and colour, are needed.

Caddis Fly Life Cycle (Complete life cycle)

The eggs hatch into tiny larvae and there are two main groups, those that build cases (cased) and those that do not (caseless); both need to construct a cocoon in which to pupate. The material used for the construction of the case can be twigs, sand grains, plant material and even small snail shells; in some cases, the shape and type of material used for the case is characteristic of a species. Those that need to be out in the faster water (*Goeridae*) attach larger stones to the side of the case for ballast. Although a case obviously gives some protection to the larva, the main purpose is respiratory, providing a more efficient exchange of oxygen from the water circulating within the case. Caseless caddis larvae are either free roaming such as the sand fly (*Rhyacophila dorsalis*) or they construct 'nets' of silk to ensnare their food; the shape of these nets varies with species and local conditions such as water velocity.

When ready to pupate, the case is anchored with silk to a firm substratum and the larva spins a silk cocoon in which pupation takes place. After a couple of weeks or so, the pupa cuts its way out and swims to the surface to emerge as the adult. Although there are occasions when imitations of the larvae can be useful, it is the swimming pupae and the adults that are of most interest to the fly fisherman. Although unable to eat solid food, adults can drink water and nectar using their simple mouth parts and this extends the adult phase.

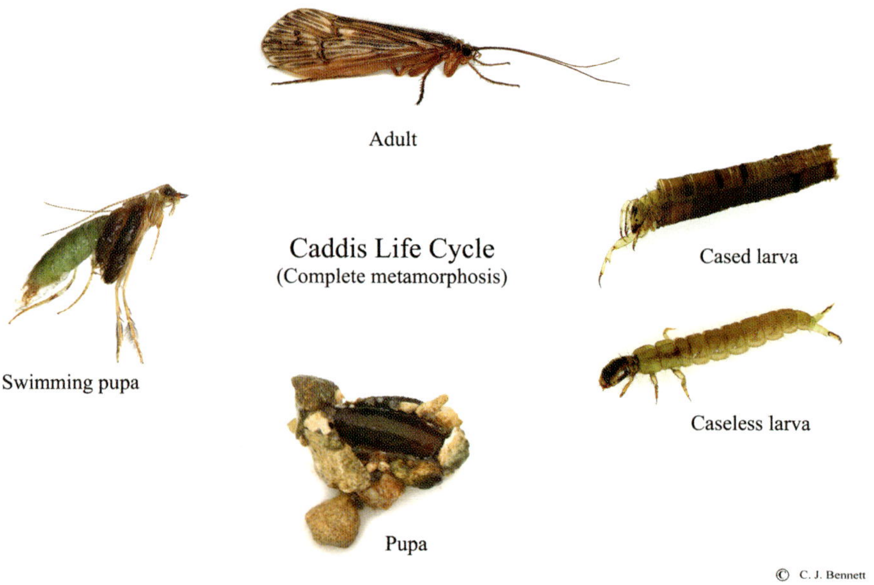

The Caperer (*Halesus* species)

The caperer is one of the largest caddis flies (up to 22mm) found on the chalk streams. It is a distinctive fly with deep veining in the rear part of its wings and is commonly seen on the water in late August and September. Its name comes from the behaviour of the females rising and dipping on the water whilst laying their eggs and on warm summer evenings large numbers can be seen engaged in this activity. Lunn produced both a winged and hackled imitation of the caperer both of which are excellent.

The Cinnamon Sedge (*Limnephilus lunatus*)

'Cinnamon sedge' is a generic name used for a group of sedges all of which are common and extremely abundant on the chalk streams from late June to September. Probably the most common is *L. lunatus*, which has blotches on the wings and a distinctive crescent moon shaped mark at the tip; hence its Latin name. Once again, Lunn designed an excellent imitation of this fly.

The Sand Fly (*Rhyacophila dorsalis*)

This is one of the earliest sedge flies to appear on the water and can be seen from April right through to autumn. It is a very common species and emerges throughout the day, but it can be difficult to identify as the colour and size can vary considerably.

The Brown Silverhorn (*Athripsodes cinereus*)

This very common sedge is found on most rivers in the United Kingdom, including the chalk streams. The adults have very long antennae, up to three times the length of the body, and a habit of flying rapidly (and in large swarms) just above the surface of the water in the evening, but they never seem to land on it. There is also a closely related species (*A. albifrons*) which has distinctive white markings on the wings and is also commonly found on the chalk streams.

The Grannom (*Brachycentrus subnubilus*)

This sedge is well-known to anglers as it is a day-flying sedge and is the first to appear on the water in April. On some rivers, like the Avon at Salisbury, they can emerge in such huge numbers that it is hard to see across the river, but on other rivers, perhaps due to heavy weed-cutting, it has all but disappeared. The larvae in their distinctive square cases attach themselves to weeds out in the main current where they filter particles from the water stream with their second and third legs. There now seem to be very few on the River Test, but as the season is still closed during the main emergent period this is probably of little interest to Test anglers.

The grannom is a small to medium-size sedge with a fawn/grey appearance and after fertilisation the eggs at the rear end of females give the body a distinct green colour giving rise to its other name of green-tail fly. The females, which are larger than the males, go under the water to lay their eggs which can often be seen covering the weed beds in large numbers. There are a number of artificial patterns representing this important fly with one pattern going as far back as the seventeenth century.

The Brown Sedge (*Anabolia nervosa*)

This is a medium-sized sedge of a mid-brown colour and it is very common on the chalk streams where it often appears in the evenings in quite large swarms. It is generally an autumn emerging species, but the odd specimen can appear earlier.

The Black Sedge (*Silo nigricornis*)

Quite a common, medium-sized sedge (11-13mm) and obviously very dark in colour. It is a day-flying insect, with adults on the water between June and September; usually flying rapidly over the water.

The Welshman's Button (*Sericostoma personatum*)

Although the common name was originally used to refer to a type of beetle, for some reason Halford used the name 'Welshman's button' to describe this sedge and the name has stuck (this highlights one of the problems with the use of common names).

Judging by the large numbers of curved case larvae that are always found in kick-net samples, this has to be one of the commonest sedge flies found on the chalk streams. It is a medium–sized day-flying sedge (10-15mm), with a distinctive shaped head; it normally appears on the water in late spring and can be seen until mid-summer.

The Stoneflies (Plecoptera)

Apart from a few species, the stoneflies are not well-represented on the chalk streams. Most of the thirty-four British species occur in stony, fast flowing and well-oxygenated upland rivers, where they are of great importance to the fly fisherman.

Like the up-winged flies, the stoneflies are a primitive group which have an incomplete life cycle (without a pupa stage). The nymphs can easily be distinguished from other larvae by their long antennae and two tails, giving them a somewhat 'earwig-like' appearance and as the name suggests, they are found amongst the stones and gravel of the river bed.

Stonefly Life Cycle (Incomplete life cycle)

When ready to emerge, the nymph usually crawls out of the water where the skin splits and the adult emerges. The adults look very much like a winged nymph and are light to dark brown in colour with a few having a yellow tinge to them. The hind-wings are a similar size to the fore-wings, which are held flat along the back at rest. They are not strong fliers and tend to fly straight to the nearest refuge.

Adult

Stonefly Life Cycle
(Incomplete metamorphosis)

Nymph

There are only three stoneflies that are commonly found on the chalk streams:

The Yellow Sally (*Isoperla grammatica)*)

This is a medium-sized fly (9-13mm), and is easily recognised by its conspicuous yellow/green wings. It is found on the chalk streams for most of the season but never in any great numbers. There are many different artificial patterns but it would not be worth carrying more than one on a chalk stream and even that might not be much use.

The Willow Fly (*Leuctra geniculate*)

This is a small to medium fly (7-9mm) which is commonly found on the chalk streams late in the season (August-November). The adults have slim bodies, brown wings and distinct whorls of 'hairs' around each segment of the long antenna. There are a number of artificial patterns that can be used for the adult, including one designed by Skues.

The Needle Fly (*Leuctra fusca*)

There are actually two species of needle fly which are almost identical, but as one of them only occurs between February and April it is of little interest to the chalk stream angler. The 'late' needle fly emerges at the same time as the willow fly and is very similar; the same artificial would therefore suffice.

Other Chalk Stream Flies

The Midges (*Chironomidae*)

The 'non-biting' midges (buzzers or plumed gnats) are probably more common than any other freshwater fly. They are found in all types of habitat from water-butts and gutters right up to the largest lakes, where up to 50,000 per square metre have been recorded. On the chalk streams, tiny adults can be seen swarming over the water in enormous numbers just before dark and each swarm can consist of numerous species in a whole range of colours; over 1,500 species have been recorded in Europe.

Being so small, they are somewhat difficult to imitate but artificial patterns can be used in a range of colours to imitate both the hatching pupa and the adult. Newly hatched adults tend to fly off the water very quickly and females returning to lay their eggs tend to drop them whilst hovering above the water.

The Reed Smuts (*Simuliidae*)

Unlike midges, reed smuts (or blackflies) are only found on rivers with a good flow. Large numbers of the larvae can be seen attached by a silken thread to stones and weeds where they filter feed with the aid of a fan of bristles held out into the current. The adults resemble tiny house flies and, like mosquitos, the female needs a blood meal before the eggs can develop. They are therefore notorious 'biters' and one species, known as the Blandford fly, has been known to hospitalise people. Although trout can often become preoccupied with feeding on the adults, they are generally too small to imitate or to even be noticed by the fly fisherman, apart from the occasional sharp reminder from one of the females.

The Crane-Flies (*Tipulidae*)

The crane-flies (or daddy long-legs) need no introduction and are a familiar and welcome sight on the river, particularly late in the season when they can provide some exciting fishing. There are over three hundred British species with wingspan sizes ranging from 15mm right up to 65mm. Although generally thought of as a terrestrial fly, many species are aquatic.

The Hawthorne Fly (*Bibio marci*)

The hawthorne fly is also known as St Mark's fly because it tends to start hatching around St Mark's Day (25th April). This early season terrestrial fly is easily recognised in flight due to its dark colour (black) and long trailing rear legs. At a time when there is often little else to bring the trout up to the surface, it can provide some excellent sport when large numbers are blown onto the water during windy conditions.

There are a number of other small black terrestrial flies that can end up on the water throughout the season and these are generally grouped under the generic name of 'black gnat'.

The Alder Fly (*Sialis spp.*)

This is a common fly on most waters with adults generally appearing in the early part of the season. It looks very much like a dark sedge, with very distinctive veining in the wings, but they belong to a totally different order of insects. The larvae are normally found in the silted areas of the river and are ferocious carnivores. The adult can be represented by a dark sedge pattern.

Protecting Our Fly Life

If we are concerned about our chalk streams, then we need to know as much as possible about their present condition and perhaps more than anything else this includes the fly life because, being at the bottom end of the food chain, losses here will affect everything above it. If we don't know what we have, then how will we know if or when we lose it? And if we do lose it, how do we put it back?

Over the past twenty years or more there has been a significant decline in fly populations, not only on our chalk streams but also on many other rivers throughout the country. 'Nature abhors a vacuum' and a pollution incident that eliminates most of the pollution sensitive up-winged flies, stoneflies and caddis flies will leave gaps which, if not filled by downstream drift from fly populations above the pollution site, will be filled by species that reproduce quickly, such as freshwater shrimp (*Gammarus*). Whilst this provides plenty of subsurface food for the trout and other fish, it gives little sport for the dry fly fisherman and this shift in the invertebrate community can be difficult to reverse. River enhancements can improve such things as egg-laying and feeding sites for existing fly

Chalk Stream Flies
(Larvae)

Chalk Stream Flies
(Adults)
Large Dark Olive
Baetis rhodani
Medium Olive
Baetis vernus
Large Spurwing
Procloeon pennulatum
Olive Upright
Rhithrogena semicolorata
Small Dark Olive
Baetis scambus
Iron Blue
Baetis muticus
Small Spurwing
Centroptilum luteolum
Blue Winged Olive
Serratella ignita
Southern Iron Blue
Baetis niger
Pale Watery
Baetis fuscatus
Pond Olive
Cloeon dipterum
Turkey Brown
Paraleptophlebia submarginata
Scarce Purple Dun
Paraleptophlebia werneri
Mayfly (Green Drake)
Ephemera danica
Angler's Curse
Caenis macrura
Autumn Dun
Ecdyonurus dispar
Large Green Dun
Ecdyonurus insignis
Yellow Mayfly
Potamanthus luteus
Yellow May Dun
Heptagenia sulphurea
Alder
Sialis spp.
Welshman's Button
Sericostoma personatum
Grannom
Brachycentrus subnubilus
Cinnamon Sedge
Limnephilus lunatus
Caperer
Halesus radiatus
Brown Sedge
Anabolia nervosa
Brown Silverhorn
Athripsodes cinereus
Black Sedge
Silo nigrocornis
Midges
Chironomid spp.
Willow Fly
Leuctra geniculater
Cranefly
Tipulidae spp.
Hawthorne
Bibio marci
© C. J. Bennett

populations, but will do little or nothing to replace a population that has been lost or greatly reduced.

Over the past ten years there has been a wide range of reasons given for the decline in fly populations; various kinds of pollution, water abstraction, increasing water temperatures, sedimentation etc., but the problem remains and we still have no answers. In many cases we don't even know when we have a problem because whilst a fish kill is usually picked up quickly, an invertebrate kill is not. The release of an insecticide into the river Wey in 2002 left the river 'looking' in perfect order whilst virtually all of the invertebrate population was lost for over 15 miles downstream. A later survey showed that most of the fish had moved off due to a lack of food.

Picture of R. Wey after pollution incident

So how do we detect these pollution incidents?

Monitoring water quality

The Environment Agency (EA) has a statutory responsibility to monitor the water quality of our rivers, taking both chemical and invertebrate samples. Whilst a chemical sample will show how clean the water is at the precise time the sample was taken, it cannot reveal what the water quality was like at any time before the sample was taken. As freshwater invertebrates have to live in the water, they are continuously sampling the water and a serious pollution incident that decimates a population will leave behind a 'fingerprint' long after the water quality has improved. For this reason, periodic samples are taken of the invertebrate community using a detailed scoring system based on each group's sensitivity to pollution; up-winged flies, caddis flies and stoneflies, which are the most sensitive, score the highest.

However, over the years and with more and more cutbacks, the regularity of this monitoring has been reduced to such an extent that pollution incidents can now easily go unrecorded. In fact, the above incident on the River Wey would have gone unrecorded had it not been picked up by an angler using the Angler's Monitoring Initiative (AMI). This is a simplified form of the EA system, developed at Leckford on the River Test and uses the flies that anglers are most familiar with and which also happen to be very sensitive to pollution. By taking a single sample once a month (taking about 30 minutes), a club or other group of concerned anglers can keep a regular check on their water quality. A serious pollution incident that might otherwise have gone undetected can then be picked up and reported to the EA. A number of incidents have been successfully dealt with using this system. AMI is now used at over two hundred sites in the UK and one-day workshops are run at Leckford and throughout the country by the Riverfly Partnership to train anglers (and others) to use this system.

The demise of the blue-winged olive

Apart from the mayfly (*Ephemera danica*), the blue-winged olive is probably the best-known fly on our chalk streams, providing good sport during the long summer evenings when large numbers of females return to lay their eggs. Whilst this fly has been seriously depleted on many of our rivers, including the chalk streams, the Wiltshire Avon still has a large population and this provides a unique opportunity to study this fly in detail. A two-year research project has been carried out which has revealed some important information.

The blue-winged olive has always been recorded as having just one generation a year with overwintering eggs, but weekly monitoring of the population size and growth rates at two sites at West Amesbury clearly showed at least two generations a year. Rapid growth in nymphs was recorded from early May right through to November, with eggs still being seen in mature nymphs in the middle of November. Monitoring the development stages of the eggs also confirmed a second generation because whilst the development in most of the

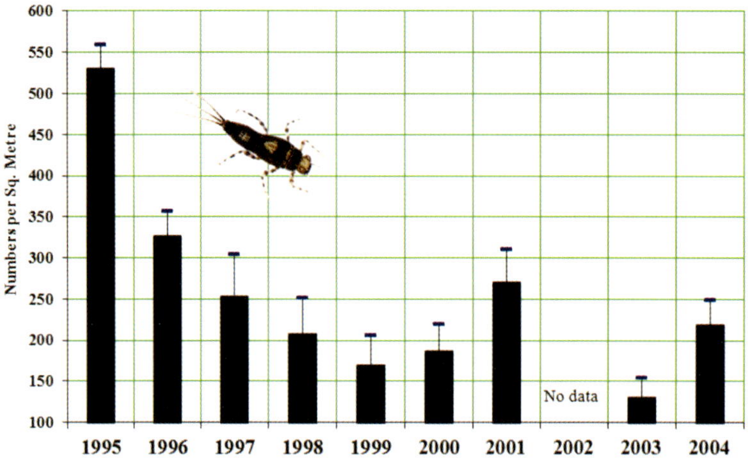

Decline in the blue-winged olive (Serratella ignita) *on the River Test at Leckford.*
(Error bars indicate 95% confidence limits)

eggs was, quite normally, suspended in the penultimate stage (to enter 'diapause'), some were hatching immediately, producing a second generation.

Monitoring of eggs in the river over the winter period showed a build-up of silt on the surface of the eggs. Whilst this had no direct detrimental effect on the eggs, it slowly undermined their adhesive quality causing large numbers to become dislodged and lost as they were washed downstream. Therefore, even under normal conditions, very large numbers of eggs are lost during the egg stage but those remaining are adequate to maintain the size of the population. However, with increased sedimentation and/or higher phosphate levels, a population could easily be decimated.

Restoring Fly Populations

Improving fly populations is not something new. Nearly a hundred years ago the world-renowned river keeper William Lunn was increasing the fly populations on the River Test at Houghton. After he noticed that most of the female olives go under the water to lay their eggs, he pioneered the use of fly boards to provide additional sites for egg-laying females. Within a short time of placing a fly board out in the main current of the river, the underside is covered in countless millions of eggs; the board can then be moved and used to restore the fly life at another site. Lunn also used large numbers of mayfly eggs to bring back a lost population at Houghton.

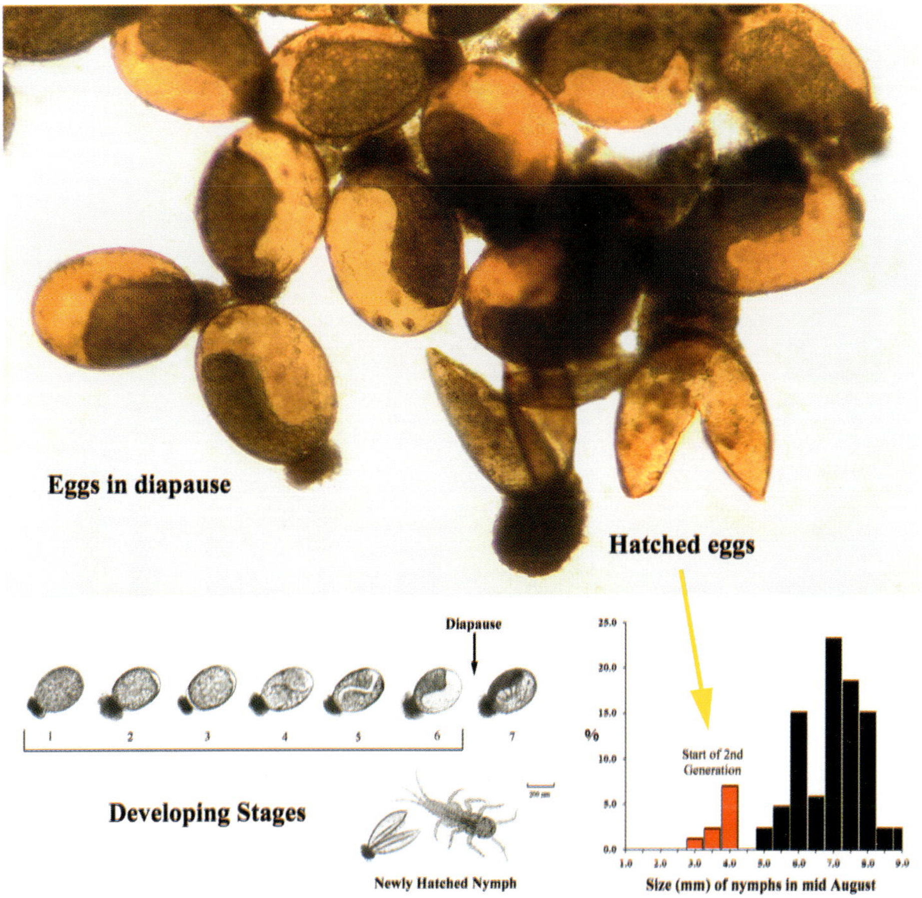

BWO eggs at West Amesbury showing most in diapause but some hatching to produce second generation

© C.J. Bennett

However, times have changed since Lunn did his work at Houghton; although we have the benefits of greatly improved technology, sensible bio-security precautions are needed to avoid the transfer of alien species that have become established on many of our rivers, such as the signal crayfish and, more recently, the killashrimp. It would be foolish to attempt to re-establish a species using material from a known infected site to one that was clear, such as one of the few remaining strongholds of the native white-clawed crayfish.

Restoring mayfly populations

The short incubation period of mayfly eggs enables a quick and easy method to re-establish this species. Large numbers of fertilised eggs are collected from females returning to the

(a)

(b)

(c)

Fly boards (a) fly board in position, (b) bottom of fly board covered in eggs and (c) female laying eggs on the board
© C.J. Bennett

water in the evening and allowed to attach to incubation plates overnight; the eggs are returned to the river after about twenty days, just before they are due to hatch. After the loss of the mayfly populations on the River Wey in Surrey and the River Wye in Derbyshire following severe pollution incidents, the populations were restored using this method; in the latter case, a full population was re-established using the eggs from just 80 females.

Restoring Blue-winged Olive populations

The above methods provided a relatively quick and easy way of increasing two important mayfly populations, but a new approach was needed to overcome the massive losses of the blue-winged olive. Therefore, part of the two-year research project on the Wiltshire Avon was to attempt to re-establish the blue-winged olive population on the River Wey. This involved keeping large numbers of eggs in small incubation chambers over the winter period which was done with the minimum of attention; only occasional water changes were needed and some were even incubated, quite successfully, in tap water. This suggests that the eggs are robust in relation to water quality and may be protected during pollution incidents. This is supported by observations on the River Wey shortly after the severe pollution incident when tiny (newly hatched) nymphs were recorded in the river.

In contrast to the huge losses of eggs monitored on the river, there were virtually no losses in the incubation chambers and three million eggs were placed into the River Wey in the spring, just before they were due to hatch. This significantly boosted the blue-winged olive population and this will be followed with the introduction of a further thirty million eggs. It thus seems that the massive losses of overwintering blue-winged olive eggs, due to

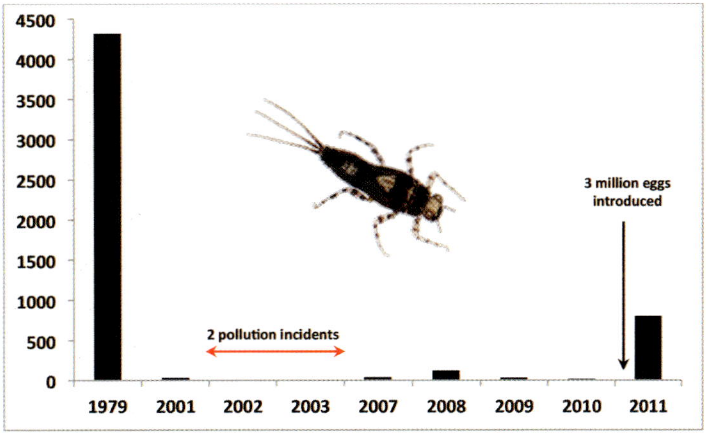

River Wey blue-winged olive population

BWO egg incubation chamber – each 'egg ball' contains around 1000 eggs

sedimentation problems, can be overcome by incubating large numbers of eggs over the winter period. Previous work has also shown that, with chilling, blue-winged olive eggs can be brought out of diapause to produce a second generation, thus short-circuiting the long incubation period.

Losses in other up-winged populations

As we have seen above, slow-reproducing species such as the blue-winged olive, where the eggs will be in the river for up to eight months before hatching, are at particular risk and even though the eggs appear to be immune to most pollution problems, accumulation of silt on the egg surface causes loss of adhesion resulting in massive losses as they are washed downstream. Many of the up-winged flies that have also suffered serious declines over the past twenty years (medium olives, pale watery and small dark olives) have similar long incubation periods and it seems probable that the eggs of these species are being similarly affected. In contrast, mayfly populations, which have generally suffered no such losses (and in some cases have even increased), have a very short incubation period of between fifteen and twenty-four days; far too short for the adhesive properties of the eggs to be affected.

The suspended development of the eggs (diapause) could also explain the reduction in the summer generations of these slow-reproducing species. The length of diapause is largely determined by water temperatures which in turn can change the number of generations in a year. Increasing water temperatures could therefore explain why the summer generations of these species are extremely reduced whilst the autumn generations have, in some cases, increased. This certainly seems to be the case with pale watery populations on the River Test, where good hatches are now seen as late as November.

Restoring grannom populations

The enormous population of grannom on the Wiltshire Avon is mainly confined to the waters below Salisbury. This is probably because adults are reluctant to fly either over or under the road bridges in the city. The huge swarms of adults that emerge below the city fly upstream until they reach the main road bridge, when the whole swarm turns left and follows the road (thinking it's the river); therefore many millions of eggs that would have been carried upstream, are lost.

With the normal downstream drift of larvae and with little or no upstream flight to compensate, populations will obviously fall, but by moving large numbers of eggs to sites above the bridges, this important early sedge could be restored to the upstream fisheries. It's interesting to note that Lunn moved large numbers of grannom eggs from the Avon over to the Houghton water after grannom were lost on the Test, but found that this was only successful where there were adequate weed beds for the larvae at the recipient site. Lunn also had varying amounts of success with other sedges.

Some General Observations

How do you know which way to go if you do not know where you are? And how can you plan for the future if you do not know the state of the present?
Sir David Attenborough *(Silent Summer)*

If we don't know the condition of our fly life, then how will we know if or when we lose them? And, if we do lose them, how do we put them back? On some rivers we have already lost them; who would have thought that, due to a serious lack of fly life, imitative fly fishing on the River Test, mecca for fly fisherman from all around the world, could now be a thing of the past.

"*There is more to fishing than catching fish*" and if we are to keep this very special type of fly fishing on our chalk streams, we need to look after our fly life and where necessary, improve it; Lunn was doing it nearly a hundred years ago. For too long we have taken it for granted.

We know so little about our fly life and the answers will not be found in endless committee meetings; the answers are out there on our chalk streams, but who is looking for them? Certainly not the large angling bodies that just seem to want to ignore the problem; so it has to be the angling clubs and the Salisbury & District Angling Club will probably be the first in the country to have a group dedicated not only to keeping the relatively good fly life that we have, but to improving it.

We know we can increase the populations of olives with the use of fly boards and we can restore mayfly populations by reintroducing fertilised eggs. By incubating large numbers of blue-winged olive eggs, we can also restore populations of this massively important fly. We may also be able to restore grannom populations to the upper reaches of the Avon by moving large numbers of eggs upstream of the road bridges which seem to be an obstacle to egg-laying females.

As we can no longer rely on the statutory bodies to regularly monitor our water quality, we must also do this for ourselves; the AMI has been highly successful right across the country and is now even being used by one group in Russia. But we must not be complacent; it needs to be expanded further across the chalk streams and above all, we need to maintain motivation. The initiative between the Salisbury & District Angling Club and the Frensham Fly Fishers to reinstate the blue-winged olive on the River Wey, will hopefully return this iconic fly to what it was when I cast my first fly there over fifty years ago; a time when you could almost walk across the water on the backs of the sherry spinners; only time will tell – but time is running out!

Chapter Four

Artificial Flies for Chalk Stream Fishing

Dennis Shaw

Ancient History

Fly design has a long history. Nobody knows who first thought of attaching some fur or feather to a hook, or when they did so. What we do know is that both hooks and silks fine enough to be used for fly tying have existed for at least three thousand years. The first known written account of fishing with an artificial fly is in *On the Nature of Animals* (circa AD 200) by Claudius Aelianus (Ælian). In the book Ælian gives a third hand account of a Macedonian way of catching fish with speckled skins on the river Astræus using an artificial fly. He describes how the fishermen fastened red wool around a hook and fixed onto the wool two wax-coloured feathers which grow under a cock's wattles (the red appendages under a cockerel's chin). It is also possible that this was the first description of a dry fly, for when describing the natural fly being imitated, Ælian says that it "*hovers on the river*". He describes how the fish seeing the fly on the surface: "*swims quietly up, afraid to stir the water above, lest it should scare away its prey; then coming up by its shadow, it opens its mouth gently and gulps down the fly, like a wolf carrying off a sheep from the fold or an eagle a goose from the farmyard; having done this it goes below the rippling water.*"

Early literature on the topic and examples of early flies are very scarce, so much of what we know about early fly design is pure guesswork with many different interpretations of the available information. It seems likely though that most very early flies differed little from the fly described by Ælian – a body of wool, silk or some natural material and a feather wing. Certainly, in the context of English chalk streams and British fly fishing in general, no surviving text has yet been found describing British fly fishing or artificial fly design during the eleven centuries that separate the comments of Aelian and the introduction of printed material in the 15th century. Early 20th century authors tended to dismiss the implications of Aelian and of other texts describing pre-medieval fly fishing traditions in continental Europe and Japan and effectively assumed that British fly fishing sprang fully formed into existence in the 15th century. This understandably convenient approach was clearly wrong and there undoubtedly was a British fly fishing tradition developed prior to the 15th century, together with an associated progression of fly design, but that history is lost to us, at least for the time being and probably forever. As Andrew Herd puts it in his seminal history of fly fishing: *The Fly* (2003):

If I am confident that there is much more to find out, then I am also frustrated to think what we must have lost. Eleven centuries is time enough for civilisations to flower and fade, let alone for a sport to find its feet. Who knows what knowledge was painfully gained, only to be snatched away by plague, war or famine? And who knows what remains to be discovered, locked away in the recesses of the great libraries, like those of the Vatican?

Nevertheless, it is only from publications in the 15th century that we can glean the first specific detail about British fly fishing and fly design. Of these publications by far the most important is *Treatyse of Fishing with an Angle*, a manuscript by an unknown author or authors, incorporated into a popular sporting volume of the time called the *Book of St Albans* by a publisher named Wynkyn de Worde. The *Treatyse* was hugely influential and very widely read in its day, serving as a basic angling textbook for about two centuries. Strangely, given the considerable detail about coarse fishing, the *Treatyse* contains very little information about fly fishing methods. It does however list twelve of the earliest trout flies, although with so little design detail that the appearance of the flies is pure speculation. It also describes the materials used in their construction. It seems that all twelve of the flies had simple woollen bodies and do not appear to have had a wound hackle of any type. Each fly had wings made from feathers of various sorts, but how the wings were attached is unknown.

There is little literary evidence concerning the development of flies for a further two hundred years, until the works of the famous 17th century British angling writers that laid the foundation of the modern sport of fly fishing and dominated the genre of angling literature until the late 18th century. These writers, Barker, Venables and Cotton, describe an advanced fly-tying culture across the British Isles, with considerable regional specialisation, that must have been the result of an extensive oral fly-tying tradition. As for the designs of the flies themselves, this is nicely summarised by Andrew Herd in *The Fly* in commenting on the work of Barker:

Barker divided artificials into two classes: 'Palmers', which had a cock or capon's hackle wound in a helix down the entire length of the body, making for a bushy pattern; and streamlined 'flies', which were winged, without a hackle. These two classes of pattern dominate the British lists until the 19th century, when fashions changed, palmers fell from favour and the standard winged fly style changed to incorporate a few turns of hackle around the base of the wings. As a result, the contents of a 17th century British fisher's wallet would have been unfamiliar to our eyes, largely because of the presence of quantities of slim dubbed flies with no hackle and almost vertical wings; a type of pattern which has no counterpart today, except for Swisher and Richards' floating 'No-hackle duns', which are a modern re-use of a very old principle.

An important point to remember is that prior to the 19th century the design concepts of 'dry fly' and 'wet fly' did not really exist. All artificial flies were fished on long rods with fixed horse-hair lines and the fly worked either on the surface or slightly beneath it. Of course, in these early days, dry-fly fishing, or more accurately, fishing floating flies, required that the flies float unaided. Chemical floatants had not been invented and so flies had to float by virtue of their design and materials alone. Even so, flies quickly became waterlogged and needed to be dried if they were to continue to float, presumably by false casting. Despite its importance to dry-fly fishing, the origin of the false cast is obscure, though it has probably existed almost as long as fly fishing itself. In the second edition of his book *The Angler's Companion*, (1853) Thomas Tod Stoddart gives the first known description of false casting with the intended purpose of drying the fly:

It is not an unusual practice, on recovering the line, and before recasting, to describe a figure of eight, twice or thrice successively, in the air with the fly-cast, in order to relieve the plumage of the hooks of the moisture imbibed. Upon this practice, or 'dodge' as one might term it, a good deal of stress is laid by the fishers of certain rivers both in England and Wales.

Later that same year, in the December 17th issue of *The Field*, one of the earliest references to fishing a dry fly (as opposed to a floating fly) appears in an article titled "The Hampshire Fly Fisher". In it the writer says:

As far as fly fishing is concerned, fishing upstream, unless you are trying the Carshalton dodge and fishing with a dry fly, is very awkward.

The statement is ambiguous because it is not known whether the 'Carshalton dodge' is a reference to false casting or to dry-fly fishing as a whole, but it is difficult to imagine the one without the other unless you are talking about the use of a blow-line.

The middle of the 19th century saw developments in fly design really get under way. One of the most important design innovations was the addition of a wrapped hackle to older patterns to improve their floating capabilities. We do not know who had this idea, but it could be argued that it was the single most important development in fly design ever. With the simple addition of an appropriately wrapped hackle, a fly could be made to float, or in the case of wet flies the hackle could imitate legs and the extra movement, or kick, of the hackles helped to convey the illusion of life. The first person to suggest that he had originated the technique of fishing dry flies as we know them today, with upright split wings and collar hackles, was Cheltenham tackle dealer James Ogden, who claimed to have done this in 1839, although he did not write about it until forty years after the event. His claim was challenged by J. W. Hills, who alleged Ogden had done this much later, writing that Ogden introduced the dry fly to the Derbyshire Wye in 1865. Interestingly, Hills states that Ogden's method was so successful that the blow-line he used was banned by the water owner and Ogden himself was attacked by his fellow anglers and driven from the water.

The first detailed written description of dry-fly fishing is by H. Cholmondeley-Pennell in the appropriately titled *Fishing with the Dry Fly* published in 1870. As well as describing the method of fishing, he also describes the dressing of the fly in detail:

The construction of the fly to enable it to fulfil its role is, first its wings, which are generally made of the whole tops of feathers, Mallard usually. Set nearly back to back and pointing upwards and outwards. Secondly its body made entirely of non-absorbent materials such as mohair and hackle.

What Cholmondeley-Pennell describes is what we now know as a Fan Wing. This early design was only really suitable for large dry flies imitating big mayflies such as *Ephemera danica* and would have needed to be dried by frequent false casting. Hence the need for non-absorbent materials and most probably they would also have been very heavily hackled. Another problem at this time was that flies were tied on gut-eyed hooks which increased the bulk and actually encouraged them to sink. Dry-fly fishing took quite a while to catch on, mainly because with the tackle available at that time, it was a difficult technique to practise. It was also very difficult to tie and fish smaller flies and so the occasions when it could be successfully practised were limited. All of this was soon to change though. In 1879 H. S. Hall began marketing his up-eyed hooks and around the same time it was discovered that a fly soaked in paraffin could be kept afloat for much longer. The stage was set for Hall, G. S. Marryat, E. J. Power, Dr. T. Sanctuary and other luminaries of the day to begin the development of the modern dry fly.

Halford & Marryat

On the 28th of April 1879 what could be described as the chalk stream dry-fly big-bang took place when Frederic Halford, on a visit to buy flies in John Hammond's fishing shop in Winchester, first met George Selwyn Marryat. Marryat at that time was already a well-known and acclaimed dry-fly man. In contrast, Halford was relatively inexperienced both as a dry-fly angler and as a fly tier. The pair became good friends and when Halford took rooms at the Houghton Mill, the two of them began to investigate and then, in

Halford's case, write about the theory and practice of dry fly fishing. A major part of this was to design a series of dry flies. Halford wrote that the motivation for the development of the series was the many discussions that he and Marryat had about the lack of uniformity in the patterns sold in the shops; even flies from the same fly dresser lacked consistency. In 1886 Halford published his first book, *Floating Flies and How to Dress Them*. Halford had wanted Marryat to be the co-author, but Marryat declined, preferring to remain out of the limelight. Nevertheless, Halford made no secret of the fact that he drew heavily on Marryat's experience and most of what he knew about fly tying he learned from Marryat. Chapter VI was titled '*Hints to Dry-Fly Fishermen*'. It was basically a set of rules for dry fly fishing. There were essentially five steps;

1 – Finding a fish feeding on winged insects.
2 – Presenting to him a good imitation of the natural insect both as to size and colour.
3 – Presenting it to him in its natural position, floating and 'cocked'.
4 – Putting it lightly on the water so that it floats accurately over him without drag.
5 – The four previous points should have been fulfilled before the fish has seen the angler or his rod.

Good advice really and still relevant today, whether fishing on chalk streams, rain-fed rivers, or even on stillwaters.

Sadly Marryat died during an epidemic in 1896. After Marryat's death, Halford continued his (their) work and after further refining his ideas, published his second book, *Modern Development of the Dry Fly*, in 1910. In it he revealed his final selection of thirty-three flies. The selection included a pattern for every common smaller up-winged fly plus three sedges, the black gnat and brown ant. The flies, though more lightly dressed than the available flies of the time, were still heavily dressed in comparison to today's flies. What Halford had attempted to do, with Marryat's help, was to produce a definitive set of flies that were exact in colour, shape and size, and which would allow the angler to fish throughout the whole season with the correct imitation. Whilst Halford's patterns did work and still do for that matter, his designs and consequently his flies were fundamentally flawed. He based all of his designs on what he observed from above and set against a white background. Halford knew that this was not how the fish saw the fly, but chose to ignore that fact. It seems to have been one of Halford's traits that once he reached a conclusion, he rarely if ever changed his mind. Additionally, he preserved all his specimens in alcohol which may have altered their natural colours, although this could have been dependent on how long they had been preserved before he used them. What he did get right was the general shape and size of his flies and with their long tails and dense hackles, achieved a balance that was not evident in earlier dry flies. This balance meant that the flies landed the right way up and cocked, something that could not be guaranteed with earlier dry-fly designs.

Halford's influence cannot be overstated and can still be felt over a century later. Despite his many flaws, most of his work was positive and for that he deserves a great deal of admiration. I also feel very envious of Halford. Not only did he achieve immortality through his work, but he also retired in 1889, at the age of just forty-five, to devote the rest of his life to fishing and his obsession with fly tying. How many of us would love to do that!

Skues

At around the same time that Halford was busy with his work, anglers like Sir Henry Cunynghame and Dr. Francis Ward were studying the dry fly as seen from below and from the perspective of the fish. Ward carried out his studies in a specially dug observation pond and published a number of articles describing his experiments, including observations about how the angler was seen by the fish. He invited the great chalk stream angler, George Skues, to use his facilities. Skues had published his first book, *Minor Tactics of the Chalk Stream* in 1910, in which he famously introduced the controversial concept of nymph fishing in chalk streams to a wide audience during the period when the 'dry fly only' school was at its peak. The deferent title of the book and it's mischievously light-hearted dedication to *"My friend the dry-fly purist, and to my enemies, if I have any"* did little to forestall the ensuing storm of bitter debate between adherents of the different philosophies which still resonates in the world of chalk stream fly fishing one hundred years later. Using Dr. Ward's facilities, Skues, with the assistance of Mr H T Sheringham (then angling editor of *The Field*), performed some important experiments later described by Skues in his book *The Way of a Trout with a Fly* (1921). In the chapter titled '*Looking up'*, Skues not only described how the fly looked to the fish, but also how the fish saw the world both above and below the water. This important work explained how a fish has a limited 'window' of vision as far as the surface of the water and the world beyond it is concerned, caused by refraction of light and how, conversely, its sub-surface vision, being unaffected by refraction, is very much better . This explained why a fish would sometimes travel a fair distance to intercept a wet fly or nymph, but would only move a short distance for a dry fly. If the dry fly is not in the fish's 'window', the fish simply cannot see it.

Although Skues is quite rightly regarded as the father of nymph fishing, he did not in any way claim to have invented it. In *The Way of a Trout with a Fly* he states:

Years ago I had the run of an old Westmoreland fly book full of hackle flies, all tied with silk bodies and a bunch of dubbing at the shoulder under the hackle. These but for the excessive length of the hackle might have been nymphs. And many patterns described by Theakston in "British Angling Flies" were more like nymphs than the winged fly they are supposed to represent.

Skues developed his own series of nymphs mostly using cock hackles "*tied as short, and setting as close as possible.* Hackles were always a problem for Skues: *It is extremely difficult to get hackles stout enough in the fibre to represent the legs of nymphs, yet short enough for the same purpose.*"

He stated that nipped hackles would serve, but every self-respecting fly dresser resents nipped or cut hackles, even though they work! He eventually solved the problem by devising a way of dressing his nymphs which gave him the required short hackle set close. His method was to tie in a bunch of cock hackles with the tips over the eye and just long enough that they could be bent back and secured to form the legs he desired. The rest of the nymph was then tied and when the thorax was formed, the butts of the hackles were used to form the thorax cover. This is a simple and clever solution to the problem. Skues' nymphs were not designed to fish deep like many of today's nymphs; they were tied to fish just below the surface, more like an emerger than a nymph. The bodies and thorax were made entirely (or contained a high proportion) of seal's fur; "*as many of the nymphs are full of lights and glistening*".

It is interesting to imagine how far Skues might have taken nymph fishing and the development of nymph fly patterns had he not been limited by the attitudes and constraints of his era. He certainly had the intellect and the imagination to go much further, but was hampered by both the uncompromising Halfordian upstream dry fly only doctrine and by the lack of scientific knowledge at that time. Skues was to be dogged by criticism all his life and in 1938 at the age of eighty, was still called upon to defend himself at a debate on the ethics of nymph fishing in chalk streams called by the committee of the Fly Fishers Club. It is said that the tough and mentally agile old fellow clearly won the day.

The Modern Era

Progress in the field of chalk stream fly fishing and fly tying was slow in the first part of the 20th Century. Quite apart from the inhibiting influence of the rigid upstream dry fly only doctrine and the lack of scientific knowledge, other factors were involved. Tackle lacked the sophistication available today and was little better than that available during the late Victorian era – split cane rods, heavy reels, silk lines and gut leaders. Anglers had limited opportunity to share knowledge and discoveries. Comparatively few books were published and access to books was limited. Social and economic pressures resulted in there being comparatively few anglers and ordinary people had little leisure time available until the great social and political changes that followed the end of the Second World War. Things only really got moving again with the technological explosion in synthetic materials that started during the war with military applications, but which developed commercially during the 1950s. These new materials had a profound effect on tackle design. In 1938 the American company DuPont patented nylon. This new material was marketed as a more effective successor to the troublesome gut and gut-substitute products used for leaders. It was not a perfect material to begin with, but manufacturers consistently improved its quality and anglers came to understand its attributes and how best to utilise them. By the 1960s nylon was universally accepted and gut became a thing of the past. In 1947, in its fiftieth year of operation, Shakespeare introduced the glass-fibre 'Wonderod' invented by Dr. Arthur M. Howald, thus initiating the era of the affordable, durable and reasonably effective fly rod. In 1949 PVC became available, thereby solving the problem of longevity which had severely hampered synthetic fly lines since they first appeared in the 1930s. In 1954 Scientific Angler patented a process for applying a variable thickness of PVC to a level-braided core, producing tapered synthetic lines that could be made cheaply and precisely.

Now anglers could get tackle that was reliable, affordable and low maintenance. Coupled to the general improvement in the quality of life of ordinary people, more anglers could spend more time on the water. Advances in entomological understanding were also taking place and the sharing of knowledge through readily available books and magazines caused fly design to advance in leaps and bounds. Some of the more important influences of the modern era are discussed below.

Marinaro

The great American angler and writer, Vincent Marinaro, was one of the first innovators of this modern period. In his first book *A Modern Dry Fly Code* (1950) Marinaro focussed on terrestrials more than on up-winged flies. One of the terrestrials he introduced was the Jassid. This is a simple fly to tie, consisting of only a palmered hackle, clipped top and bottom, and a flat wing made from a Jungle Cock nail feather. The rationale behind the design is that when trout eat small flies they only need to open their mouths a little bit in order to suck the fly in. If the fly is dressed with a conventional hackle the trout is not able to do that. Trimming the hackle top and bottom is the obvious and simple solution. The Jassid is a fly which has fallen out of favour in recent years. Why this should be so is beyond me because it was and still is one of the finest small flies you can have on the end of your line.

Another style of fly Marinaro introduced was his thorax or 'Thor-X' style dry fly. The main design feature of the thorax style fly is that the wings are tied in at the mid-point of the hook shank and two hackles are wound to form an 'X' configuration. The thinking behind this design derives from the observation that a fully hatched natural dun rides upon the surface of the stream supported only by its legs and with its body entirely clear of the water.

Coupled to this was a belief that the wings of a fly are a much more important feature to the fish than the body. Thus the aspiration was a fly that emphasised the wings, elevated the body above the water and rode on the very tips of the hackle. Indeed, the ultimate theoretical, although impractical, design aim of this type of thinking would be a fly that sits on only six hackle points representing the six legs of the insect. Although these propositions may be interesting and understandable in the context of an attempt to precisely imitate natural flies, to my mind the concepts underpinning the 'Thor-X' style are flawed. I believe that many dry fly patterns work well precisely because the body of the fly is on or in the surface film. I think that this signals vulnerability to the fish, that something has gone wrong for this fly compared to the other flies around that have fully and successfully hatched and are poised for flight on the tips of their toes. Fish are suckers for an easy meal and what could be easier than a fly wallowing trapped in the surface film? In fact, in practice, the 'Thor-X' design does not achieve its aim anyway because the fly rides on its body in the same way as conventionally tied dry flies. Marinaro-style thorax flies are rarely seen these days because their relatively complex dressing is no more effective than the easier-to-tie traditional-style dun patterns.

Marinaro's second book *In the Ring of the Rise*, published in 1976, contains some of the best photographs of trout taking flies ever published, clearly showing the different rise forms. The book also contains photographs of flies seen from below, exactly as the fish sees them. In it he also describes a rather complex style of tying a widely spread hackle fibre spinner wing. There are simpler styles of spinner wing available today, but Marinaro insisted that the wings had to be fixed widely separated so that they gathered and condensed light exactly as the natural spinner's wings do.

Sawyer

The legendary Frank Sawyer developed several nymphs for chalk stream fishing whilst working as a river keeper for the Services Dry Fly Association, the most famous being his Pheasant Tail Nymph. The Pheasant Tail Nymph is the finest example of effective minimalist design in fly tying. Take a hook, some copper wire and a few pheasant tail fibres, add the genius of Frank Sawyer and the result is arguably the deadliest nymph ever devised. He also gave us the Grey Goose Nymph which is essentially the same fly, but tied with grey goose herl instead of pheasant tail fibres. Writing for *The Masters on the Nymph* (1979) Sawyer said:

Since I started fishing with the nymph I have evolved patterns to imitate all members of this swimming group (Ephemeroptera) and, indeed, had success with them. But I found there was no need for any exact likeness of one or another and that if most of the details and characteristics of several could be incorporated in two patterns the fish could be taken consistently on them. General shape and colouration, together with the right size, is of greater importance than an exact copy. My two universal patterns, as I call them, are the Pheasant Tail and Grey Goose. The Pheasant Tail serves for the dark-coloured nymphs and the Grey Goose for the lighter ones ~ Both artificials have proved to be effective throughout the season.

Sawyer also said that "*if no response to either is obtained I considered myself beaten.*"

There are profound lessons for all would-be fly designers in both the words and the designs of Frank Sawyer!

Swisher & Richards

In 1971 a landmark publication from American authors Doug Swisher and Carl Richards significantly influenced the design of chalk stream flies. As well as the by now obligatory excellent photographs, *Selective Trout* also introduced several new fly designs including No-Hackle Duns, Paraduns and Wiggle Nymphs. As mentioned earlier, No-Hackle Duns are in some ways a throwback to the earliest fly designs because, as their name suggests, they have no hackles. Of course, in the modern era there are floatants that keep these flies floating for long periods, which was not the case in earlier times. Swisher and Richards believed that legs provided little or no attraction to the trout, suggesting that the main trigger points were the wings and the body. As they put it:

The most deadly pattern to evolve from our study is the no-hackle fly. Observation of our photographic efforts indicated that legs play a very insignificant role in the outline of most mayflies. This fact prompted a close-up study of standard artificials, where we noticed that hackle was a ridiculous imitation of legs. It was not only too bushy, but also obscured the outline of both the body and wings instead of being the least significant feature as it should have been.

Although their answer was to eliminate the hackle altogether, this would have caused stability issues, so to overcome this they tied the No-Hackle Dun with very widely splayed tails which acted as outriggers to stabilise the fly. The wings were made of various feathers such as duck quill, turkey flats and hen hackles.

Paraduns were tied in a similar way, but had parachute hackles. The intention of the hackles though, was to assist in the positioning of the fly on the water rather than to aid flotation and consequently they were kept as sparse as possible. Of course, parachute flies had been around for a long time. As usual, nobody knows who invented them, but the strongest contender is the unknown fly dresser supplying the now long defunct Glasgow angling shop, Alex Martin, which sold parachute flies in the 1920s. But it was Swisher and Richards who popularised the design.

The Wiggle Nymph was their attempt to imitate the undulating movement of many species of nymph. These were made by tying the abdomen on a piece of fine wire created by cutting the bend off a hook. This was then attached to a loop of wire or nylon knotted to the bend of another hook on which the thorax of the nymph was tied. This seems to be a good idea and the fly does work in practice, but no better than conventionally tied nymphs. Perhaps it does not achieve the correct type of wriggle.

Clarke & Goddard

In the UK, Brian Clarke and John Goddard published several important books that introduced a number of unique designs. Amongst these was the G & H Sedge – a sturdy, durable sedge pattern designed by Goddard and Cliff Henry. This pattern employs spun deer hair which is clipped into a shape that imitates both the body *and* the wings of a sedge (caddis) fly. Spun bodies were nothing new, but Goddard and Henry's design introduced an interesting development of the concept by incorporating the wing profile as well. Goddard, in collaboration with Brian Clarke, also introduced the upside-down Paradun. This was their answer to Marinaro's Thorax dun because they also sought to create a fly that rode on its hackle and which had prominent wings. Their solution was quite different to Marinaro's though. In this design, the wings are tied on the under-side of the hook and the parachute hackle is tied on the top-side of the hook. The tails are tied in well round the bend which helps the fly to land the right-way-up, which is, of course, upside-down with the hook pointing up. Like Marinaro's design, the concept seems sound, but in reality it works no better than conventionally tied patterns and given the complexity of the dressing, it is no surprise that it never really gained popularity as a fishing fly.

Patterson

There was a better solution to the upside-down fly; the Funneldun. The Funneldun is a simple design by Neil Patterson. He wanted a dry fly that would float on its hackle and tail, but with the hook point uppermost where the fish could not see it. Although the design is simple it is also most ingenious. A small ball of dubbing is tied in at the hook eye, then hackle is tied-in and drawn backwards (funnelled) over the ball of dubbing and the eye. Then the tails are tied in. Patterson states in his book, *Chalkstream Chronicle* (1995), that there are three things that are crucial here:

First, that you use a good bunch of stiff hackle-fibres for the tail. Secondly, that you tie a turn of silk underneath the hackle fibres to splay them out. And thirdly, that you find the exact position on the hook bend so that the tails are far enough round to topple the fly. But not too far round to make the end of the body touch the surface.

To finish the fly, a slim tapered body is dubbed on and then finally a 'V' from what will be the underside of the hackle is clipped out. Patterson's design is an effective and easy-to-tie dry fly which, as an added bonus, can be tied using the cheapest of materials. For some reason, I guess possibly tradition, the Funneldun is not as popular today as it should be.

Betters

Another historically important fly dresser who has contributed greatly to fly design is Frans Betters who designed the Haystack and the Usual, both simple but very effective no-hackle dry flies. Both flies consist of a slim tapered body with a clump tail and wing, the only difference between the two being the materials used. The Usual is tied using snowshoe rabbit's foot under-fur for the body and guard hairs for the wing and tail. The Haystack, which was originally tied to imitate the Isonychia mayfly on his home water, the Ausable, was tied using deer hair for the wings and the tails and had a body of dubbed natural fur. Al Caucci and Bob Nastasi introduced a variation that they called the Comparadun, the main difference being that the tails, tied from hackle fibres or microfibetts, are longer and split. A further variation was introduced by John Juraceck and Craig Mathews. They added a tail made of 'Z-Lon' and called their variation the Sparkle Dun. One important and often overlooked design feature of the Haystack and its derivatives is in the construction of the wing. Although tied in initially as a clump, the deer hair wing should be manipulated so that, when viewed from the front it, creates a full 180° semi-circle. Properly tied and by varying the tail materials, colour and size, you have a simple, stable imitation of a dun, a spinner or an emerger.

Christie

Another tweak to the popular parachute style of fly is Roy Christie's Reversed Parachutes, a design he conceived in 1976, originally as a midge imitation.

This is what Roy says of his design:

The reversed parachute has its origins as an emergent midge on Walthamstow's reservoirs in 1976. The design consists of a parachute hackle set outside the bend of a larval hook, about a third way into the bend. This allows the entire weight of the hook to hang from the hackle and ensures that the imitation hangs through the surface film, pulling the tippet through the meniscus on impact. It has proven astoundingly successful across the world when tied to imitate any creature stuck in the surface film.

As well as being reverse tied with the hackle at the bend, Roy's unique way of wrapping the hackle on a loop of nylon makes it virtually indestructible. He wraps two or three turns round the loop, then through the loop for two or three turns and then repeats as necessary. Finally the loop is drawn tight, trapping the hackle very securely. Roy also designed the Avon Special Emerger which is also reversed tied. On this fly the hackle is conventionally wound on the hook at the bend, but when it sits on the water the body of the hook penetrates the surface and the hackle sits like a parachute hackle on the water. Both flies are designed so that the hook sinks the tippet, which is an important feature for Roy.

Moutter

The Paraloop is another variation on the parachute theme. The Paraloop design is normally associated with Ian Moutter, but after Ian designed it, he discovered that Americans Jim Cramer, Ned Long and Bob Quigley, to name but three, had also had the same idea. Several people coming up with the same design is not uncommon in fly dressing. The Paraloop is tied on a post which can be Kevlar, GSP thread, flexifloss, or materials with similar qualities. The hackle and post are tied in either at the tail of the fly or at the thorax, the hackle is wound up the post and back down and then tied off at the tie-in point. The rest of the fly is tied and then the hackle is pulled over and tied-off. What Moutter wanted was a fly with a profile similar to that achieved by trimming the hackle on the underside. He achieved that goal and the design as it developed became so much more. Many tiers now prefer the Paraloop to the parachute.

Van Klinken

I cannot leave parachutes without mentioning Hans van Klinken and his Klinkhåmer Special. Van Klinken came up with this pattern in 1984 and although he found out later that others had had the idea before him, he is the one most associated with the style. The Klinkhåmer Special was originally designed to imitate a large emerging caddis sitting as deeply in the surface film as possible, but has been developed so much that now that it is more generally used, particularly in the United Kingdom, as a generic emerger. Van Klinken introduced two design features into this fly which set it apart. The first was to bend the hook so that he had a straight shank where the wing, thorax and hackle were tied in and a deeply penetrating curved shank for the abdomen of the fly. A hook of the correct shape is now marketed by Partridge Hooks as the 15BNX Klinkhåmer Extreme hook. The second was to tie the hackle off at the base of the post. This made tying the parachute hackle much easier than the traditional method of tying it off at the head. Many flies are tied and sold as Klinkhåmer Specials, but they are tied on the wrong shape of hook. The shape of the hook is critical to the design principle of this fly. Although primarily famous because of his Klinkhåmer Special, van Klinken is also responsible for many other great patterns, particularly CDC (Cul de Canard) flies. In the 1980s whilst experimenting on the length of wings on his CDC flies, he discovered that short wings caught better than longer wings and floated almost as well too. In the process he also discovered that leaving the thick stem of the CDC feather as part of the wing was desirable. Many anglers believe that it is the natural oil in the CDC feathers which makes them float. This is not the case; the oil only helps keep the feather from becoming waterlogged and it is the structure of the feather that makes it float. Each fibre is covered with tiny barbules which trap air. When CDC flies sink it is because the CDC has become matted, preventing the barbules from functioning properly. In order to make it float again you have to dry the CDC feathers. What van Klinken discovered was that when he included the thick stem of the CDC feathers as part of the wing, they took longer to become matted, could be dried more quickly and fluffed up better. The fly he was working on when he made this discovery was his 'Culard', a small sedge pattern consisting of a ribbed herl body with a short CDC wing and a blue dun collar hackle.

CDC Flies

Most anglers today think that CDC is quite a new medium but CDC flies have been around for a lot longer than most anglers think. According to Marc Petitjean in a chapter in Leon Link's book *Tying Flies with CDC* (2003), the first CDC flies were tied in the 1920s. Petitjean identifies two men, Charles Bickel and Maximillien Joset as being the first to tie flies utilising CDC. Joset called his flies Moustiques. Moustiques were a simple design, being little more than a spider type fly with a hackle of CDC. It is not certain, but they were most likely fished as dry flies. In 1977 Aim Devaux designed the Moustique Devaux. He basically took the Moustique and added a second hackle behind the first CDC hackle, then after wrapping the second hackle, stroked the fibres forward over the eye and fixed them in this position with several thread wraps over the base of the fibres. This fly is very similar in design to Neil Patterson's Funnel Dun, the main difference being that the Moustique Devaux is not designed to fish upside down. The most important development in popularising CDC flies came in the early 1980s when Slovenian angler and fly dresser Marjan Fratnik designed the 'F' Fly. This is an easy–to-tie,

Artificial Flies - 1

Ælian's Fly
(*Author's guess*)

Medieval Flies
(*Author's guess*)

Fan Wing

Palmer

'Fly'

17th Century Flies

A selection of Halford's flies

A selection of Skues' flies

Artificial Flies - 2

Jassid
(*Marinaro*)

Thor-X
(*Marinaro*)

No Hackle Dun
(*Swisher & Richards*)

Paradun
(*Swisher & Richards*)

Wriggle Nymph
(*Swisher & Richards*)

G & H Sedge
(*Clarke & Goddard*)

Upside Down Paradun
(*Clarke & Goddard*)

Funneldun
(*Patterson*)

Haystack
(*Betters*)

Usual
(*Betters*)

Reversed Parachute
(*Christie*)

Avon Special Emerger
(*Christie*)

Paraloop
(*Mouter*)

Moustique
(*Joset*)

Moustique Devaux
(*Devaux*)

durable fly that is a very effective fish catcher. The fly is nothing more than a silk body and a wing of two to four CDC feathers tied in down-wing style – simple, but extremely effective.

Oliver Edwards designed a great dry fly which, except for the Coq de Leon tail, is made entirely of CDC. The method of construction involves some clever cutting and manipulation of the CDC feathers. The end result is an effective and durable fly design that can be tied in a variety of sizes to suit the different species of up-winged flies.

Today the most famous exponent of CDC flies is Marc Petitjean who has designed many flies made almost entirely of CDC, including dry flies, emergers, nymphs, wet flies, streamers, salmon and steelhead flies. Leon Links' book is subtitled '*The Fisherman's Miracle Feather*'. I think that is a pretty accurate description.

Materials & Fashion

There have been many influences on the design of flies specifically for chalk stream fishing. Fashion and tradition have had a huge impact. For many, many years the greatest influence was the 'upstream dry fly only' doctrine and 'exact imitation' theories of Halford, Marryat, Hall, Sanctuary, *et al.* It took a very long time for different approaches to penetrate and indeed, much of the fresh thinking came from America and Europe, where the dry fly only school's theories were less influential or even entirely ignored. Different styles of fly have also risen and fallen in favour – the earliest flies, which were mainly hackle-less, were replaced by the hackled flies of the Halfordian and pre-World War Two eras, which were in turn replaced by the hackle-less flies of the late 1940s and 1950s, which have remained popular to this day. Flies made with soft bodies or with hard bodies have come and gone and come again, according to the fashion of the time. The availability of materials has also been a driving force in fly design. Our forebears did not have the synthetic materials we have available today. Dubbed bodies made from pig's wool, mohair and various animal furs such as mole, water rat and rabbit/hare held sway in the United Kingdom for many years. Then seal's fur became available and was the material of choice. Now seal's fur is a politically incorrect material to use and mohair is making a comeback. The invention of synthetic materials has revolutionised fly design, particularly with regard to dry flies and emergers. We now have materials to make bodies and wings that are lighter than water and non-absorbent and these, coupled with modern floatants, allow us to make dry flies and emergers that will float using the merest wisps of materials. Another influence has been marketing; yes, even in fly design we are subject to the influence of clever advertising. On many occasions over recent years a wonder material has been discovered and a host of flies or patterns have been designed to utilise it. In many cases the 'wonder material' is more than likely a batch of something or other that some enterprising dealer has found lurking in the back of a warehouse somewhere. Fly tying is such a small niche industry that virtually no materials are designed and manufactured specifically for it, so when a new, cheap and plentiful material is 'discovered' and a fly-tying application for it is invented, a suitable price-hike is usually worked into the equation too! The list of synthetic materials available today is mindboggling, but many are very good and can be utilised in a multitude of fly designs. The experienced fly dresser will soon learn to sort the wheat from the chaff, but the less experienced will have a steep and possibly expensive learning curve.

Selecting a Fly

All these different fly designs, patterns and styles are only effective when used at the appropriate time and in the appropriate place and for the average fly fisherman this can often be a perplexing and confusing dilemma. It need not be so though. What fly to use at any given time or on any given water is simply a case of making some simple observations. I would strongly urge the beginner to acquire a basic understanding of entomology because it is helpful when discussing what flies are evident, what the fish are taking, or what flies you would expect to see on a given water at a given time of day or year. But, it isn't absolutely necessary to know the difference between a large dark olive and a medium olive at 50 metres or what a *Baëtis fuscatis* or *Ephemera danica* is, or whether it has two or three tails. What you do need to know is that the flies on the water are a sort of brownish-olive colour, have upright wings and are about a size 14. It really can be that simple. As you approach the water look for clues that help you make an informed choice. Look for signs of flies in the air. An obvious example would be the hawthorn fly (*Bibio marci*), especially if it's a windy day. The hawthorn fly is a poor flyer and is easily blown onto the water. If there are no obvious flies about in the air, carefully (so as not to spook any fish) look for signs of flies on or above the water. Take your time, the flies might not be obvious. Hawthorn flies, for example, are very easy to spot in the air with their bulbous thoracic area and long gangly legs, but in the water they actually sit very low, semi-submerged, and can be hard to spot. If you cannot see any obvious flies, can you see rising fish? Look carefully at the rises. Is the fish actually breaking the surface taking something off the top, or is the rise more like a bulge in the water surface. If it is a bulge, then it is likely that it is taking emergers. An obvious rise form is a bold, slashy rise, usually in the evening and most likely to a sedge. With experience you will soon become quite adept at spotting even the less obvious flies and you will learn to interpret the different rise forms.

If there is no sign of flies or rising fish, try looking at the fish themselves. Are they lying close to the bottom, maybe moving to the side occasionally? If so, then they are taking nymphs as they drift by and it is time for a weighted nymph. Are they actively moving about in the middle or upper layers? Then it is most likely that they are intercepting emerging nymphs and an un-weighted nymph might be the answer. But what if the fish are lying motionless, with no obvious signs of feeding? Well, that is the time to take a guess at what they might take or expect to see. Remember, a trout is basically an opportunistic beast and just because there is no sign of feeding does not mean that they will not take a tasty morsel if it is presented to them properly. If you cannot see any flies in the air or on the water and can see no sign of fish, then your last option is to 'read-the-water' and look for places or features where you might expect a fish to be lying. Just because you cannot see it does not mean that it is not there. On chalk streams this is often, wrongly, called 'fishing the water' by the ill-informed and is frowned upon by some. However, even Halford said that he was '*a strong advocate for floating a cocked fly over a likely place, even if no movement of a feeding fish has ever been seen there'*. But the one thing you should never do is fish right through a beat standing bolt upright, whipping the water to a foam with repeated, mechanical casting over all the water. That is bad practice on any water, not just the chalk streams and is sure to ruin your chances for the day and the chances of anyone following you. It is far better to just wait a while. Almost always something will happen that gives you an idea of what is going on and how fish can be caught. If being patient is difficult for you, there are still some clues for you to look for. Look under the leaves of trees and bushes. The males of most species of up-wings hatch first and seek refuge in trees and bushes, usually for that day, but it can be for up to a week. They hide there waiting for the females to emerge later in the day, so if you find flies under leaves there is a reasonable chance that the females of those flies will hatch at some point later in the day or in the evening and you can be ready for them. One last place to look is spider's webs, not only can you find what has hatched that day, but in many cases you can find what has been hatching for several days. And, of course, don't forget word of mouth. A friendly tackle shop owner, a river keeper or a fellow angler are all sources of information that you ignore at your peril.

Six Flies for Chalk Streams

Before you think about what fly to put on the end of your leader, you will need some flies in your fly box to choose from. Arthur Ransome in *Rod & Line* (1929) said:

> *Some of the best fishermen who have ever lived have not needed more than six flies.*

So with those sage words in mind, I commend to you six flies: two dry flies, two emergers and two nymphs. These flies have been selected because of their fundamental design characteristics rather than the specific pattern employed. The pattern given for each is for reference. Each fly has been selected because it is easy to tie and with the beginner in mind. For those that do not tie, each style is readily available for sale in most tackle shops. This small selection will enable you to fish the entire season with an appropriate fly to cover any situation.

CDC & Elk:
Hook – TMC102Y #11 – #19
Thread – Brown 6/0
Body – CDC
Wing – Fine Tipped Deer Hair
Designed by Swiss fly-tyer Hans Weilenmann, this pattern has gained a reputation second to none. This is what Hans says about his design:

Every fly fisherman has to believe in something. For me enticing fish to take a fly hinges on the concept of 'triggers'. Offer a fish the appropriate positive triggers and it is more likely to think 'food!' Based on this philosophy, I designed the CDC & Elk, which has become my staple dry fly, in 1992. In this pattern, I combine the proven wing silhouette and buoyancy of Al Troth's Elk Hair Caddis and the dubbed body look and straggling filaments, which suggest a multitude of components from sprawling insect legs, trailing nymphal shuck, crippled wings, etc. achieved by wrapping a Type 1 CDC feather around the hook shank. Ever since the early nineties, the CDC & Elk has taken fish consistently across a multitude of waters and several continents. It is a pattern deceptive in its simplicity and versatility. From its beginning as a modified Elk-hair Caddis it slipped into the slot as the go-to fly for a multitude of mayfly hatches, a general search pattern to cover hatchless periods, an emerger pattern, and a wet fly.

The original design of this pattern can easily be varied to create a cripple/emerger or a spent fly pattern by simply altering the style of the wing. Or, you can add legs to it to turn it into a Daddy Longlegs pattern. It is a truly versatile pattern that can be used all season long with complete confidence. There is even a Paraloop version of it designed by Paul Ainsworth.

Split-Wing CDC Dun:
Hook – TMC102Y #11 – #21
Thread – Brown 8/0
Wings – CDC tied upright and split
Tails – Coq de Leon (Pardo Claro) tied 'outrigger' style
Body – Fine Synthetic Dubbing

This is my variation of a style of fly popularised by Marc Petitjean. I simplified it by using a fine synthetic dubbing for the body. Tied in a range of colours and sizes this fly can be used to represent every up-winged fly you will encounter throughout the season. Although it is designed as a dun and I think that the fish sees it as a dun as it approaches its window of vision, when it is within the window, I think that the hackleless design and position in the surface film may make it appear more like an emerger or possibly a cripple. This is an unsupported theory, but given that most of the fly is in rather than on the surface, I think it is quite a plausible.

Iwi Emerger:
Hook – Varivas iwi F-2000 #18
Thread – Yellow UTC70
Shuck – Pale dun under brown Z-lon
Body – Pale morning dun turkey biot quill
Wing – Pale dun Z-lon under a single CDC feather
Hackle – Grizzle dyed yellow. Clipped underneath.

This is another fairly easy pattern to tie and is based on a simple emerger design. The shuck and wing should be kept fairly fine on this style of fly. The single strand of CDC over the Z-Lon is there to add to the illusion of life, not for flotation. The floatation should come from the Z-Lon wing and the hackle. On this style of fly I prefer to clip the hackle underneath so the fly will sit as low as possible in the water, just where the fish expect to see hatching insects at their most vulnerable. As with the CDC Dun, it is tied in a range of sizes and colours to match what is hatching.

Klinkhåmer Special:

Hook – Partridge 15BNX Klinkhåmer extreme #16 – #20
Thread – Brown 6/0 and Danville's Spider Web
Wing-post – White crinkly poly yarn
Hackle – Red game cock hackle
Body – Brown/olive fine synthetic dubbing
Thorax – Peacock herl

A deadly pattern discussed above. For those who are not familiar with the Klinkhåmer hook, be aware that it is very big for its designated size. Size 20 may sound small, but in reality it is roughly equivalent to a standard size 14 hook.

Sawyers Pheasant Tail Nymph

Hook – Standard or 2X nymph hook #12 – 18
Thread – Reddy-brown copper wire
Tail – Tips of the pheasant tail herls used for the body
Body – 2 – 4 pheasant tail herls twisted together with the wire
Thorax cover – pheasant tail herls

What more can I say? It is simply one of the best weighted nymphs you can put before a trout.

Gold Ribbed Hare's Ear Nymph (GRHE)

Hook – Standard or 2X nymph hook #12 – #18
Thread – Yellow 8/0
Tail – Hare's mask guard hairs
Rib – Fine or medium flat gold tinsel
Body – Hare's mask blended dubbing
Thorax – Hare's mask blended dubbing, darker than the body
Thorax cover – Any dark grey or black feather fibre

No-one knows who invented the GRHE, but I for one will drink a toast to that person. This is the 'Mr.Versatile' of the fly fishing world and it has been around for a very long time. You can tie it as a simple un-weighted nymph, or as a weighted nymph by winding on an under-body of thin lead wire or by tying in a small bead at the head or thorax, or you can add a game hackle to it, or a parachute hackle, you can even treat it so that it floats without a hackle. Whatever you do to it, you can be sure that it will excel.

Mixed Fishery Freedom

It is not very well known, but there are some places on the chalk streams where you can fish upstream or downstream and with any fly you want, or even with as many flies on your cast as you want. These are usually the lower stretches and they are often designated as coarse or mixed fisheries and are not subject to restrictive rules. They have plenty of trout and grayling in them though. A word of caution before I proceed; it is up to you to ascertain any rules and regulations relating to where you are fishing and ignorance is not an excuse. If you do not know, do not fish until you do! But, if the rules allow it, you can have some fun and experiment to your heart's content. Try using spider patterns like Stewart's (Baillie's) Black Spider or a Partridge and Orange. Even if the rules allow downstream fishing, I would recommend that you still fish spider patterns upstream. If you fish them downstream the hackle tends to collapse under the pressure of the water and the fly appears lifeless. Fishing upstream allows the hackle to move, creating an illusion of life that is more attractive to the fish. Lures, or streamers as our American cousins call them, can also be used. Lures like the Woolly Bugger, a fly attributed to Russell Blessing and originally tied as an imitation of the Dobsonfly, is one of those flies that has developed from being a simple imitation of a particular insect to a fly that is universally acknowledged to be a killer lure in virtually all situations anywhere in the world. A useful variation, particularly appealing to chub, is to add rubber legs to the dressing. The extra 'kick' from rubber legs is something that fish seem to find irresistible. Other lures worth trying include Bob Church's Black Chenille, a Minkie or a Matuka-type lure.

An insect that is often overlooked in the United Kingdom and particularly in the context of chalk streams is the grasshopper. Flies imitating grasshoppers are popular in America, but for some reason have never become popular here. But, if you hear some grasshoppers chirping in the adjacent meadow, it is well worth giving an imitation a go on a chalk stream. They are particularly good at bringing up big fish! Some grasshopper patterns are quite complex to tie, involving glue and foam and all manner of unfriendly techniques. One that does well is a variation of Hans Weilenmann's CDC & Elk; simply tie the standard pattern on a size 10 – 4 X hook and add a bunch of six pheasant tail fibres, knotted once, to each side of the fly to represent legs. This pattern has many advantages over traditional hopper patterns. It is easy to tie, floats well and above all, is easy to cast. It is a strange quirk of chalk stream etiquette in some circles that terrestrial insects, such as ants and daddy longlegs are deemed acceptable, but grasshoppers are not. Grasshoppers can be effectively imitated using a hook no bigger than that commonly used to imitate a big mayfly and the addition of legs is considered acceptable when imitating, say, a hawthorne fly. Why grasshoppers should be frowned upon is thus a bit of a mystery.

The Future

Fly design has come a long way since that first Macedonian fly in 200 AD. Many fads and fashions have come and gone and many obstacles have stood in the way and have gradually been overcome. Where will fly design go next? Tackle seems to have reached a pinnacle of development. Sure, there may be innovations to come, but nothing of the magnitude of glass or carbon fibre rods, plastic fly lines or nylon. Tackle using these materials is so effective that improvement is hard to imagine. The same is true of fly tying materials, where the options now available allow the construction of virtually any conceivable design. Undoubtedly, there will further 'wonder' materials invented or discovered, but will they really do a better job than the materials we have now? I have my doubts. Perhaps the one place where there is room for improvement is in the matter of hooks. Maybe wire as strong as tempered steel and as fine as gossamer is just round the corner. Or maybe plastic hooks, clear plastic! Now that would be the holy grail of hooks! Or, more modestly, perhaps we could agree on a properly defined and universally accepted hook scale (Ha! Who am I kidding?). But in the area of fly design itself, things will continue to move forward and this will impact upon the chalk stream fly fisherman and the flies he uses, regardless of where the developments take place. Much inspiration has recently come from Eastern Europe, particularly with CDC dry flies and deep nymphs, together with new techniques for fishing them. Scandinavia is also a place that I predict will produce significant developments. There seems to be an abundance of talent and imagination in that region and they are producing some innovative patterns and styles of flies that merge realistic and traditional tying techniques to create unique designs. These flies are usually called 'semi-realistics'.

One such tier is Ulf Hagstrom from Sweden. Ulf has designed several unique patterns, the 'Uffe's Killer' and 'SRM' emerger being two outstanding examples.

'Uffe's Killer':
Hook – Partridge 15BNX #12 – 20
Thread – Colour to match body.
Tails & Body – A varnished and 'reversed' feather.
Hackle – Dry fly hackle in colour to match the hatch.
Wing – TMC Aero (sometimes colored with marker to match the hatch), poly yarn or similar

Ulf says of his 'Uffe's Killer':

The different approach with this fly compared to many other popular patterns meant to imitate the adult mayflies is the way it sits on the surface, just like the real mayfly sits with only its feet touching the surface this fly has nothing but a sparse hackle on the surface creating a very realistic footprint on the water. The fly is very light and lands perfectly every time you cast it. At a first glance it might look fragile but it is a whole lot more durable than it looks...

The last few years I have started to tie it in smaller sizes as well, using an olive dyed partridge feather for the body makes an almost perfect large dark olive imitation and bright yellow partridge feathers works perfect for sulphurs.

SRM emerger:
Hook – Partridge 15BNX #10 – 20
Thread – Sheer 14/0.
Tails – Microfibetts, synthetic quills or any other synthetic tail material.
Body –VN nymph skin
Hackle Post –Yellow foam
Hackle – Good quality rooster.
Legs – Golden Pheasant tail 'Veli auti style'

His 'SRM' emerger was the result of a request seven years ago to tie a realistic looking mayfly emerger. As he tells it:

Two years earlier I had experienced one of the biggest mayfly hatching I have ever to witness. It was for a hatch of the Ephemera Vulgata that we had come but we were fortunate to see 3-4 other mayfly species hatch at the same time also. After having fished a big drake imitation with some success I started to watch the fish feed and I found that every fifth take or so was duns on the surface being taken, but the other four takes were to something just underneath the surface; the emerger. When a mayfly nymph reaches the surface it will stop there for a duration of time, sometimes only a second and sometimes much longer, to catch its breath so to speak before starting to break free of the nymphal prison. And boy is it in trouble hanging there because the trout loves an easy prey! What I saw was that it was actually the emerging nymphs of the Leptophlebia that was being taken much more often than the drakes. My own conclusion was that these nymphs hung, still for several seconds before starting to emerge compared to the drake nymphs who started almost as soon as they reached the surface. The drake nymphs were hardly ever taken and [it] was the same with the adult Leptophlebia. And I will say that the SRM emerger is designed with this behavior clearly in mind.

I think that these patterns probably represent the next trend in chalk stream fly design and are an attempt to meld a greater degree of exact imitation with features that give the impression of life. Both patterns are complex to tie, but it might be worth the effort. Viewed from the side or from below the SRM emerger in particular, has an almost perfect come-and-eat-me look to it. Ulf achieved this by choosing to tie it on the same hook as the Klinkhåmer Special which gives it an excellent profile and position, just below the surface. The legs add an extra degree of vulnerability to the appearance of the fly. 'Veli auti style' legs are made using a single Golden Pheasant tail fibre which is pulled sharply at a right angle from the stem. This causes the fibre to have a small curly bit on the end which looks remarkably like a foot and is an excellent imitation of a nymph's leg. As appealing as these semi-realistics are though, I am reminded of the words of John Geirach in his book '*Trout Bum*' (1986):

I think five year old kids and game fish view the world in much the same way, both are capable of intense, single-minded observation, but they see the essence of a thing rather than the details.

The one proven constant in successful fly design is that the best flies are simple, giving the illusion of life rather than being an exact copy, which can often seem lifeless. Sawyer's Pheasant Tail Nymph, Hans Weilenmann's CDC & Elk, Frans Betters' Haystack, Vincent Marinaro's Jassid and many more eternally popular and effective flies all have two things in common – they are simple to tie and use minimal materials. They rely on good design and good choice of materials rather than complexity and exotic, fancy ingredients. To put it another way, the best flies catch fish, not anglers.

Chapter Five

The Madness of the Mayfly

Peter McLeod

There is no hatch of insects that creates quite as much hysteria among chalk stream fly fishermen as *the* mayfly (*Ephemera danica).* Also known as the 'green drake', this large insect can drive both fish and fishermen mad. More literature has been written about the mayfly and its life cycle than nearly any other insect. This up-winged member of the Ephemera genus has a life cycle that culminates in prolific hatches that traditionally start in the month of May, from which it takes its name. When this occurs the trout in the rivers where mayfly are found throw caution to the wind and zone-in on this veritable feast. In the early 1900's there were very few mayfly hatching on our chalk streams and F. M. Halford nearly excluded it from the *Dry-Fly Man's Handbook* because he felt it had little significance. However, he hoped this would change and had the forethought to include it. How right he was! Why mayfly numbers have increased over the last century from a mere trickle to the most significant hatch of the year seems to be down to reduced river flows and an increase in sediment. Mayfly nymphs live in sediment beds and an increase in this type of habitat would logically result in increased numbers of mayfly.

In *A Summer on the Test*, John Waller Hills wrote: *The coming of the mayfly is more than an incident in the fisherman's year. It is an event of nature.* This annual phenomenon is nature's way of plugging a gap in the trout's diet and its abundance also allows them to fully recover their condition after the winter. By the beginning of May the hawthorne fly is no longer about and hatches of iron blue duns and olives happen so rapidly they are hardly a substitute. Were it not for the mayfly, there would be very lean pickings for the fish. The mayfly hatch is very much connected to temperature and in recent years we have seen the hatch on the southern chalk streams extending further into May and early June. This timing could also be connected to the temperatures experienced during the winter months. Mayfly will continue to hatch throughout the season and on the Avon some river keepers see them as late as September, but not in any density. The wonderful thing about this hatch is that when it arrives in force, the mayfly will come off in any weather. At the height of the mayfly hatch, also known as 'duffer's fortnight', fishermen are drawn to the rivers in droves and it is true to say that many of them only fly fish at this time. This leads to a situation in which enthusiasm is not necessarily matched by expertise or by familiarity with the rules of the fishery.

Nothing is quite like a warm evening in late May with a gentle breeze drifting through the meadows. There is the odd slashing rise as some of the younger, more inexperienced fish attack the duns lifting off the surface of the river. You look up among the trees and see the mayfly spinners bouncing up and down in their courting dance while you wait for them to move to the water and for the rise to begin. Swifts, swallows and chaffinches swoop across the water meadow, sometimes skimming so low they almost brush the grass as they join the banquet. After a while the female spinners flit back to the water's edge and expel their eggs, falling exhausted into the water. The rise begins in earnest and the fish lose all their inhibitions. That is the magic of the mayfly that we look forward to every year.

Life Cycle & Habitat

The life cycle of the mayfly has been described by Dr. Cyril Bennett in his chapter on the entomology of chalk streams, so I only intend to summarise it briefly to illustrate the practical significance of the various stages to fly fishing. There are three species of mayfly in the United Kingdom; *Ephemera danica*, *Ephemera vulgata* and *Ephemera lineata*, all of which look extremely similar and can be essentially treated as one species from the fisherman's perspective. As Dr. Bennett points out, only the *Ephemera danica* occurs on chalk streams and is most commonly found in the southern region on rivers such as the Avon, Test, Lower Itchen, Kennet, Lambourne and the Frome. I would be remiss if I did not mention the Wye and Derwent in Derbyshire and some of the rivers in Norfolk that also have extensive hatches, but this is by no means a definitive list. Many other rivers have hatches of these remarkable insects, but it is the density of hatch that dictates if they have an impact on trout feeding habits and consequently on angling.

I should explain here that the term 'hatch' is commonly used by anglers to refer to at least three different things concerning mayflies (or any other flies for that matter). Firstly, the term is used to refer to the entire period during which mayflies hatch out in abundance (normally a period of about three to four weeks), as in 'the mayfly hatch is the highlight of the angling year'. Secondly, it is used to refer to a specific hatching event on a particular river at a particular time, as in 'there was a great mayfly hatch on the Avon this evening'. Thirdly, the word is used to refer to the process by which the insect progresses through its life cycle from nymph to imago, as in 'before mayfly can hatch, the temperature must be right'. The context will tell you which meaning is intended.

In *The Keeper of the Stream*, Frank Sawyer expressed his belief that the mayfly hatch was subject to five year cycles. He thought that, like all living things, in-breeding of stock eventually caused the gene pool to degenerate, leading to less successful hatches. On the Upper Avon he attempted to circumvent this by introducing females from another river every year and this proved relatively successful. A female mayfly lays somewhere in the region of 6,500 eggs, and those that survive develop into nymphs that live in burrows in the silt. They have large mandibles and strong front legs, not unlike a dragonfly nymph in miniature, that make it easier for them to dig their burrows. There is some conjecture as to how long the nymph stage of the cycle lasts, but it is commonly thought to be one to two years. Some nymphs might hatch after only one year, explaining why some mayflies are smaller than others. The nymphs, at the appropriate time dictated by conditions and temperatures, ascend in the water column by swimming to the surface and breaking their way through the surface film, with some clambering out onto vegetation and others remaining on the surface of the water. Here they split their shucks and emerge head and thorax first leaving their mouth parts behind and become duns or sub-imagos. This is known as the 'emerger' stage of the cycle. The duns need some time for the characteristic flag-like wings to dry before they can take to the air and find shelter amongst the trees and reeds. You may find that this will take considerably longer in wet weather as the duns flutter on the surface, desperately trying to dry their wings before heading aloft. You should therefore never discount a wet day during the mayfly hatch, as often these fluttering duns can prove irresistible to the fish. Once hatched, the insect can survive without food for a couple of days.

The sub-imago moults during a further stage into a fully fledged imago or 'spinner'. The imago has longer legs and longer setae than the sub-imago and the wings become polished and transparent. The body normally takes on a cleaner, creamier appearance. The spinners then perform an aerial mating ritual during which they dance together in cloud-like columns, the late afternoon sunshine glistening on their wings and making them appear to 'spin' up and down through the air. The males and females bind in mid-air and then fall to the ground in a lovers' embrace. After mating, the females take flight once more and descend back to the surface of the river to lay their eggs in the archetypal bouncing action that releases the eggs. They then collapse exhausted in the surface film where they are referred to as 'spent spinner' or 'spent gnat'.

Each phase of this cycle represents a valuable opportunity to fool a trout as they will feed on each and every stage. Many of these stages are ignored by fly fishermen and there is no room for this narrow-mindedness; every day is a school day. Even though this is one of the oldest forms of fly fishing, I believe that anglers should keep one eye on technological developments and modern entomological understanding and the other on the history and traditions of our sport. The aim should be to become rounded fishermen.

Trout behaviour in relation to mayfly – reading the signs

Trout behaviour changes dramatically over the course of the mayfly hatch. When the hatch first starts trout are either completely ignorant of the bonanza that is about to begin or they have forgotten about it. During the first few days trout will sometimes completely ignore mayfly as they drift down the river and rises tend to be sporadic. At this point, if fishery rules permit, you will frequently find that imitating the nymph stage is more effective than imitating the emerger or adult. The nymphs leave the cover of the river bed in their push towards sexual maturity and are surprisingly strong swimmers, often being described as 'agile darters'. The trout target these nymphs as they become increasingly active. After all, they are a substantial mouthful.

As the hatch progresses there is increasing activity in and on the surface film. This catches the trout's attention and they begin to zone-in on the emerger stage. The mayfly emerger is a phase greatly overlooked and underestimated by anglers. While the fisherman's attention is on the insects beginning to amass in the trees, you will often see bulgy rises as the trout lift off their holding spots and grab an emerger as it drifts past. As the insects attempt to struggle free, firstly from their shucks and then from the surface film, they are at their most vulnerable and the urgent struggling often sparks the predatory instincts of trout and other fish. It is thought that, to begin with, fish are intimidated by the size of these hatching insects. They are, after all, three or four times the size of the usual insects they feed on. Slowly the fish gain in confidence and begin to attack the winged adults on the surface, often producing that incredible slashing rise that gets the blood flowing. Frank Sawyer believed from his observations on the Upper Avon that before the fish '*abandon themselves to an orgy of feeding*', the trout have to re-learn every year that these insects are good to eat.

After a few days their instincts to attack this plethora of food fluttering about above them overcomes their timidity completely and the full fever sets in, with trout feeding voraciously and occasionally coming clear out of the water to catch an escaping mayfly. At this point, the angler does not need to present his fly with any great accuracy because often the fish will move a considerable distance to intercept a drifting mayfly. As the days pass however, the fish slowly become sated and what I call 'the glut' sets in. This normally coincides with the prolific hatches we all dream about and the fishing becomes more challenging. To achieve success the angler will often have to present the fly in exactly the right line and, in some cases, have the artificial in the correct numbered sequence. The fish will only take every fourth or fifth fly that comes over him, a phenomenon I think of as the 'dinner queue'. The reason this occurs is that the mayfly, being a large insect, actually takes a little time to swallow and ingest, a fact that many fishermen fail to take into account. It is important to spend time observing the rising fish rather than just blundering straight in. A few minutes sitting on the bank and taking stock can often mean the difference between success and failure. Sometimes a fish in this phase gently sips the fly off the surface and often has its dorsal fin and the tip of its tail out of the water, a feeding behaviour I refer to as 'sharking'. The rise form is a lovely classic ring, with the fish hanging high in the water column looking for the next meal.

Finally, the fish become increasingly wary. Sometimes they have been pricked or caught and released and perhaps remember the experience, or they have just had too much exposure to fishermen on the banks and flies aimed at their heads. Trout in this phase become what John Goddard and Brian Clarke refer to as 'educated'. Many of the bigger fish become educated faster as they clue in to what is going on before their smaller brothers. Keep a close eye out for other hatches such as pale watery duns or black gnats. The fish have been dining on lobster for a couple of weeks and might now prefer a burger. There is very little room for error in this phase and the wrong fly pattern or a duff cast can put the fish down. When this occurs, if you have the patience to wait for fifteen minutes or so, you will often find the fish will start rising again. Let them eat a few naturals first before resuming the attack so that they can relax. You may also come across fish which remain static regardless of hatches and flies, both natural and artificial, floating over their heads. These fish are completely gorged and simply cannot eat any more. Yes, it happens, even to trout!

Tackle setup

When it comes to fishing mayfly patterns, I find it is important to adjust your normal rig. When I first started fishing chalk streams as a child, the normal setup was something like an 8 ft. 6 in. rod with a 5 or 6 weight fly line to match. Tackle technology has moved on dramatically since then and lighter rods have been developed that are more than capable of dealing with windy days and large fish. I changed to an 8 ft. 6 in. 4 weight and then later to an 8ft. 3 weight which had the precision and power to do the job in hand. Many would still say that the 8 ft 6 in. 5 weight would be the standard rod for English chalk streams at mayfly time and there is nothing wrong with that, particularly in a strong upstream wind. These days it is really down to personal preference.

A reel on a chalk stream is rarely required to be more than a line storage device, so take your pick. I prefer to go classical with a nice ratchet check and exposed rim that I can palm if need be. It makes a nice noise and I personally love the sound of a singing reel.

Where fly lines are concerned, a standard floating line is employed and I like one with a long forward taper that improves accuracy and also produces a nice light presentation on the river surface. There has been long debate about colour of fly lines and their visibility to the trout. Goddard and Clarke conducted detailed studies on this, concluding that the colour of the fly line is less significant than the 'flash' of the line, which you can either buy into or not, but I have veered towards using 'Camo' fly lines which are normally green or buff in colour. I have really picked this up from fishing for trout abroad, where guides will tell you it makes all the difference, but on chalk streams many anglers use white or pink lines and still seem to catch their share of fish.

In my view, it is the leader that is key. The usual leaders I use on chalk streams in this age of light fluorocarbon tippets and micro flies are discarded during mayfly time in favour of old-style nylon 'Profil' leaders, with a length of about 9 ft and tapered to a 5 lb breaking strain point. The reason for this is that many mayfly patterns are tied with extended wings and when cast using fine flurocarbon, can twist horribly. A twisted leader loses strength quickly and although I would normally choose fluorocarbon over nylon because it has the same density as water and sinks well, this advantage is outweighed by the twisting phenomenon. Although Skues might have given anything for the properties of fluorocarbon in a leader for nymph fishing, when it comes to using it with a bushy dry fly you will also find that when the drift has ended and you draw back the line to recast, the fly is sucked under and drowned by the sunken tippet. Not only can this be very annoying, but it takes longer to dry the fly by false casting before it can be presented to the fish again. A nylon leader lifts off more easily. Although a length of 9 ft is usually sufficient, I will add a section of tippet material and lengthen it to 12 or even 15 ft for a particularly shy fish. The trade-off here is manageability because the longer the leader, the harder it is to present the fly accurately, especially at short range when there is not much fly line out of the tip ring. Tapered leaders can make a big difference in short range casting because they turn over better. Tapered leaders are expensive yes, but an easy way to conserve them is to add tippet material as they become shorter. A great little gadget on the market right now is leader rings; tiny little brass or chrome rings that are tied onto the end of a leader allowing level pieces of tippet to be added easily and without continually shortening the tapered section through tying blood-knots. Using leader rings will allow a tapered leader to last through nearly the whole period of the mayfly hatch.

When using nylon leaders or tippet material, it is vital to employ some form of degreasing agent to counteract the shiny nylon surface and to slightly reduce nylon's propensity to float. I very much favour the old concoction of Fullers' earth mixed with glycerine. This will drop the leader into the surface film, hiding it from the fish.

Keeping the fly afloat is also vitally important and for this there is no better substance than the old favourite, Gink. A trick I sometimes employ is to soak flies in Gink the day before I go fishing so that it dries properly before the flies are used. This can greatly improve 'floatability' and avoids the problem of getting Gink on the leader while applying it to the fly. After a fish has been caught the fly is often waterlogged and saturated in slime. Having washed the fly in water to remove the slime, I find that squeezing it in old-fashioned amadou or shammy leather blots out the moisture, which is necessary before re-applying floatant.

Last, but not least, flies. Everyone has their favourites, from classical patterns with split duck-feather wings to modern hackle representations such as the Shadow Mayfly. The traditional split duck-feather mayflies are the worst offenders when it comes to spinning and causing twisted leaders. In the last six or seven years there has been a move away from them towards hair and hackle wing patterns. Parachute patterns have become especially popular. I favour mayfly patterns with some form of detached body. Many patterns on the market today catch more fishermen in the tackle shop than fish on the river, but the only fly I have stopped using completely is the Grey Wulff, mostly because the great Lee Wulff never intended it to represent a mayfly. Others disagree and this fly will catch fish during mayfly time. My favourites are Oliver Edward's Mohican Mayfly, Paul Proctor's Loop Mayfly, Mrs Cox's Mayfly and I do keep a few Shadow Mayflies in my box as I find them particularly effective at dusk. Shadow Mayflies are the easiest to control and require less effort in the half light, when sometimes you are casting at a splash. I have also had considerable success with the plastazote bodied pattern which has a detached body formed from plastazote etherfoam. I first bought some of these because I thought they looked cool and there are obvious benefits to a fly that does not sink. I later found out that they are more than just a gimmick and can be huge fun to fish, something discussed later. When it comes to flies representing the nymph stage, you can't go wrong with Richard Walker's Mayfly Nymph. Charles Jardine recommends having both weighted and un-weighted versions of this fly because the depth at which they are fished is important. It is also imperative to have an emerger pattern and for this I am fond of Paul Proctor's Mayfly Emerger which has proved deadly for me.

When considering fly patterns it is also important to consider where you are fishing. Different river systems have different densities of hatches and also mayflies of different sizes and grades of colour. For example, the mayfly that hatch off some of the Norfolk chalk streams are very creamy in colour and are larger than those I have seen on the Test and Avon systems, whilst mayfly hatching on the Avon are greener in colour and it can be important to take this into consideration when choosing patterns. As a general rule on size, I reduce the size of the fly the harder the fish are to catch. Often, the more educated a trout is, the smaller the mayfly pattern needed to fool it. I normally vary between a size 8 and a size 12 hook, but will go down to size 14 or even size 16 hooks if necessary. There is nothing quite as exciting as finding a trout that has seen hordes of fishermen and hosts of artificial flies and then having the satisfaction of being able to fool it. Granted, this can be easier at mayfly time than at other times of the year and it is also possible to catch the bigger fish because they become caught up in the excitement of the hatch.

Observation, different rise patterns and takes

When you arrive on the river bank look for signs the hatch has started and if it has, note the stage the hatch has progressed to. I always start by inspecting the undergrowth along the river edge to look for nymphs that have crawled out and are hatching. If you see a number of shucks then it is likely the mayfly have hatched to the sub-imago stage. I then begin to look in sheltered areas next to the trees to see if the dance of the mayfly has started. Peering into eddies is also a good indicator because you will often see shucks trapped by the current in the swirling waters. Look for fish and see how they are behaving. If they are lying low and occasionally flicking from side to side with the white of their mouths showing, then they are probably munching the nymphs as they attempt to swim to the surface. If the fish are coming up and head-and-tailing with hardly a break of the surface, they are clued in to the emergers as they try and struggle free. Another good indicator is the level that the swallows are flying at in the meadows. As the hatch progresses and the duns morph into spinners you will see the birds begin to swoop ever closer to the ground. When the hatch starts in earnest you will see them dive and dip as they grab the bounty erupting from the water's edge. Waterfowl will also start to take notice, with ducks and moorhens beginning to take their share and their chicks skittering across the surface to intercept drifting mayflies.

Eventually, the first rings will begin to appear as the female spinners begin to dip into the water's surface to lay their eggs. At this stage observation is particularly important and you should not rush in. I look for a fish that is beginning to rise consistently. At first you will see the 'oncers', fish that take a fly and then do not rise again for some time. When you have found a fish that is rising continuously, watch it for a while before carefully moving into position. I like to creep up as low as possible using the vegetation on the bank as cover. Don't forget that the higher you are in relation to the fish the easier it is for that fish to spot you in its 97°cone of vision. This phase requires an up-winged dry fly pattern.

At last the fish will calm down, hold station and rise consistently. This can be a clue that they have now begun feeding on the spent gnat and are just mopping up the carcasses as they drift down the river. The bigger fish learn this very quickly; a dead mayfly tastes just as good as a live one and is an easy meal, requiring little expenditure of energy. The spent gnat is another facet of the life cycle of the mayfly that the fish take a little while to become accustomed to. First, they learn that live mayflies taste good and that is what they look for. Sawyer felt that, to begin with, they did not even realise the spent gnat was the same insect. Eventually, they get the message and begin to feed on the easier option. A flat-wing spent mayfly pattern can prove deadly for the bigger fish that refuse to rise to an up-winged pattern and I for one, have had some incredible evenings fishing only spent patterns. It is important to note that it is worth fishing the spent gnat for a couple of weeks after the main hatch has finished. The trout become accustomed to savouring these delicacies and their enthusiasm for an easy meal takes some time to subside.

Rises can take many different forms. There is the 'sip', where the fish barely breaks the surface and merely sucks the fly through the surface film. There is the 'slash', which occurs as the fish comes up aggressively sideways before crashing down on its victim and as the tail comes across the surface you will see a torrent of water projected sideways. This is normally a smaller or less experienced fish that has become excited about the prospect of a gorging. Another rise I am particularly fond of I call the 'tail slap'. Here the fish will attempt to drown the fly before eating it. Finally, there is my total favourite and the most spectacular of all which I like to call the 'Free Willy'. Here the trout launches itself bodily out of the water as it attempts to take an airborne fly that it has been tracking. All of these different forms can indicate the mood of the fish and how reckless, or cautious, they might be in accepting an artificial.

Presentation of the fly and casting

When presenting the fly, first think about where you are going to do it from. As mentioned before, stealth is everything. Find a suitable spot from which to cast and make your way slowly to it. Keep as far back from the river as you can, walk slowly, try not to thump the bank and keep your face down. While guiding in Norway one of my mentors told me that fish can see a pale human face like a flash from a mirror, so since then I have always stalked with my face looking to the ground. Once you are level with your chosen spot, only THEN move to the river bank. I have watched many fishermen march up the bank to a rising fish and start thrashing away. They then wonder why the fish does not rise to the fly – normally because 'Elvis has left the building!' Try and present the fly from as far away as you can manage comfortably without over-stretching your casting ability. How far this is differs entirely from fisherman to fisherman, but if you have stalked the fish properly then it is possible to get pretty close. Stealth is particularly important when wild trout are your target. Wildies will see you a mile away and ping off, normally scaring a large chunk of the stretch above you.

Accuracy in casting will greatly improve your chances and I have found that before going fishing it helps to practice. A saucer on the lawn is a good idea, or like I did as a teenager, you can upgrade to practising on the cat. The closer you can drop the fly (hookless of course!) the more likely you are to get a strike from a cat. I admit it is a little unorthodox, but I can safely say that those years spent casting at cats has greatly improved my accuracy! Casting a large bushy fly into the wind is not that easy sometimes and there are a few techniques that I have found help. The size of the loop you are casting will dictate how effectively the line will cut into the wind. If you use a little more wrist action in your cast you will find the loop of your cast will tighten up significantly, punching the line through the wind. Where the line goes, the fly will follow. This is particularly helpful when trying to drop a fly on the nose of that annoying trout rising under a bush on the far side.

If you find that you are catching up because of tailing loops or the fly is landing too hard, relax the wrist in the cast and the loop will open up. This has the fantastic side-effect of causing the fly to parachute upwards, and if your length of line is correct, the fly will drop like a feather. A few other interesting tricks include casts I call the 'Bend-it-like-Beckham' cast and the 'Kick-back' cast. If you are casting up the near-side bank to a fish rising above you with a side cast, grabbing the line as the leader is extending and pulling backwards slightly will kick the fly to the left and drop it away from the leader. This is particularly useful if you are attempting to cast around some obstruction between you and the fish. You do, however, have to be very careful with this one because if you let the fly drift too long you will find it becomes caught up in the obstruction you were trying to avoid. The Kick-back is similar, but is used with an overhead cast. If you are struggling to turn over a heavy fly, grab the fly line and pull backwards just as the leader is unfurling. The fly then turns over properly and drops neatly onto the water. The last cast I advocate is the 'Whip' cast. This is where the rod is cast back and forward on a short line for three or four false casts before your main cast. This will dry large mayfly patterns that tend to become saturated.

When presenting a mayfly imitation, a very important consideration is drag. Although a common problem in chalk stream fishing, it is amplified by using such a large fly. A drag free drift can be the difference between success and failure. When casting at a fish immediately above you, drag is not much of an issue because the fly, leader and fly line are usually in the same current lane and the fly drifts down naturally. The line can simply be retrieved by hand so as to stay in contact with the fly as it drifts towards you. This is not the case when casting upstream and at an angle across the river. Many river fishermen do not understand the significance of drag. When a fly is cast across the river, invariably the faster current in the centre of the flow creates a belly in the line which in turn causes the fly to drag. As a general rule, fish do not like a fly that is dragged over their noses because it looks unnatural. There are a few tips that can help combat drag. The most common is the upstream mend. As the line is cast out, an upstream flick of the rod tip in a circular motion will put an upstream mend into the line and give you a few vital seconds of drag-free drift. Alternatively, you can try the squiggle cast; as the line is shot out through the rings and just before it connects with the surface, drop the rod tip and waggle it from side to side. This puts wiggles in the line on the surface of the water and will create enough slack to allow the fly to drift free.

Positioning of the fly is also important. During a prolific hatch you will often find that a fish will not move to the left or right to take a fly and will take only those that drift directly over it. A trout's life depends upon using as little energy as possible for maximum returns of food. If there is no need to move – it won't. I would liken a trout rising in a prolific mayfly hatch to a human lying in a lazyboy chair in front of the television with a cooler of beer on the side table. The human is unlikely to get up and go to the fridge for a beer when all that is necessary is to reach out to the side table and the same goes for the fish. It is therefore vitally important to gauge the mood of the fish and present the fly accordingly. Fortunately, it is easy to see if the fish is moving off its line to take flies or not.

I will quite often cast off one knee to make my profile lower to the rising fish. Strip off the amount of line you think you will need BEFORE you begin casting. If you cast and strip off line at the same time, it will take longer and it is more likely you will spook your quarry with all that false casting. Always try to make your first cast your best and I find that false casting off the line of the fish to gauge the length before dropping the final cast on target works well. By doing this you have presented the least amount of opportunity for the fish to spot you. If the cast has not gone according to plan then don't pick the fly and line up off the surface before it has passed the fish, otherwise you will almost certainly spook it. When you do lift it off, take in the slack line with your other hand and bring it off smoothly and crisply. Too many times have I seen fishermen thrash it off and then wonder why the trout is making for the next village. Try and land the fly about 18 inches above the fish to give the fish time to see the fly. This should be taken as a guide and not a rule because sometimes the fly will be taken after a much longer drift, as long as you have managed to avoid drag.

Striking is also slightly different when mayfly fishing. Mayfly patterns are large and you have got to give the fish time to turn on the fly. It pays to wait a fraction of a second longer and hook them squarely.

Advanced Mayfly Techniques – the fun stuff

The simple guidelines set out above should work on most fish during mayfly time. However, not all fish are the same. Sometimes you find a difficult one and something different has to be tried. There is nothing more annoying than finding the perfect consistently rising fish, carefully stalking it, making a perfect presentation after slipstreaming your back cast through a gap in the trees, getting the fly in the right position, in the correct current lane and in the correct order in the dinner queue and....... nothing happens! The fish continues to feed; in fact it gives you the fin as it obnoxiously gulps the fly in front of, to the side of and directly behind your artificial.

The first thing to do is to change pattern and perhaps drop down a size. If the fish has not spooked, it might be that it has seen twenty-five Grey Wulffs that day and can tell you if it came from Farlows or Robjents. If the fish can learn that natural mayflies are good to eat then, over the same period of time, they can also learn that Grey Wulffs are not, particularly in this age of catch and release. In your irritation do not be lazy – grease the fly and degrease the leader. Once again attempt the perfect presentation. If you pull this off and there is no reaction from the fish, then on your next cast dump the fly unceremoniously on top of its head. Not only will this make you feel better but it will often trigger the fish's aggressive instincts and cause it to take the fly.

Another technique that works really well on wider, slower stretches of chalk stream is the 'stripped mayfly'. A trout cannot stand the prospect of food escaping. It is a little like a dry fly version of Sawyer's induced take. Cast the fly above and to one side of the fish and as soon as the fly alights, strip in some line by hand or even just raise the rod to make the fly wake over the fish. This will often induce a primeval reaction in the fish and can produce some stunning takes. I have developed this one stage further to the 'stripped plazote-bodied mayfly' technique. The etherfoam in the tail is impossible to sink which makes this pattern particularly good for this. On some of the lower stretches of the Test and Avon this technique has proved deadly and I have seen fish bow-wave right across the river to intercept a stripped plazote-bodied mayfly.

Even if there is a heavy mayfly hatch, do not be afraid to change fly patterns to something other than a mayfly imitation. It often amazes me that fishermen will cling to mayfly patterns just because mayflies are hatching when they are quite evidently not catching any fish on them. A favourite of mine in this situation is the Daddy Longlegs. This gangly terrestrial can prove just too irresistible to finicky trout. It is important to ring the changes and if very large does not work then try very small. Size 16 CDC Olives or F-Flies can be fatal to an educated trout.

Another unorthodox technique I have successfully used in the past I call 'using the trees'. A rising trout looks upwards to feed and those that live close under the banks (normally the large and clever fish) eat quite a number of flies that fall off the undergrowth on the bank directly into the water below. If you are struggling to present your fly to such a spot without drag, cast very lightly directly into the bushes or rushes above the fish. Then very gently pull the fly off. Granted, this is risky because you can get hooked up, but you will be amazed how often the fly just drops off onto the head of a waiting fish that snaffles it instantly. I once landed twelve fish in a day on the Wissey in Norfolk during a prolific hatch using this technique and I only lost three flies!

The mayfly hatch is a natural phenomenon that should be marvelled at. As one of the main events in the chalk stream calendar, I would urge my fellow anglers to pause on the river bank and take it in. We have all witnessed anglers become overwhelmed by the madness and throw bank etiquette to the wind, which only detracts from the enjoyment of others. After all, chalk stream fishing is not all about catching fish. It is the feeling of being enveloped by nature that makes us go in the first place. Ensure your tackle is organised and appropriate for the task and that all your accoutrements are easily to hand. Be stealthy, move slowly up the bank and acquire a good position before beginning to cast. Observe the hatch, see what stage it has reached, and choose your fly pattern accordingly. Take your time over the presentation of the fly and have drag at the forefront of your mind. Lastly, keep an open mind. If you are struggling with a particular fish be prepared to try something completely different. Armed with some of these ideas I hope that the reader will gain as much magical enjoyment from the mayfly as I have.

Chapter Six

Seasonal Tactics

John Stoddart

Fly fishermen need the equipment and the skills to use it, but to a large extent these change little throughout the season. By contrast, the environment in which they enjoy their sport changes all the time and they must know what to expect at any time of the year. The conditions in and around the river, the flies that are interesting to the fish, the problems the angler needs to solve, all vary as the months pass. I have met fly fishermen who profess little knowledge or even interest in entomology, but even a rudimentary understanding of the main fly groups will enhance the fishing experience, enabling considered choices of fly to be made. Fish will feed on what is abundant on the day and imitating what is abundant will give you the best chance, even if from time to time a fish takes an artificial fly that is quite different to the naturals actually on the water. What follows is a description of the features of the changing seasons on chalk streams. Of course, there are no clear boundaries between the seasons and the one glides seamlessly into the next; mayflies will continue to trickle off the water long after their peak time in May and early June; crane flies will appear earlier in the summer than their autumn peak; all of it varies and can be unpredictable, but some general trends can be observed.

Spring

In the early season sport is often slow, the weather is still cold and little growth has occurred in the marginal bank vegetation, leaving the angler exposed. The rivers can still be in flood, the water is often high and coloured and the banks are wet. Weed growth has not yet begun in the river, though some weed hangs on through the winter and provides a refuge in the shallower water. The wind can be a deciding factor; the cold east and north-east winds will put off the angler, the flies and the fish. Nevertheless, sheltered places may still see trickles of flies, even in the wind. There are always some flies hatching somewhere and even during warm spells in the depths of winter, small numbers of large dark olives and midges will hatch. It is often said that in early season the best sport is to be had in the middle of the day from mid-morning to late afternoon, but experience shows that mornings and evenings can also be productive at times.

In spring fish gather in the gravelly shallows between any weed beds that have survived the winter. Fish will often only be active in limited areas so search out the rises; they may be difficult to see in the high, roiling water. The deeper, slower water is often unproductive for the dry-fly fisherman. These places are best left to mayfly time and beyond. This is the usual picture, but as I write, in spring of 2011, exceptionally high temperatures and low water levels have advanced everything by about three weeks and have caused an algal bloom to discolour the water in many of the streams. Each year is different, but the general rule is cold and wet.

The flies of spring are olives, grannom, hawthorn flies, alder flies and midges. Close observation should reveal what the fish are interested in and artificials need not be over-elaborate – imitations of the general outline, colour and size of the fly will be successful.

Olives are part of the up-winged fly group and for the less experienced they can be described as mini-versions of the mayfly. There are many varieties in different sizes and shades of colour and some are present in all seasons. The large dark olive is the first to put in an appearance in spring, with significant hatches in March and April. Large dark olive hatches almost always occur from midday to early afternoon and this is when the angler has his best chance. Large dark olive spinner falls, which occur later in the day, are so sparse that the trout don't often get excited about them. Medium olives of various species appear later in April and in early May. These olives hatch throughout the day and into the evening. All olive hatches tend to occur in the faster moving water with little activity in the slower, deeper sections. Many flies have been devised to imitate olives, both modern and traditional: Kites Imperial, Greenwell's Glory (dry), the Gold Ribbed Hare's Ear (dry) and the more general Adams patterns all serve well. Modern CDC flies in small sizes make excellent imitations of the olives and the body colour of these patterns can be varied to suit the hue of the naturals. All these patterns will imitate any of the olives and the angler need only vary the size to match the natural insects hatching at the time.

Walk by the rivers in Salisbury city centre on a warm lunchtime in early April and clouds of small caddis (sedge) flies will be skittering low over the water and filling the air. Tourists swat them away from their lunches, but anglers smile at the thought of the sport to come. It is the season's opening show and it can excite the trout or leave them cold, but it is a joy to the fly fisherman after the harsh winter months. It is not so for everyone – a friend living by the river (not an angler) was for years disturbed by these 'dirty creatures'. After my explanation of their origins, character and local importance they are now allowed to crawl on her ceilings and curtains, but every year she forgets their name and has to be reminded: 'grannom'. The grannom is often dismissed as being of no interest to the trout. It is true that the adult form is seldom taken (although should you want to try it, it can be successfully imitated by variants of the CDC and Elk in the right size), but the emerging pupa is taken with gusto, particularly on the Nadder where the trout seem particularly keen on this fly, often jumping from the water to try their luck with the adults. The trout's preference for the emerging pupa can lead the angler who tries to imitate it into controversy over fly selection. On many chalk stream fisheries, particularly in the upper reaches, there is an 'upstream dry fly only' rule in force, either permanently or at least from the beginning of the season until the end of June. The most effective imitations of emerging grannom pupa are emerger fly patterns like the Klinkhåmer and Shuttlecock-styled patterns. These are designed to ride low in the surface film with at least a portion of their construction beneath the surface. For some, this disqualifies them as 'dry' flies. Others hold the view that as long as some reasonably substantial part of the fly is above the surface, then it is a dry fly. The debate goes on and on. One solution is to head for the lower reaches of the rivers which are often designated as 'mixed', 'open' or 'coarse' fisheries with more flexible rules. Some of the best early season trout fishing can be had on these lower reaches, which are often stuffed with trout. As a bonus, they are also amongst the most beautiful stretches of the river. Trout in these reaches are often stocked fish that have survived and have moved downstream in the winter floods. Although survival rates of stocked fish are thought to be low, those that have over-wintered are strong and eager. There are also good numbers of wild trout in these stretches.

As spring progresses increasing numbers of black flies; hawthorn, alder and black gnat, will appear. Hawthorn flies are terrestrial insects that spend their larval stage in the grass roots of the meadows and after hatching, live amongst the bushes and trees. They arrive on the water as a result of aerial incompetence. They are blown or fall there and are then taken by the trout. The fish are not always interested in them, but on the right day they can be important. They are easily identified by their black colour and distinctive body shape with its disproportionately dangly legs. Black-hackled and bodied artificials (sometimes incorporating the dangly legs) in sizes 14, 16 and 18 will cover these occasions. Alder flies are sedge-like aquatic insects that frequent the slower marginal sections of rivers and are also found on stillwaters. Dark coloured sedge imitations in the appropriate size will work for them.

Midges are present at all times and although usually associated with stillwater fishing, are also found on the rivers and streams more or less continuously, including during spring, although they are more abundant in the late summer and autumn. After hatching from the egg, these insects have three stages to their life cycle. The first is the larval stage, thin, hair-like 'bloodworms' that can be successfully imitated on stillwaters, but which chalk stream fishermen do not generally try to imitate. It is when the larva transform into pupa, tiny, nymph-like creatures and then rise to the surface film to hatch into adult flies that they become important to the river fly fisherman. Both the pupa and adult flies can be imitated with small, dark, sparsely dressed patterns, with CDC emerger patterns and micro-flies (size 20 or smaller) being particularly successful. In spring, when fish are rising but you can see no flies on the water at all, the culprit is often tiny midges. Now is the time to put on your spectacles, attach a 7X tippet and try out that size 26 fly you bought out of curiosity but have never been brave enough to use! Don't worry that you cannot see the fly on the water after you cast it out. You will have a rough idea where it is and if a fish rises anywhere near it your instincts will take over. But if you really cannot bring yourself to enjoy fishing invisible flies, an alternative is the Griffith's Gnat in size 18. This highly visible fly is an excellent representation of a midge mating ball and will often be taken by fish feeding on hatching midges.

Two skills above all others are required in all seasons but particularly in early spring, and they are concealment and observation. Many anglers really do not grasp how important concealment is. I see anglers taking no heed of their own impact on the environment as they wander upright along the bank. As a local bailiff remarked to me recently, "You'll even see them wearing a big white hat!" Every creature in the region spots them and departs quickly. Certainly, the fish see them and if they do not immediately scatter, at least stop feeding in nervous anticipation of what the big white hat is going to do next. Skilful fishermen crouch in what little marginal vegetation exists, stand back from the water, keep low and blend in. When I look at the return books the effect is clear; concealment is crucial to success and those anglers who take care to hide their presence catch almost all the fish.

Don't start casting the instant you arrive, using the fly you left on the line at the end of your last outing. Take your time and consider your options before starting to fish. Watch the water for any fly life or fish movement. Coloured water will perhaps help the angler to stay out of sight of the fish, but will also keep the fish out of sight of the angler. Surface movement may be the only indication of feeding fish so look carefully for the less obvious rise forms. Look in the air above the river and under the trees, look at any cobwebs, they might contain recent fly corpses and this can help tell you what can be expected on the water. You must observe much and fish little.

Catch returns indicate that the wild fish are the first to react to the warming weather and the new food supply. Stocked fish introduced to the river in the early season congregate in the deeper water and take their time to learn what can be eaten and how to eat it. Stomach contents of introduced fish show that they have eaten leaves, grass and pieces of stick as they struggle to learn what should replace their previous diet of hatchery pellets. Following the stocking truck will therefore not help you find the feeding fish. Research with dye-marked fish indicates that stocked fish respond to the fly fisherman's efforts three to four weeks after their introduction and from then on provide good sport.

Chalk streams in spring may be uninviting when it is cold and the river is swollen, but as the season develops the warmth brings on the bank side growth and the water weeds stir into life, thickening into banks and stretching green tendrils along the channels. Wildlife appears and the colours of spring, greens and yellows, are at their best. The meadows are sprinkled with flowers, the marsh marigold stands out boldly with its yellow-orange flowers, the hawthorn is white with blossom and the pink, stumpy stalks of the butterbur look almost alien. It is a vibrant time and it is good to be out in the countryside. The fish can be difficult and the hatches of fly sporadic, but it is a joy to be fishing again after the winter lay-off. If no flies are hatching and no fish are rising, a nymph can be fished to the deeper lies when and where the rules permit and the nymphs of the up-winged flies can be imitated by nothing more complex than a Sawyer's Pheasant Tail Nymph, the traditional pattern sometimes now weighted with a gold bead to get it down through the swollen water column more quickly. If the water is coloured it is unlikely that you will see fish feeding, so considered casts with nymphs to likely lies is the way to produce results. Other nymph imitations that are effective in this situation are the Gold–ribbed Hare's Ear Nymph and weighted caddis imitations.

Early Summer

The early season is left behind as the mayfly start to trickle off the water in early May. From mid-May through to late June or thereabouts, mayfly dominate the scene and as that is the subject of an entire chapter elsewhere in this book, we will leave the clouds of dancing insects, the boiling rises and the flailing anglers to arrive at the altogether more tranquil circumstances of the high summer.

High Summer

By the end of the mayfly period the fish have fully recovered from the struggles of winter and early spring, they have put on weight and the stocked fish have learnt their trade. The rivers are quieter and anglers who gathered in large numbers for the mayfly circus have departed. The water is lower and crystal clear and the air is filled with fly life throughout the day and into the evening. The bank-side growth is high, helping to conceal the fisherman and providing ample resting places for the flies. The thick cover makes it easier to observe activity on the river without being seen yourself and you can move in closer to the rising fish, but it may also make some of the river inaccessible and casting difficult. Nettles, brambles and even wasps' nests all test your determination. Waders may be more use as protection from nettles than for wading. After the experience of the mayfly feasts, the fish are sated and have become wary of the anglers' offerings. Sometimes they will rise slowly to the angler's fly, circling and backing downstream to inspect it closely before making a decision to leave well alone. This can be frustrating, but a change of pattern or size of fly will often fool them into a take. Ranunculus and other weed in the river may now be close to or at the surface, making the water difficult to fish. The weed is important to the health of the river because it holds back the flow of water, keeping levels up and providing a home for the insects on which the fish feed, but a balance must be struck. If the abundant weed is not cut, fishing can be impossible, but too much cutting can reduce the insect habitat and fish cover. For the angler, the summer weed cuts are a mixed blessing, but it is possible to cast carefully between the rafts of cut weed floating down the river, line held high to avoid the drag of weed and the fish will often be excited by food liberated during the cut. With warmer weather and lower water levels, the fish move to deeper water and the shallower water will usually only hold fish in the late evening. Shady places under the trees and overhanging vegetation will be where the trout are to be found. Fish will be rising in the shelter of the dense cover and casting can be tricky.

Every type of fly will be around and the angler will need to experiment to find the right pattern. Terrestrials will still be present in large numbers and the terrestrial food basket will be supplemented by caterpillars, ants, aphids and beetles that fall in or have been blown onto the water. Olives, of course, are still present. Blue-winged olives will have joined their relatives, along with smaller olives and spurwings. The yellow May dun, first seen in spring and early summer during the mayfly hatches, becomes noticeable again during August and is to me the most beautiful of the up-winged flies. It is never found in abundance, but stands out clearly with its brilliant, sulphur body and wings as it rises over the water. It is perhaps of questionable interest to the trout, but it is one of the most glamorous flies. The old explanation for the trout's lack of interest in this fly is that it is bitter tasting, but it is more likely that the trout see so few that they never develop the habit of eating them. There are exceptions though and I have found yellow imitations of the dun to be taken fairly readily on the Nadder. The larger caddis or sedge flies also appear and can provide dramatic late evening sport. Among the small flies, the midges are joined by the reed smuts and Caenis.

Let me give you an example of the difficulties that can confront you on a summer's day. Some time ago I encountered a typical summer fish rising under the cover of an overhanging thorn bush, strung with brambles, which just brushed the water. A strand of barbed wire crossed the river, just a foot or so above the surface and a yard above the bush. The fish rose steadily right under the bush where the current was rapid. A bank of weed was breaking the surface directly between me and the fish. Every attempt I made to put the fly over the fish resulted in the fly being pulled away from the bush by a combination of the current and the line catching on the exposed weed. How to get the fly over the fish? Clearly the solution was to get enough line into the space above the bush to let the fly drift unimpeded down the current lane and under the bush, but I just could not get this right on the first occasion.

Giving the fish best for that day, I moved on, but I often thought about that fish in its almost impregnable lair. Returning to the spot on another day, I found the fish in the same place and again rising right under the bush. This time I tried a low sideways flick to create a loop of line under the barbed wire and the fly was free to run the few feet straight down under the bush. A splash and a plump one-and-a-half pounder was the happy result. This delightful wild fish was returned to his bush to grow into a two pounder for next season. The incident exemplifies the challenges and pleasures of difficult summer fishing – you may work harder to catch fewer fish out of difficult lies, but the challenges and great satisfaction when you successfully meet them, more than compensate you for your trouble.

Exploring the deeper sections and the hatch pools with weighted nymphs such as Sawyer's Pheasant Tail Nymphs or rough bodied Gold Ribbed Hare's Ears in the larger sizes with bead heads and perhaps a lead under-body, can be worthwhile in hot summer weather. These flies can get down to the fish in this sometimes turbulent water. Where nymph fishing is permitted, it can be at its most exciting when nymphs are cast to fish seen feeding below the surface. Raising the rod as the fish turns to the drifting nymph requires careful timing and acute observation and learning the practice of the induced take – lifting the nymph in the water just as it approaches the fish – will improve your chances of success.

Dragonflies and damselflies will be seen busying themselves around the reeds throughout the summer, though it is unlikely that the adults form part of the river trout's diet. The nymphs may certainly be taken and both are important to the stillwater angler, but many clubs set size limits on the dressing of nymphs and in this way exclude most dragonfly and damselfly nymphs from legitimate imitation and use on chalk streams.

The evening and the hour that approaches darkness can be the most rewarding of the summer period. Fish, often the larger ones, will start to feed under cover of dusk. The 'evening rise' is a famous phenomenon that has often been described. Sometimes evening rises will begin and end in a short time, so you need to be on the water waiting and the timing of the rise may vary from river to river and from day to day. There may be several short evening rises to different species and at about the point of darkness, fish will often rise for half an hour or so, stopping as quickly as they started when full darkness falls. The evening rise is often to spinners; females returning to the water to lay their eggs and then die on the surface. The blue-winged olives do this and are still fairly plentiful on the Avon in the rippled and more oxygenated water. Returning blue-winged olives will almost invariably interest the trout and can be successfully imitated using artificials such as the Sherry Spinner. The bodies of the returning blue-winged olive spinners are reddish-brown to orange in colour. Artificials tied with a reddish-orange body, spent wings and the three tails of this fly will be effective. These 'trigger' features are often exaggerated to produce the required response, an example being extended tail dimensions which also help to float and balance the fly on the water. Flies can be modern CDC or Klinkhåmer-style designs or more traditional patterns like the Orange or Ginger Quill. All will imitate the blue-winged olive spinner effectively.

It is often very difficult to work out what insects the fish are taking in low light conditions. Frequently the fish are interested in tiny flies, often in emerger form, just beneath the surface. These very small flies, midges, Caenis and reed smuts, can induce extreme selectivity in the feeding behaviour of the fish which sometimes concentrate on them to the exclusion of all else. In this situation, the best hope is to try the very small 'micro' patterns. At the other end of the scale, the late evening can also bring hatches of large sedges and big, bushy patterns such as the Humpy can bring spectacular takes from the bigger fish. This is a time when drag can become your friend rather than your enemy – sedge patterns skated or twitched across the surface in the manner of the natural fly's fluttering attempts to escape the surface after hatching can cause aggressive responses from the trout and they will sometimes charge right across the river to take the fly. The large numbers of adult sedge flies that are often seen flying over the water in the evening are rarely the focus of the trout's attention. It may be that they are too difficult to catch whilst they are on the wing and the trout instead concentrate on the hatching pupa which will be taken at or below the surface.

Summer can be frustrating, but on chalk streams the angler enjoys the advantage that, in good years, the water remains clear and is kept topped up by the river bed and valley-side springs discharging constantly cool water into the stream. On a chalk stream the angler can enjoy success throughout the season, though in summer he must choose his time to fish with a little more care.

Autumn and Late Season

September marks the beginning of autumn and the trout season has only a few more weeks to run. On most chalk streams the trout season ends on 15th October. The days are shorter, the valleys and hills take on their autumn colours after the harvest and the temperatures drop as the sun gets lower in the sky. On the river things start to turn full circle. The vegetation dies back, the cover is reduced and the greens fade to yellow and brown. Autumn winds and heavy rains can flatten what little cover remains. The angler is once again exposed, but the fish, although now wise to the angler's ways, show a marked increase in activity. Feeding picks up as the weather starts to cool and the trout prepare for the long winter and for spawning, by packing in the food. Some of the stocked trout can be coloured and ripe and can be seen cutting redds and attempting to spawn as early as October, but the wild trout spawn from Christmas onwards under the protection of the closed season.

The grayling have become more active and have fully recovered after spawning in spring. They provide good sport through the autumn alongside the trout and then on into the winter after the trout season closes. At the end of the trout season many clubs and syndicates relax the rules for the fly fisherman who wants to continue to pursue grayling. He is often permitted to use two-fly rigs. These include the New Zealand style, with a dry fly above and a nymph below attached by a short length of line to the eye or bend of the dry fly, but the typical two-fly rig used to fish for grayling in the deeper pools where they tend to congregate in the first, crisp days of autumn is a heavy nymph on the point and a lighter one on the dropper.

The flies of autumn include all the terrestrials mentioned in the context of summer, but as the temperatures drop, the variety and numbers of these flies start to decrease. The terrestrials are supplemented by increasing numbers of crane flies, 'daddies', that are very alluring to both trout and grayling, particularly the bigger fish. The larger crane flies are land based and their larvae originate in grassland, only being blown onto the water after hatching into adult flies, but some of the smaller crane flies are aquatic, the larvae spending their early days in the soggy margins of ponds and rivers. Although the crane fly is much more important on stillwaters, an artificial can sometimes be very effective on chalk streams and is a relief to the short-sighted angler, who can return to bigger hook sizes and large, highly visible patterns.

The olives of various species continue to be important, with the blue-winged olive hanging on well into September. Other small species, such as the pale watery, continue to put in an occasional appearance. Further generations of the large dark olive, last seen in early spring, make a return appearance throughout September and October, having been very sparse or entirely absent in the summer months.

Large species of sedge flies, such as the caperer, appear in September and October. The caperer is for me another of the stars of the fly world for its size and rusty red-brown colouring. Large sedge patterns, up to size 10, in darker colours can be employed to imitate this fly. The CDC and Elk, with a darker wing and heavier dressing than usual, is particularly effective.

Sub-surface feeding continues unabated during the autumn and while the nymphs of the up-winged flies are of most interest to the chalk stream fisherman, they are not by any means the whole of the underwater diet available to the fish. Shrimps and water lice are taken, along with quantities of water snails. The fish tend to switch their attention to shrimps in particular at this time of year, so shrimp imitations, like the famous Sawyers Killer Bug, are a good idea. Water snails are of most interest to stillwater anglers, but are also found in the rivers. Snails do not just cling to the bottom or onto vegetation, but will float to the surface to breed and it is then that they may preoccupy the feeding trout. Larger trout will also feed on fry, including their own offspring, and in some rivers crayfish also add to the trout's diet. Fish obtain more energy for effort expended from these bigger meals. However, the strictest and most restrictive of the codes adopted by some chalk stream anglers and fisheries excludes imitations of these additional 'non-nymph' foods from the angler's choices, at least until the end of the trout season, but they undoubtedly form a substantial part of the trout's diet, particularly of larger fish and where the rules permit, imitating them will be successful.

In autumn the water may be difficult to fish as leaves start to fall and cover the surface. Other debris may also be floating down the stream and sudden heavy spells of rain will quickly raise the level of rivers such as the Nadder, which are affected by spates to a greater extent than other chalk streams. The run-off from roads and farmland can also colour the water. In recent years the early autumn periods have been dry, with the rain and winds not arriving until November and consequently autumn river flows have been low. Usually autumn sees more water in the river.

The days being shorter, hatches occur more often during the full daylight hours than is the case in summer, when evening hatches predominate. Notwithstanding this, the sedges continue to be flies of the evening and large sedge patterns will still be best employed at dusk. As autumn advances the dry-fly fisherman's days are numbered. As the temperatures fall, most of the surface life will disappear with the exception of occasional large dark olives and midges. It is thus sub-surface food and nymph fishing which is likely to be of most importance towards the end of the season and the angler might find that he can return to fishing the shallow runs as he did in spring, only now using nymphs, but this depends upon how fast the water is flowing. Although chalk streams maintain a reasonably constant temperature, they can and do fall below 10°C, when trout become very much less active. In the severe winter of 2010-11, on the very coldest days, a thin film of ice covered the slower reaches of the Nadder, demonstrating that in extreme conditions chalk streams are not immune to temperature change, even if they are cushioned from its worst effects by abundant supplies of ground water at a constant temperature. The grayling remain active in conditions of extreme cold and falling water temperatures and, due to the very sparse surface fly activity during winter, are usually targeted using specialised nymphing techniques.

The chalk stream trout fisherman is a privileged person. He has access to water full of insect life and feeding fish, sometimes of a good size and weight. He can enjoy peaceful and beautiful stretches of the river and is protected from crowds of anglers on most waters by the beat systems employed by most fisheries. Compared with the coarse angler, he travels light, needing only what he can carry in his pockets. His quarry is not the size of a carp, pike or tench, but is quick, opportunistic and fights hard. We know that we could catch trout more easily with worms or maggots dangled downstream and perhaps that way we could also catch the big trout for which a tiny up-winged fly is barely a snack; but our knowledge of the seasons, the fly life, our ability to imitate and trick the trout into taking our artificial offerings, our codes which limit our ability to take the trout too easily, all contribute a little art and some morality to the primitive thrill of catching wild creatures.

Chapter Seven

Presenting the Upstream Dry Fly

Ian May

Developed as a major chalk stream tactic over 150 years ago, the practice of fishing the dry fly is regarded by many as being the very pinnacle of chalk stream fly-fishing skill and sometimes takes on the appearance of being something approaching a 'dark art'. This is an illusion that belies the fact that the dry fly works in two-dimensions, whereas fishing the sunk fly requires consideration of a third dimension – depth – and this method could therefore be considered every bit as skilful, or indeed an even more demanding discipline, than fishing the dry fly.

Historically, opinion has been divided, sometimes strongly, as to the 'rules of engagement' that should apply whilst fishing the dry fly. The gospel according to the late F. M. Halford and his dedicated band of followers, deemed the practice of speculative fishing or 'covering the water' as unacceptable in the extreme. Put into real terms, this means that the 'ultra-purist' dry-fly angler should, in order to maintain his (or her) integrity, be seen to cast only to visibly rising fish. In view of the fact that here in the 21st century we face a serious and regrettable decline in numbers of up-winged flies hatching on our chalk streams, one does wonder if an afternoon's dry-fly fishing following the purist ideal to the letter might amount to little more than a pleasant stroll along the riverbank. It is my view that, whilst always being delighted to happen upon free-rising fish that are sitting 'on-station' lazily sipping down surface flies, I see no problem with fishing strategically to fish that, although not visibly surface feeding, can be seen, and are in a position which allows a dry fly to be drifted over them in the hope of enticing a positive response. This approach allows us to target visible fish 'between hatches' and adds a valuable extra dimension to those sparse fly days that can, and often do, occur, particularly when fishing during the early season period when many chalk stream clubs and syndicates insist upon dry fly only. This more open minded and speculative approach also works particularly well at those times of the season when fish are feeding in an opportunistic fashion on terrestrial insects such as flying ants, beetles, hawthorn flies and crane-flies.

Although tackle for chalk stream dry fly fishing is very much a matter of personal choice, there are a few important considerations that can make a big difference to your ability to make a good, efficient delivery and presentation of a dry fly, and in successfully landing any fish subsequently hooked.

Rods

With so many different rods on the market, it is little wonder that confusion often arises regarding the ideal 'weapon of choice' for fishing a dry fly on a chalk stream. Not only are there a number of different materials to choose from (carbon fibre, bamboo/cane and glass fibre) with different grades of quality within each material, there is also an enormous variety of lengths, flex actions and cosmetic finishes. Personal preference is paramount here, because there are anglers who gain extreme pleasure from the specific attributes that are associated with fishing with a split cane or glass fibre rod. The easy progressive build-up of rod loading as the line is tensioned when the back cast is initiated, the eternal wait as the line moves up and away from the angler, the reverse flexing of the rod as the tension and weight of the backward moving line loads the rod, ready for the relaxed and easy forward cast and characteristic, unhurried delivery are all things of joy to those who choose to fish with cane or glass. Such a rod action also affords handy protection for fine tippets and light hook holds, which is more than useful when playing a fish. On the other hand, there are those who would not consider using such a rod due to its weight and 'slow action', much preferring a state-of-the-art, 'sub three-ounce' sliver of carbon that sits light in the hand and produces a Mach 2 line speed with associated arrow pointed, dynamic micro-loops. These rods allow the fly to be landed 'on a sixpence' in any awkward, squally, early season wind and all with a minimum of rod flex and operator effort, except perhaps while dealing with the noticeably less forgiving action in attempting to protect fine tippets and light hook holds when playing a large fish. Most people sit somewhere between the two extremes and for them there are many rods that will fit the bill admirably. Something with perhaps a middle to tip action that will allow an easy tightening (or widening) of the loop whilst casting and also have enough 'give' to allow a fuller, more forgiving flex when the fly is taken and a fish hooked. There are many rods available that fit this description, the majority of which are very affordable. Rod length is an important consideration and I would recommend a rod of 8 ft 6 in to 9 ft in length wherever possible, with a shorter rod of 7 ft to 7 ft 6 in long being selected if fishing on narrow streams or carriers or where there is an abundance of overhead obstructions. A longer rod offers better line (and hooked fish) control, but can prove to be a burden if used where the stream width is narrow or where there are obstructions overhead. A last point on rods is that it is wise to ensure that the finish is not 'over-glossy' as this will increase the risk of the rod flashing and possibly alerting fish to the angler's presence if the water is clear or the conditions are bright.

Reels

It is often said that fly-fishing reels are nothing more than line storage devices that have no other purpose in fly fishing and whilst agreeing that reel selection does not assume the same importance as rod or line choice, there are a few considerations to take into account when choosing a reel. Firstly the reel should ideally be a large arbour model, where the line is stored on the reel in the largest diameter coils possible. A narrow arbour reel can allow the line to be wound onto the spool in small, tight coils and significantly increases the risk of these coils remaining in the line whilst fishing (this can however, largely be avoided if sufficient backing line is used to increase the diameter of the spool's arbour before loading the fly line). A large arbour reel will also allow the line to be retrieved more quickly than is the case with a narrow arbour model. It is good insurance to use a reel that has a high quality drag system that can be finely adjusted to protect light tippets when playing a strong fish and that also remains reliable if the reel becomes wet whilst fishing. It is also a benefit if the reel is of sufficient weight to actually balance the rod in the hand whilst fishing. Lastly, it is wise to avoid reels that are overly bright and shiny because, like the rod, a highly polished reel can flash in sunny or bright conditions.

Lines

If ever there was a component of a carefully selected and well balanced fly-fishing outfit on which to spare no expense, it is the fly line. There can be no greater cause of frustration than a line that continues to retain a 'memory' and as a result, sits on the water like a coiled spring. Line memory is the term used to describe the result of a line that has been wound onto a reel in tight coils and retains the same shape, in varying degrees, when the line is pulled from the reel. If this happens, presentation can be completely upset because the ability to position the line, leader and fly on the water with any degree of consistency is lost. It is generally accepted that higher quality (and therefore, usually more expensive) fly lines are less susceptible to this problem and it really does pay dividends to buy a line that is of sufficient quality to avoid this. Good buoyancy is another important quality that will help considerably with good fly presentation because a line that sits 'on' rather than 'in' the water surface will be less susceptible to the influence of the flow when presenting a fly across tricky current lanes and can be picked up with noticeably less surface disturbance when lifting the line off the water to make a mend or to recast. Line colour is a much-debated point and opinion varies on what the fish can or cannot see when the line is lying on the water. I have seen enough fish caught in clear, shallow water with light, bright and fluorescent coloured lines to be of the opinion that these lines do not 'put the fish down' simply because of their colour. That said, my preference is for a slightly darker coloured, drab line because I find a bright coloured line far more visible whilst in the air during casting and suspect that the fish can probably see it more easily too. A final, but important point regarding fly lines for dry-fly fishing is the technique of 'over-lining' the rod. This is when, by using a line that is one (or on occasions two) line weights above the rod's recommended AFTM rating, one is able to load the rod more efficiently with less fly line outside the rod tip, which helps considerably when making short, accurate casts with a minimum of false casting.

Line & Dry Fly Floatant

Maintaining a high floating fly line is a 'must' when fishing dry flies on a river. Even when using a high quality line, the ingression of water into the line-to-leader connection (whether nail or needle knot, or braided loop) and the reduction of the line's general buoyancy through gradual wear and tear means that it is occasionally necessary to apply a treatment to prevent this from affecting the line and leader's performance in the final presentation of the dry fly. There are a number of proprietary products available, with my choice being the green-labelled Mucilin treatment (which contains silicon) that is applied by means of a felt pad that sits on top of the wax-like substance in its small, round plastic container. I also use the same product (applied sparingly between thumb and forefinger) to treat wing posts, collar and parachute hackles and tails, to give varying degrees of floatability to the majority my larger dry flies, but recommend using one of the more fluid treatments, such as Gink or Dilly-wax, to apply a float enhancing treatment to the absorbent bodies, hackles and tails on smaller flies. CDC oil, used very sparingly on the various parts of delicate CDC flies, makes up the trio of treatments that I carry whilst fishing dry flies. Other extremely useful substances that complete the armoury are the hygroscopic powders that are used for drying waterlogged flies, firstly in the form of the sealable container in which you place the fly, close the lid and shake and also the brush applied 'Frog's Fanny' that works minor miracles on waterlogged CDC flies that need to be dried and re-treated intermittently if they are to fish with the correct amount of buoyancy.

Leader Sinkant

Another important potion that is required in order to enhance dry-fly presentation is something to sink the last two feet of tippet directly above the fly. Again, there are a number of commercially available products that fit the bill, but I prefer to make my own. By using a mixture of Fuller's Earth powder, clear glycerine and green Fairy Liquid, a very efficient line sinkant can be produced. When mixed and kneaded together, the result is a plasticine-like concoction, through which the line can be drawn in order to degrease it. This helps to ensure that the tippet section sinks and remains sunk, which is a most important element in any dry-fly presentation system. It is my experience that submerging the final section of the tippet has a very definite bearing on the fish being fooled into taking the dry fly. This is particularly apparent when fishing on flat, riffle-free, glassy water often found on the chalk streams where it is difficult to disguise the leader to fly connection without submerging it.

Leaders and Tippets

As the system component that links the fly line to the fly, the leader has to serve a number of purposes and demonstrate certain characteristics in order to successfully fulfil its function. To be fully effective, the leader needs to transmit the energy generated by the defined stop of the rod tip at the end of the casting stroke. This energy travels through the system by means of an unfurling, travelling loop, which moves down the line and leader and ultimately 'turns over' the dry fly. To do this effectively, the leader ideally needs to be constructed in such a way as to allow thicker, heavier line to move, or turn over, a thinner more flexible line. It therefore needs to be stiff enough to ensure the full turn-over of the fly and flexible enough to allow the fly sufficient free movement to maximise the drift distance and to minimise or negate the effect of drag on the fly. These profile and stiffness criteria can only be met by using a tapered leader of which there are many variations, with the two main types being knotted and knotless. Knotless leaders are available in both single strand (monofilament) and multi-strand construction, which includes both braided and furled leaders. Knotted leaders are constructed by joining varying lengths and thicknesses of leader material together to form a complete leader.

Let's look briefly at the braided and furled types of leader that are the first choice of many chalk stream dry-fly fishermen. Braided leaders are produced by weaving together single strands of material to form a multi-strand leader. These are manufactured to include a tapered profile and have a suppleness and flexibility that surpasses most conventional single strand leaders. Furled leaders are also made from multi-strands of material, but are constructed in the same way as rope or twine. The leader is created by looping material back on itself and spiral twining it to form the taper and then twisting it to form a single strand. As is the case with braided leaders, the benefits are a thin, supple, knotless leader that casts smoothly and turns over well, whilst also offering a degree of stretch when tightening into a fish. They also tend to be less shiny and therefore less conspicuous than single strand nylon leaders because of their multi-strand construction and textured surface, which also assists in the application of floatant. Some of the disadvantages are that braided leaders, and to a lesser degree furled leaders, are hollow because they consist of multi-strands and water can become trapped between the strands. This can attract dirt and can also be the cause of casting spray, which can prove to be a real problem by disturbing fish on glass-flat water. Both braided and furled leaders tend to be difficult to mend when on the water as they are more supple and are heavier than nylon because they pick up water. Both types can also be noticeably more expensive than single strand nylon tapered leaders, with furled leaders costing up to as much as three times more.

Monofilament tapered knotless and knotted leaders (see fig.1), are widely used when fishing dry fly on chalk streams. Leader material, profile, flexibility, length and construction are all important factors that need to be taken into account when considering the use of this type of leader. The combination of these characteristics will have a significant bearing on casting, dry-fly presentation and ultimately, fish-catching success rate.

Leader Material

Most of the important properties of a leader are dependent on the type of material used and its thickness. The most commonly used materials are nylon and fluorocarbon. In recent years line manufacturers have introduced a number of blended nylon materials, such as polyurethane and polyethylene, which have been developed and marketed as new, 'improved' line materials. Some of these new lines are labelled as 'co-polymers' and their improved qualities are excellent strength-to-diameter ratios and a comforting degree of stretch. Different materials have different properties which can provide different benefits in various fishing situations. Fluorocarbon has a refractive index that is closer to water than that of nylon and consequently it is noticeably less visible than nylon when in water. Fluorocarbon also has a higher specific gravity than nylon and is therefore heavier. Consequently it sinks more readily, which can help presentation of the tippet-to-fly section of the leader, but can also cause problems when fishing small dry flies because it can upset their buoyancy. Care should also be taken when knotting fluorocarbon, which has a greater slickness than nylon and will sometimes require different (or adapted) knots when joining pieces together to form a leader or when tying on a fly. Particular care should be taken when joining different materials to each other (eg. fluorocarbon to nylon) when constructing knotted leaders or tying a tippet to a pre-made leader of a different material because their differing properties may result in a noticeably reduced knot strength. Hence it is of the utmost importance to use a suitable, proven knot that will give a high level of security and to pay close attention to properly lubricating and carefully tightening the knots.

Leader Profile and Flexibility

The profile or shape of a tapered leader will have a bearing on the leader's performance when fishing dry flies. Many commercially available standard knotless tapered leaders (see fig. 1- A) start from a pre-determined butt diameter and breaking strain, reduce through the transition taper and then run down to a stated diameter and breaking strain at the tippet end. One of their main advantages is that because there are no knots in their make-up, they are slightly less prone to tangle than knotted leaders. Knotless tapered leaders are manufactured by a process of extrusion which controls the diameter at specific points along the leader, but is less precise in the geometry and diameter of the leader between these points. Generally, the only information given on the packaging of these leaders is butt end diameter, tippet end diameter, length and breaking strain, with a basic recommended usage (i.e. trout leader, saltwater/bass leader etc.). This makes it difficult to assess the diameter and breaking strain of the leader at some other point along the continuous taper without using either a micrometer or an accurate line gauge and referring to the manufacturer's guidelines to compare diameter to breaking strain. This can be problematic if the leader becomes shortened through the continued addition of new tippets because an inefficient or inappropriate leader profile can result. A useful way to ensure that the leader is more consistent in its performance (and to save a few bob) is to add a micro ring to the end of the leader at the outset and then add to this a length of tippet that is of a lesser diameter and breaking strain. This works well because it both allows greater control of the tippet's characteristics and avoids the eventuality of having to replace the entire leader once the thin tippet section has been lost. My use of standard tapered leaders is mainly as a component part of a self-made leader system. I quite often use a shop-bought leader as the butt section and add on varying lengths of appropriate material to create the length and stiffness that I require. More specialised knotless tapered leaders (see fig. 1-B & C) are available and these are designed to turn over flies that require certain characteristics from the leader if they are to be presented correctly. These, unlike standard tapered leaders, are manufactured in a way that accurately positions the varying steps and gives the defined taper profiles required for differing presentation situations. According to Charles Ritz in his book *A Fly Fisher's Life* (1959), the ideal is to have the longest forward taper possible while still retaining control during the presentation. He subscribes to the 60/20/20 profile, where the 60% is strength, 20% is taper and the final 20% is terminal tippet (see fig. 1-B). The 50/20/30 profile (see fig. 1-C) is recommended when fishing very small dry flies and midges. The longer tippet section will still allow a smooth transition through the leader and tippet because the fly is nearly weightless, but also has the added benefit of allowing the lightest of flies to drift without excessive drag. This is an important point because experience suggests that fish feeding on small flies do have a tendency to pay more attention to unnatural drift.

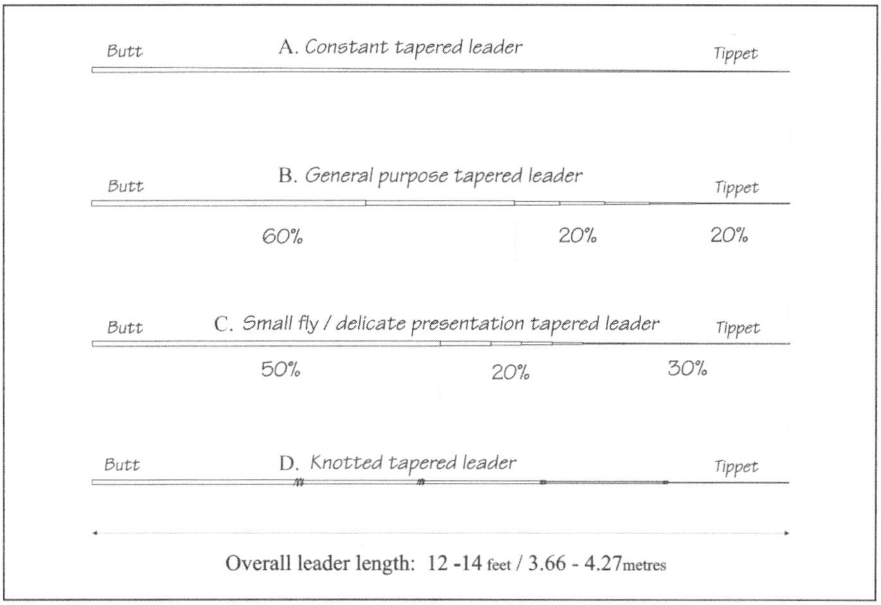

fig 1. Leader profile diagram (not to scale)

Knotted tapered leaders are constructed by joining varying strengths and diameters of line together to form a continuous length of tapering leader (see fig. 1-D). The advantage of constructing tapered leaders in this fashion is that it allows greater freedom to vary most of the important leader characteristics such as length, profile, flexibility and material. A knotted leader also gives the additional advantage that the knots used to join the line segments can assist in the formation of the S-curves that are used to minimise or reduce drag (more of this later). Shop-bought knotless leaders are noticeably more expensive than self-tied leaders (but if you consider the time saved by not having to tie them, they probably aren't). A quick and reliable knot that I use to join lengths of nylon monofilament and fluorocarbon together is the four turn water knot (see fig. 2).

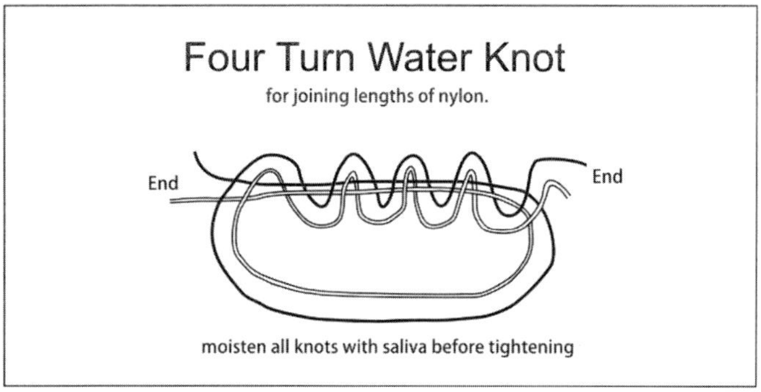

fig 2.

Charles Ritz also states in his book that, in order to give a good continuation of energy transfer from fly line to leader, the diameter of the leader butt should be at least 60% of the diameter of the end of the fly line. This works well, particularly if the leader is joined to the fly line with a needle knot, which is my preferred method (see fig. 3), but this can become excessively bulky if the leader used has a butt-end diameter that is too thick.

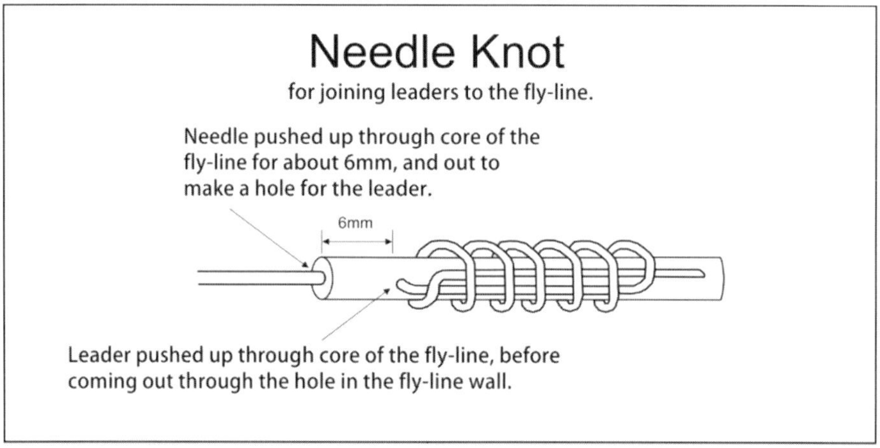

fig. 3

The leader length can have a considerable bearing on your ability to make a good presentation to your target fish. If you use too short a leader you may well find that the fish become 'aware' of your intentions and begin to lie low or simply make an ungainly dash for cover. This could simply be a result of the short leader causing the much thicker fly line to land too close to the fish on the delivery of the cast, even if the fly itself is presented well. On the contrary, if you attempt to use a leader that is too long, you may find that you are unable to turn over your chosen fly (especially if it is a large, wind resistant pattern) or that you simply don't have the space or casting skill required to get an ideal presentation. Either way, the outcome is likely to be the same, Fish -1: Fisherman – frustrated! A commonly held view is that the leader should be the same length as the rod. This is rarely the case because the usual rod length is 8½ to 9 ft and the average leader length is seldom, if ever, less than 10 ft and more often than not between 12 and 14 ft and sometimes longer. There are exceptions to this, such as when using a shorter rod, particularly in confined areas and when making very short casts, when a longer leader can prevent a useable amount of fly line from being extended from the tip ring.

Drag

Drag is the movement of the fly in response to the movement of the line to which it is attached. Therefore, drag is the unnatural movement of the fly in directions different from the path that the fly would take if it were untethered. Fish can detect the presence of drag and it is this unnatural movement of the fly that is probably the single most common reason for the rejection of a fly whilst fishing on flowing water. Over the years many fly fishermen have explored the subject of dry-fly presentation and the effect that drag has on it. The late George Harvey, an eminent American fly fisherman, spent many years experimenting with leader design in his attempts to perfect his dry-fly presentation. Whilst looking into the relative importance of leader diameter and stiffness and its effects on drag, he experimented by attaching live insects to short lengths of leader material and drifting them over feeding fish. He observed that there was no noticeable difference between the numbers of un-tethered insects taken compared to those with leader material attached and concluded that fish were not discouraged from taking flies with a leader attached, provided it did not affect the natural drift of the fly. With this said, a refusal may not always be because the fish has been alerted by the unnatural movement of the fly when drag begins to take effect. It may be that the fish has decided to accept the fly and has applied its well-tuned senses to anticipate where the fly will be in relation to the projected timing of its rise and interception, but the position of the fish's eyes in relation to its mouth results in it being unable to see the fly in the moments before taking it. This, coupled to the inertia generated by the fish as it makes the rise, can mean that it is unable to make a late change of direction during the moments prior to interception if the path of the fly has changed due to the effect of drag. So, not every refusal is due to the fish not liking the fly, or indeed, its poor presentation.

Drag Recognition and Reduction

It is never time wasted to take a few moments to look carefully at the water you are about to fish and to plan how best to cast in order to minimise drag. Drag most commonly occurs when you cast over a number of different currents and the differing speeds of water flow affect the speed and direction in which the fly line, leader and fly travel. These complex currents occur for a number of reasons and often form lanes across the river or stream. They can be a result of the water being held up by a weed bed, or by other in-stream obstructions such as a rock or boulder or where the current passes under a bridge, through hatches or where some other man-made stream obstruction creates adjacent areas with differing rates of flow. Bends in the river course often contribute to the formation of differing speeds of current. Although sometimes tricky to fish, these areas are commonly favoured by fish that take advantage of a food delivery service which allows them to move without hurry, intercept passing edible items and move back to their position in the quieter adjacent flow easily. This phenomenon alone justifies the pursuit of the mastery of a variety of presentation casts and techniques that allow the fisherman the essential benefit of a completely drag-free drift, or at least a drift with minimal drag.

So what can be done to avoid or minimise drag whilst fishing the dry fly? Firstly, apply the earlier concept of observation before casting. Take a moment or two before casting to plan how and where to make the cast in order to minimise (or at least reduce) the potential effects of drag. Advantage may be gained by getting closer to the target fish, ensuring a better look at the potential for a drag-free drift. Being closer allows observation of any previously unnoticed current lanes and micro-currents. It may also mean that there are fewer current lanes for the line and leader to cross and therefore the potential for drag is reduced. There may also be the added benefit of seeing the target fish taking natural flies and both improving the chances of selecting the most suitable imitation and more accurately gauging the fish's rising position. Secondly, ensure that your tackle is set up properly, with a clean and well-prepared line and a suitable leader that is stiff enough at the thicker end to ensure an easy turnover of the fly and flexible and supple enough from the middle to the tippet to allow the dry fly to drift with sufficient freedom to avoid drag. The leader should ideally float along its entire length apart from the last couple of feet of tippet, which should submerge for a well disguised presentation. Dry flies fished in a rapid or turbulent flow should ideally float higher in order to reduce the potential effects of drag. Flies fished this way will normally be of a collar hackled construction, with the extent of the hackle determining the amount of buoyancy of the fly. Consequently, the fly will sit up on the tips of the hackle and therefore keep a large part of its body above the surface of the water. This will make it less susceptible to the effects of drag. When fishing on the more steady, glass smooth, unbroken water often found on the chalk streams, the fly will often be a sparsely dressed pattern that sits low on the water surface or in the surface film and will therefore be more at the mercy of any current lanes that are present. To deal with this, other drag prevention measures must now to be put into practice both during the cast and whilst the fly is on the water. This brings us to a consideration of the casts and other fly presentation techniques that will help to minimise or prevent drag.

Overhead Cast

The overhead cast is the stock-in-trade cast in the dry-fly fisher's armoury and when coupled with the static and jump roll casts, can be extensively adapted to produce almost every conceivable presentation cast that the chalk stream fly fisher could need. The overhead cast can be adjusted by way of narrowing or widening the loop (see fig.4) which will allow the fly to be presented into, across and with the assistance of the wind in virtually all wind conditions. It is fair to say that there are relatively few places where a dead straight line between the rod tip and the fly will not produce almost instant drag because the resulting tight line will very quickly restrict the fly's natural drag-free drift. A very workable way to prevent this tight line is to overpower the forward cast slightly. This produces a slight 'bounce back' of the line as the loop unfurls completely and then recoils due to the excess of energy. This results in a series of small wiggles or S-curves in the line and leader as it lies on the water. These provide a small, but useful, amount of slack, preventing a tight line and helping to produce an extended drag free drift. If wind conditions allow, a combination of a 2 ft to 2½ ft wide loop with a slightly overpowered delivery is my 'go to' cast in the majority of conditions. The slower moving 'not too tight' loop gives me ample opportunity to see where and how the fly will land and the bounce back gives me enough slack to prevent the instant drag scenario.

fig. 4 Overhead cast

Upstream Aerial Mend Cast

There are two ways in which to make a mend in the line. It can be performed in the air, during the cast, or after the line has landed on the water. My preferred cast for dry fly fishing is the 'aerial mend', where the rod is stopped on the forward stroke, the rod tip is moved sideways to create the mend and is then returned to a position pointing towards the fly as it lands on the water. The aerial mend creates less disturbance on the water and reduces the risk of drowning the dry fly when pulling it into position whilst 'wet mending'. The aerial mend is very useful in creating an extended drag-free drift where there are distinct current lanes of varying speed. Fig. 5 illustrates the fly being presented to the fish positioned in the slower current lane. The end of the fly line has been positioned in the quicker current lane between the angler and the fish, but with the mend having been made in the air, it has landed with a distinct angled shape (position **a**). The quicker movement of the flow in the current lane where the mend has been placed moves the line through position **b** to position **c**, whilst the fly moves a shorter distance due to the slower flow. This provides an extended drift and helps to prevent the fly being dragged unnaturally off line before it reaches the target fish.

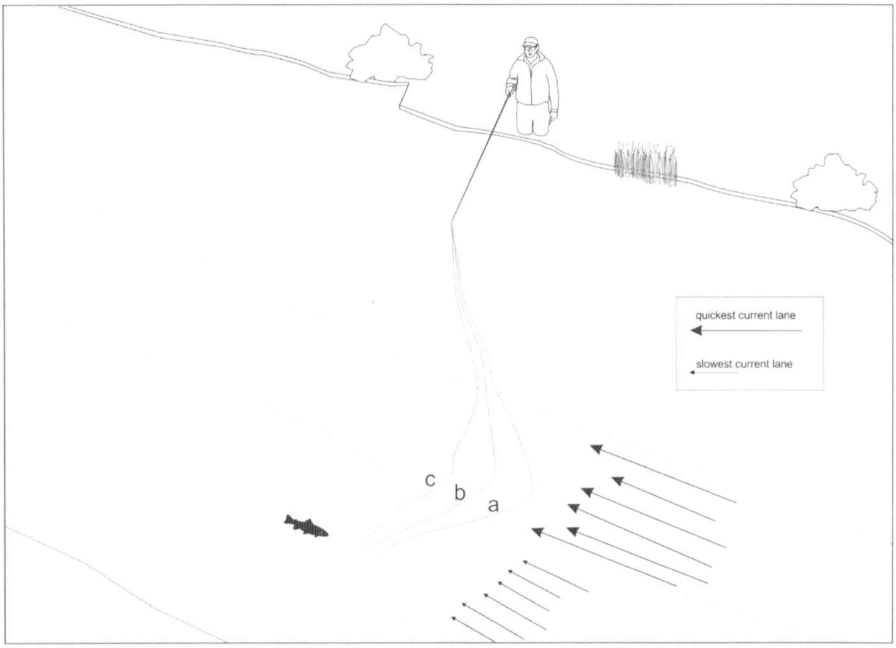

fig. 5 Upstream aerial mend cast

Upstream Reach Cast

Similar in execution to the aerial mend cast, the 'reach cast' is most efficiently performed by making a standard overhead cast during which line is shot forward into the cast to avoid the fly, leader and line 'bouncing back'. Upon making the stop on the forward casting stroke, bring the rod upstream to position 1 (in fig. 6) in one fluid motion as the line is being shot. Since the line is shooting as the reach is made, the line length will increase to compensate for the upstream sideways movement of the rod and the fly will continue to its intended target. The line will then be at a slight upstream angle from the fly to the rod tip. Follow the movement of the fly from **a** through to **c** with the rod moving from 1 through to 3 at the same speed as the current. This will give a drag-free drift with little or no slack line on the water, which allows a quicker response when the fish rises to the fly.

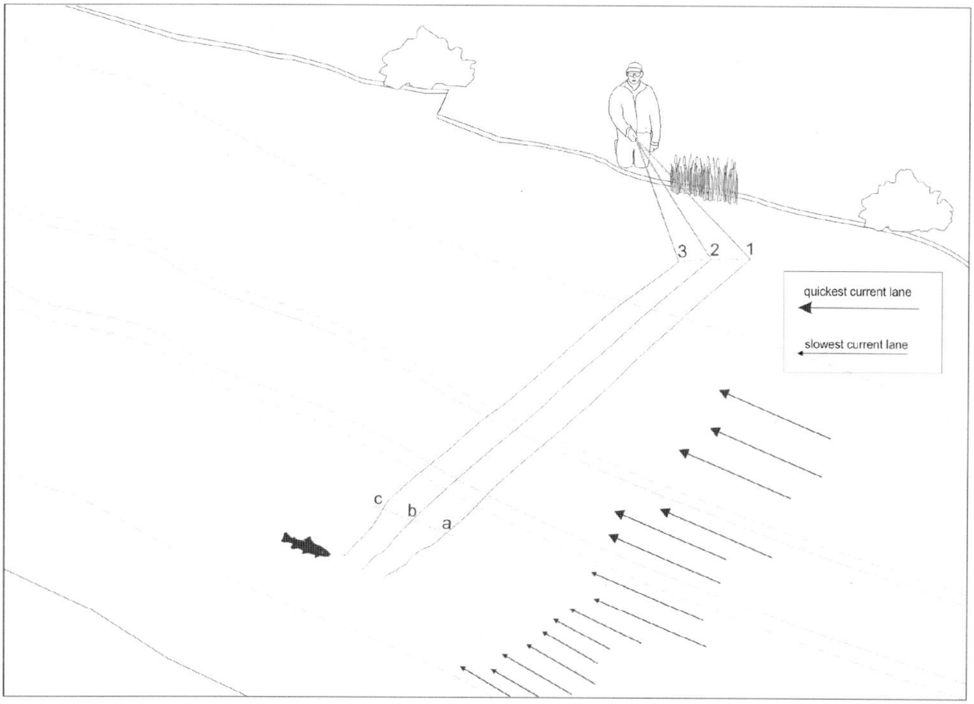

fig. 6 Upstream reach cast

Wiggle or Serpentine Cast

If fishing in an area where there are a number of current lanes that are flowing at different rates (as in fig. 7), then a more premeditated, exaggerated sequence of S-curves will help to minimise or avoid drag. The 'wiggle' or 'serpentine' cast is executed by making the forward overhead cast and as the moving loop passes the rod tip, the rod tip is wiggled from side to side. The line and leader will land on the water with a sequence of S-curves that will mirror the number and size of movements made by the rod tip. Adjustment can also be made to the distance between the S-curves and their distance from the fly and/or rod tip by adjusting the timing of the application of the wiggles. With practice, this cast can be tailored to provide anti-drag casts in all but the most complex of current situations. The formation of these S-curves aids in fighting drag by supplying slack line that can be taken up with minimal resistance to the drifting fly. The more S-curves there are, the more slack there is in the line and leader, which allows a longer drift before drag occurs.

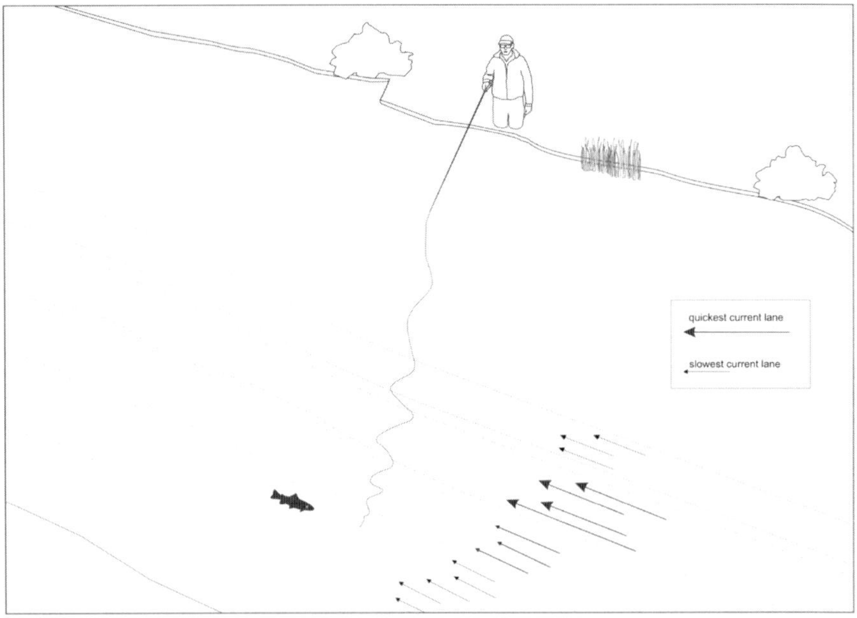

fig 7. Wiggle or serpentine cast

The Upstream Hook Cast

The 'upstream hook cast' is an extremely useful presentation cast when the angler is positioned downstream, directly behind the target fish. The danger here lies in 'lining' the fish with a cast that positions the line directly over the fish's head. The cast is executed with the rod in a horizontal plane, parallel to the water's surface and with a high line speed. The delivery is made by an abrupt stop of the rod, with the rod tip being intentionally bounced back slightly, or alternatively, with a sharp tug on the line from the non rod-holding hand, both of which will encourage the fly and tippet to kick round to approximately a 90° angle to the fly line lying on the water. This then allows a presentation during which only the fly drifts back over the fish.

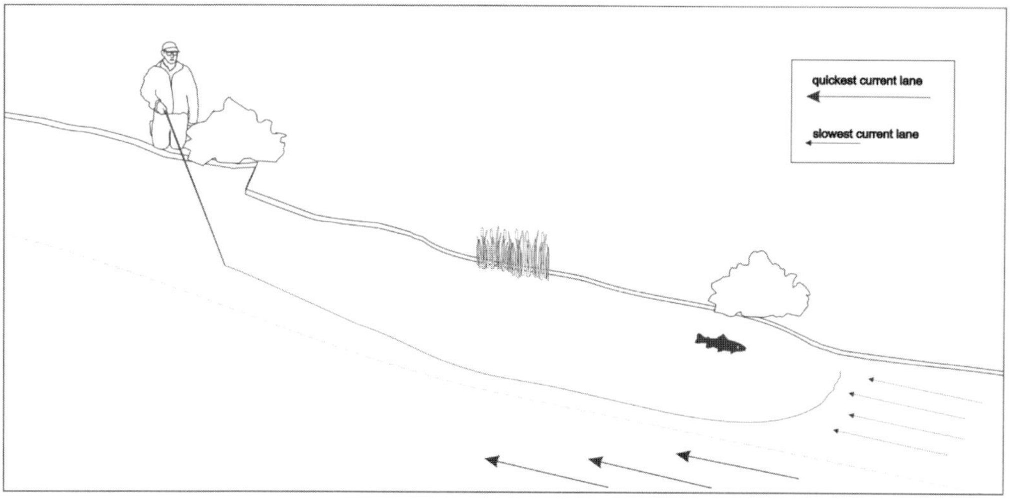

fig 8. Upstream hook cast

Fishing Back Eddies

Whilst chalk stream etiquette often dictates that the fly should be fished upstream at all times, there is the odd occasion when a little lateral thinking can be responsibly applied. Fig. 9 shows the fisherman in position **A**, making an upstream cast to a fish from the traditional downstream position. It is however, not uncommon to see fish that are positioned facing into the flow created by a back eddy. This often happens in hatch pools where the current has reversed and is flowing back towards the hatches at the head of the pool. In this situation, a fly cast 'upstream' from position **B** can be viewed as a legitimate tactic in my opinion and does not offend chalk stream protocol in any way.

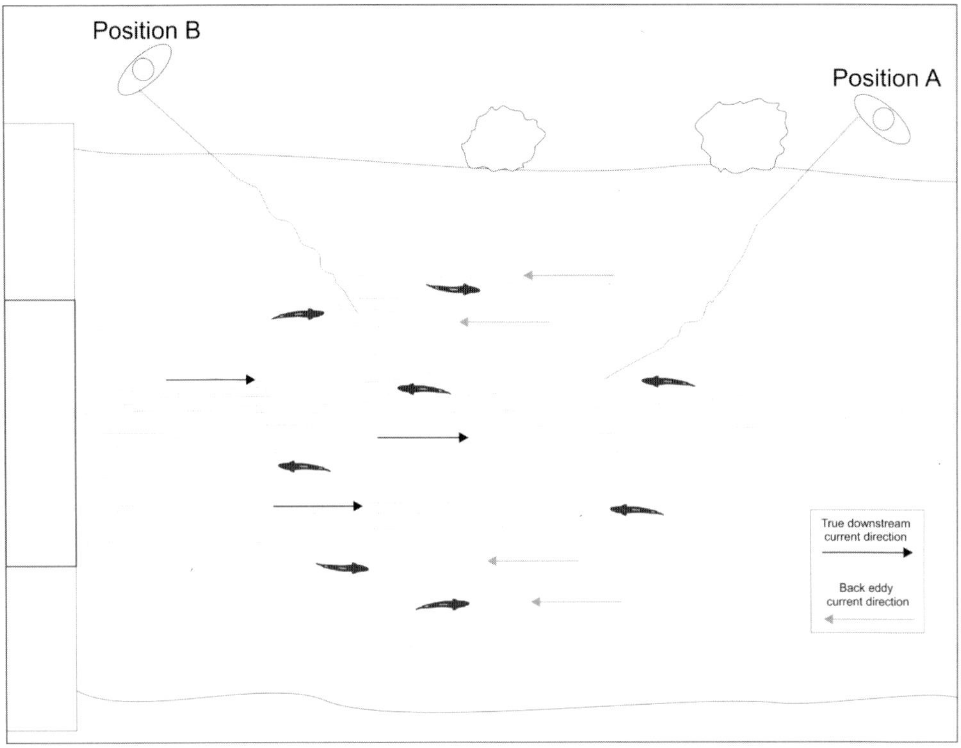

fig 9. Back eddy flow

Chapter Eight

Chalk Stream Nymph Fishing

Alwyn Lindsey

In Defence of the Nymph

For me, the essence of fly fishing a chalk stream is very simple: it is to find a fish, work out what the fish is feeding on, match that with an appropriate artificial and present the fly in a manner consistent with the way the natural food would appear to the feeding trout. Successfully using hard won knowledge and taking the time to deduce the natural feeding behaviour of a trout or grayling is the most satisfying aspect of the sport for me. You watch your fish, you consider the options, you crunch the evidence and you crack the puzzle. It is for that reason that I am often frustrated by the 'dry-fly only' dogma that persists on some chalk stream beats. Even where the rules allow for other methods, there sometimes exists an ethos that not only should anglers always fish the dry fly, but that doing so represents the practice of the highest art of the sport, all other methods being inferior, less skilful and in extreme cases, immoral. While I accept that any angler is perfectly at liberty to confine himself to fishing the dry fly, he is, in my view, not only denying himself the opportunity of catching more fish, but is also disregarding what is arguably the most skilful and challenging branch of chalk stream fly fishing: sight nymphing.

Don't get me wrong. I love to fish the dry fly and like all anglers I find casting a floating fly over a rising fish and seeing that fish take my artificial to be the pinnacle of the sport. But I say this purely because of the sheer aesthetic beauty of the whole process and not because I believe it to be more difficult or in any way technically superior to other methods. That is why, if favourable conditions present themselves, I always fish the dry fly and why, when fish are not rising, I impatiently await the next hatch so that I can once again tie on a surface pattern. But it can be frustrating that having cracked the puzzle and having deduced, for example, that the rise form you are seeing is not the result of a trout taking adult up-wings, but of the fish taking nymphs just below the surface, you are compelled by the fishery rules to fish the 'wrong' fly and must proceed to cast your dry-fly pattern at a trout that is feeding on nymphs. I am not saying that you will not catch that fish, but I will suggest that if you do, it will be more by luck than judgement. Consequently, where the rules permit, I fish a nymph when I find a trout either not rising at all or where I have deduced that a rising fish is actually feeding on nymphs. For me, this approach has more integrity and actually, on a chalk stream, can involve a great deal more skill than fishing a dry fly. Fishing a nymph well will generally catch you more fish than fishing a dry fly, not because it is easier but because fish tend to spend a great deal more time feeding sub-surface than they do taking adult flies off the top.

On his beloved Abbots Barton water on the Itchen, the famous G. E. M. Skues accidentally discovered that his waterlogged and sunk surface pattern was often intercepted by many more fish than when it was afloat. Perhaps because of the controversy this practice generated, Skues described the use of the 'sunk fly' as a 'minor tactic', meaning that it was to be used in extremis when no fish were rising and when the dry fly was simply impractical, rather like when a ghillie on a salmon water might allow spinning when the river is in spate.

If Skues can be considered the father of chalk stream nymph fishing, its sons are Frank Sawyer and Oliver Kite who practised and promoted the altogether higher art of 'sight nymphing', with Sawyer in particular bringing to the sport some of its most important and enduring fly patterns. The efforts of all three of these master anglers and writers helped to establish that the artificial nymph has a rightful place on the chalk stream and in doing so opened up the sub-surface world to the angler.

There are broadly two approaches to nymphing on a chalk stream: targeting fish that you can see and targeting those that you cannot.

Blind Nymphing

Fishing the nymph 'blind' involves casting nymph patterns upstream into likely spots, leaving the fly to dead-drift downstream and then watching carefully for a signal that a fish has taken the fly. This can be a sharp jab of the fly line or leader butt, or the merest pause, or perhaps even a flash of colour in the water suggesting the movement of a fish. Unlike fishing the dry fly, where a taking fish must be given a modicum of time to turn away with the fly, a take when fishing this method should be met with an instant lift of the rod. It is amazing how often a response to what seems to be a tiny and unsuspicious sign will be met with a hooked fish, so the golden rule is to respond immediately to any signal, no matter how unconvincing it may seem. The angler who shoots first and asks questions later will profit far more than the angler who requires proof of guilt beyond reasonable doubt before raising his rod.

A key consideration in this method is to read the water and carefully cover the likely looking lies. Good river-craft can take a while to perfect, but the basic principle is that fish will lie in areas that are well oxygenated, provide cover from predators, and offer a constant supply of food that doesn't require a disproportionate amount of energy to intercept. 'Creases' in the water, where slow water meets fast, are sure to hold fish and will be a hotspot in any river. Trout and grayling will lie just off to the sides of well oxygenated faster water waiting to intercept nymphs and shrimps as they are carried downstream by the current. Ideally, a nymph should be dead-drifted right along the crease where it will surely be grabbed by a waiting fish. The same principle applies to pools in the river where fast water coming into the pool brings with it an abundance of food that fish can easily pick off in relative comfort and without having to fight against powerful currents. Areas in front of or behind sub-surface obstructions like tree trunks and stones provide fish with shelter from fast-flowing water. In these areas, they can wait for food to come to them and only have to expend energy in venturing out into the faster water when a meal is presented. There will always be fish holding tight to banks where there is good cover and a very reliable supply of food, especially on the outside bends of rivers where the current is pressed against the bank, often creating welcome undercuts and forcing food hard into the bank where it is funnelled towards the waiting fish. Channels between bars of ranunculus also tick all the boxes for the hungry chalk stream fish. The weed provides cover from predators and is home to all manner of aquatic insects and freshwater shrimp. These channels often look devoid of fish, but the angler should not be fooled. The fish will be hiding amongst the ranunculus ready to intercept any food that appears in the channels and they should therefore be readily fished.

Once likely holding positions have been identified, care should be taken in presenting the nymph in the right way. As is the case with the dry fly, it is important to avoid drag – a fact often ignored by anglers fishing nymphs. A nymph under the influence of drag can be every bit as off-putting to a trout as a skating dun pattern. Aside from the need to perhaps vary the choice of pattern so as to try fishing at different depths, the main challenge facing the angler is detecting a take and hooking the fish. Some anglers choose to use modern bright foam indicators, but these are rarely, if ever, necessary on chalk streams and are far better suited to rain-fed rivers where nymphing without a foam indicator is often impractical because turbulent currents can make it extremely difficult to see either the end of the fly line or the butt section of the leader. Turbulent currents can also compensate for the disturbance that a foam indicator often makes on the water surface. Using an indicator on a chalk stream can be counter-productive and can lead to spooking the fish. It is not recommended unless the water is coloured or when difficult light conditions or poor eyesight exclude other options. It is far better to use a little Mucilin to grease up the butt section of the leader. This can be highly visible on the surface film, is less likely to spook fish, provides less resistance when a fish takes the fly and reduces the chances of the fly being ejected before the angler can strike. It is also much easier to cast and leaves the angler less prone to tangles.

Care should be taken not to flog the water by repeatedly casting over the same spot. It is not only unproductive, but it can render sections of river useless for many hours, thereby spoiling sport for other anglers. The better and more productive approach is to try just two or three casts to each likely spot before moving on. Generally, if a fish is going to take an artificial nymph, it will do so at first or second sight of it.

The blind nymph method can also be the difference between success and failure in deep hatch pools where the turbulence of the water often makes the spotting of fish impossible. Most hatch pools have back-eddies running to the sides of the main flow and it is here where many fish will position themselves. If a heavy nymph is cast upstream into a back-eddy and is then given slack line it will be carried upstream towards fish that are facing directly towards the angler. Stopping the line at different intervals will force the nymph to lift and this will often produce a solid take. Especially good lies will be under overhanging trees and tight against walls and undercut banks. This method is truly 'blind' in that takes are generally felt rather than seen.

Whilst blind nymphing can be incredibly successful, it is by no means the most challenging method of nymph fishing. In truth, the angler who possesses some basic river-craft skills, who can cast with reasonable accuracy and who can learn to detect takes can catch a lot of fish and while the method has its place, it is in the technique of sight nymphing that the angler can elevate his skills to an altogether higher level.

Sight Nymphing

The first challenge in sight nymphing is simply to find a fish. For the angler fishing a dry fly this is usually the least of his worries because the fish betrays its location with a rise. The nymph fisherman may also be blessed with this luxury where the rise form indicates a trout taking nymphs rather than emerging or adult flies. The most obvious of these is the classic bulge rise form, but also the classic head and tail rise can often be a sign of a trout taking nymphs, particularly if there are no insects to be seen on the surface. It takes considerable practice and time spent on the water before an angler is able to distinguish between different rise forms.

In most instances however, the angler has to locate a non-rising fish that is positioned on the river bed and while chalk streams run clear like pure gin, the existence of even large fish occupying a lie can easily be overlooked. While the late and great Major Oliver Kite was said to possess extraordinary eyesight and could spot fish unaided in any kind of light conditions, we mere mortals need the help of a good pair of polarised glasses. This vital piece of kit will open up the underwater world for the angler, but equally, fish can still be overlooked even with the best lenses that money can buy. Trout and grayling are masters at blending in with their surroundings and the angler needs to train himself not just to look, but to see. Often, simply by staring into a likely spot that at first appears devoid of fish, the angler will suddenly see his quarry. Tell-tale signs can be shadows on the riverbed or slight displacements of water, both of which can betray the presence of a fish. Light coloured sections of chalk and gravel on the riverbed are also good places to look for fish and often it is possible to spot the tail section of a fish just poking into the top of a gravel patch. The trick is to take one's time, rather than just glancing at the water and then quickly moving on if there is no obvious sign of a fish. Invariably, rushing will result in many fish going undetected or worse still, shooting off and spooking other fish.

Once a fish has been located, the angler should attempt to get as close to it as is practically possible, whilst always maintaining a downstream position and using as much cover as the surroundings will allow. A slightly side-on angle to the fish will also provide better visibility than being directly downstream and will reduce the possibility of lining the fish. The first cast should be upstream of the fish, the distance upstream being determined by the depth at which the fish is lying, with the aim being to get the fly to approach and pass the fish at more or less that depth and a foot or so to the side of it. The initial approach should be to dead-drift the fly and often the fish will take a well presented nymph first time. There are some angling writers who describe the take as being the opening of the fish's mouth and urge the angler to look for the tell-tale white 'blink' of the mouth. I find this to be extremely difficult and only possible in the most favourable of light conditions. My approach is simply to watch for the movement of the fish. As the fly comes close to it, a taking fish will move in the direction of the fly and on taking, will immediately move back in the direction of its lie. It is at that precise point when the fish changes direction to move back that I strike. Rarely will you be able to see the fly itself and so you will not be certain that the fish has moved because of your fly and often the fly will not be precisely where you thought it was. Light refraction makes this judgement even more difficult. For these reasons, any movement of the fish when your fly is in the vicinity of the fish should be met with a lift of the rod and more often than not, a fish will have taken. If the fish does not take after two or three dead-drifts, the angler should employ the 'induced-take' method.

The induced-take method relies on the fact that the raising of a sunken fly through the water column on any kind of water is often irresistible to trout and grayling. When fishing wet flies down and across on rain-fed rivers, fish will invariably take at the end of the drift as the flies start to ascend and the same is true when fishing nymphs upstream on chalk streams. Frank Sawyer knew this and exploited it to great effect, and Oliver Kite described the technique as the 'Netheravon Style' in his classic *Nymph Fishing in Practice*. The tactic is simple to describe, but is extremely difficult to master. Again the nymph is cast the required distance upstream of the fish with the aim that it passes slightly to the side of the fish. The angler must judge when he feels that the nymph is just slightly upstream of the fish. He then raises the rod in order to pull the nymph towards him. This will make the nymph ascend and travel slightly across stream towards the angler. The desired distance for the nymph to travel is ideally no more than one or two feet. If a fish is going to take your nymph, the chances are that he will do so within a few casts. If he doesn't, you can try a few more drifts with another pattern, and if that doesn't work, move on, perhaps making a mental note of its location in case you feel the urge to try again later. As with any kind of chalk stream fly fishing, repeated casting over the same fish is both unproductive and inconsiderate. On some occasions, a nymph fished with an induced take action will pass the lie of the fish and as it travels downstream towards the angler, the fish will suddenly turn and follow. When this happens, the angler should continue to lift the rod and keep the nymph travelling towards him. Very often, the fish will follow the fly right into the bank and will take at the last second. The challenge facing the angler in this situation is how to strike because the rod tip will already be held high with considerable slack line trailing from it. An effective response can be to perform a very aggressive roll-cast which will throw out the trailing line and hopefully gain a hook hold. This will not work every time but it is more likely to succeed than the alternative of frantically trying to strip line and reposition the rod for a more orthodox strike.

Flies and tackle

The easiest tasks for the chalk stream nymph fisherman are tackle and fly selection. I favour as long a rod as I can get away with on my chosen beat, bearing in mind the thickness and height of the surrounding vegetation. A longer rod is helpful in reaching over the bank-side growth and also helps to cushion what are often quick and sharp strikes. My 'go to' rod, unless fishing narrow or overgrown beats, is a 9 ft middle-to-tip action rod for a 5 weight line. For leaders, I generally use the short butt section of a tapered leader to which I attach a length of level tippet. The butt section gives me turnover and will float easily when greased up, while the level tippet cuts through the surface film and allows the fly to sink more readily than if a whole tapered leader were used. I aid the sinking process by applying a degreasing agent along the length of the tippet.

The choice of fly is again very straightforward and is most often dictated by the depth of water. Unlike dry fly fishing, where there can be many patterns for different hatches and even a number of different patterns for fishing different stages of the same hatch, a handful of nymph patterns tied in different sizes and with different weights will serve the angler well for the entire season. Two patterns that I would be happy fishing almost exclusively throughout the season are Sawyer's Pheasant Tail Nymph and the Gold Nugget Hare's Ear, the latter having caught me fish on all kinds of rivers both in the United Kingdom and overseas. The

Pheasant Tail Nymph is the epitome of chalk stream nymphing tradition and in a branch of the sport that vigorously clings to tradition, Frank Sawyer's simple yet genius pattern was a huge innovation when introduced in the 1950s. Tied out of only pheasant tail fibres and copper wire, the pattern is suggestive of many kinds of nymph and is naturally prone to cut through the surface film, allowing the angler to target fish at different depths. A fish taking nymphs close to the surface can be targeted with a small Pheasant Tail Nymph cast only two or three feet upstream of it and in instances where fish are rising to nymphs, I have had much success by applying a little floatant to the nymph so that it sits in the surface film. For fish lying in deeper water, a cast further upstream will allow the nymph to sink to the required depth by the time it reaches the fish. The best approach with virtually any nymph pattern is to fish small. For the two patterns mentioned above a size 14 is about as big as I will go and more often than not, a size 18 is the order of the day. I tend to carry a few other patterns to cater for other situations and I especially like a small Copperjohn which sinks even more readily than the Pheasant Tail Nymph while offering a similar profile. I also use a Peeping Caddis for deep water fishing and this fly is especially useful when fishing hatch pools in the manner described above. Although it is a much larger and heavier pattern than anything else you will use on a chalk stream, it has its place and of course, imitates the natural food that occupies the river bed. Spoon a chalk stream trout and you will undoubtedly find cased caddis which is exactly what this pattern is designed to imitate.

Although not nymphs, freshwater shrimps form a huge part of the diet of chalk stream trout and grayling and where permitted, good representations of these creatures can be an important weapon in the chalk stream angler's armoury. Sawyer's classic shrimp pattern was his famous Killer Bug (or Grayling Bug to give it its original name). Again, the tying is very simple, comprising only copper wire and the now legendry (and extremely rare) Chadwick's 477 mending wool. The pattern accounted for many grayling, trout and even salmon for its inventor. Another shrimp-like pattern is the Czech Nymph. This heavily weighted nymph is typically fished in a team of three, with the flies lobbed (rather than cast) upstream and allowed to trundle downstream very close to the stream bed. A long rod with level leader is used with the fly line not touching the water. Takes come on the dead drift and, more frequently, when the flies ascend downstream of the angler. To my mind, this method is quite rightly seen as out of place on a chalk stream and should be limited to use on rain-fed rivers in cold conditions when targeting grayling that position themselves close to the stream bed. The Killer Bug on the other hand is considered to be very much part of the chalk stream tradition, especially during the grayling season. Most chalk-stream anglers have a soft spot for it, me included. While patterns like the Czech Nymph or the Killer Bug will catch fish, I find that they are usually too large to be considered an accurate representation of the freshwater shrimp. It is far better to use a size 18 or 20 olive-coloured pattern tied with PVC skin to provide a more accurate drab sheen to the fly.

Deeper lying fish will often need the fly to be presented lower in the water and while the Pheasant Tail Nymph will sink, it is sometimes necessary to use a fly with more weight. The traditional solution to this problem is to use a pattern tied with a lead wire under-body, but another effective way of achieving this is to use bead-head patterns. These can be anathema to some chalk-stream anglers and while I personally draw the line at the kind of gaudy ironmongery that passes for a 'fly' on the stillwater trout scene, I see no ethical problem in incorporating a small bead within a representative pattern like the Pheasant Tail Nymph or Hare's Ear to give the necessary weight to the fly. Some argue that the bead-head provides a 'flash' element to the nymph and that this is more akin to a lure than a traditional nymph pattern. While I wouldn't dispute that copper and brass beads offer some 'flash' that fish almost certainly find attractive, I fail to see the problem in this. Do we not design patterns to attract fish and is 'flash' a new phenomenon in fly tying? I would argue that the use of wire and tinsel ribbing is scarcely different and provided that the pattern is designed to suggest the natural insect life found in the chalk stream, it should be considered fair game.

Another pattern worth carrying on the chalk stream is a buzzer. Although buzzers tend to be identified with reservoir trout fishing, chironomids (midges) abound on chalk streams, particularly on slow stretches of water where a layer of silt has accumulated. In such areas buzzers can be fished in the same manner as they would be fished on a stillwater, using a very slow retrieve. Again, small patterns are best and a few simple patterns in black and olive can salvage a difficult 'dog-day' on the river.

Ultimately, the choice of pattern is significantly less important than the manner in which it is fished. Almost to exaggerate this point, Oliver Kite designed his Bare Hook Nymph which amounted simply to a length of copper fuse wire wrapped around a bare hook. Kite took vast numbers of fish on this rather unattractive pattern and its success lay in its profile, which is similar in size and shape to the natural nymph; its weight, which allowed Kite to easily target fish at the correct depth when sight nymphing; and the movement that Kite imparted to it with his Netheravon Style. The lesson, as is the case with many other methods of fly fishing, is that good presentation is far more important than precise imitation. Presentation is everything in nymph fishing and for me, fishing the nymph on a chalk stream can be exhilarating. The angler who expands his horizons beyond the dogma of the dry-fly only approach will discover a whole new dimension to his fishing. Success with a nymph requires all the attributes of a good angler; acute observation, river craft, skill and sheer practice. When done well and thoughtfully, nymph fishing rightfully takes its place amongst the finest traditions of chalk stream angling.

Chapter Nine

Expeditions after Grayling

Jan Szakowski

For many chalk stream anglers, fishing for trout and fishing for grayling is something done simultaneously. Generally speaking, both species inhabit the same type of water and eat the same sort of food. The same tackle, the same flies and the same methods will work on both of them. When both species are in season virtually all anglers target either of them indiscriminately as opportunity allows and this is particularly true when fish are rising to a hatch of insects. In a rise, anglers fish to the rises and are happy when a fish takes the fly, regardless of whether it is a trout or a grayling. Very few anglers can tell the difference between a grayling rise and a trout rise without actually seeing the fish itself and I am not sure there really is a difference. Many anglers believe that if there is a bubble left floating on the surface after the rise, then this indicates that the culprit is a grayling. Sometimes this is correct, but it is not conclusive. Trout and other fish can also leave a bubble and I think these bubbles are a consequence of a very gentle and unhurried rise to an insect trapped in the surface film. Trapped insects are very appealing to all fish, including grayling. Of course, one of the big advantages of fishing a chalk stream is that the water is often clear enough to allow the angler to identify the fish he is casting to if the light is good enough and so, in those conditions, it is possible to specifically target a particular species. That said, I don't know anyone who will pass up a cast at a 2-lb brown in order to cast to a 10-inch grayling or vice versa.

For all their similarities, trout and grayling are different species and so there are differences in behavior which the angler should know about. For a start, trout prefer their own individual lies, although these are sometimes quite close together and they will defend their territory against rival trout of the same size or smaller. As a result the angler can concentrate specifically on each trout in turn without worrying much about the effect on other trout in other lies. Grayling also sometimes occupy individual lies, but they also have a tendency to shoal together in a favoured depression or pool where conditions particularly suit them. This tendency to shoal is more pronounced in the later months of the year after the trout season has closed, but it can happen anytime. When grayling shoal, the angler has one major conflict to consider in deciding upon his approach. On the plus side, shoaling seems to give grayling a greater feeling of safety, making them easier to approach and creating a higher level of competition for food amongst members of the shoal, making it more likely that the fly will be hurriedly grabbed. On the minus side is the problem of how to pick them off individually without disturbing the others.

In general, grayling are more tolerant of disturbance created by the angler than trout are and are less likely to scatter if the angler clumsily reveals his presence. This is not to suggest that the angler can abandon all attempts at concealment and still expect to catch grayling. It is just that grayling are slightly less 'spooky' than trout. They also seem very reluctant to leave a prime lie once they have found one and when disturbed they will return to feeding quicker than trout do. When wading, the angler will find that grayling hold position very close to the angler, especially when the light is poor.

Grayling are predominately bottom feeders and have evolved a body shape suitable for a fish that spends most of its time flush against the stream bed feeding on nymphs or shrimps. But grayling, like most fish, are also opportunists and if a fat, juicy dun flutters past trapped in the surface film, they have no hesitation in rocketing to the surface and nailing it. They feed where the most attractive food is to be found and if that happens to be on the surface during a heavy hatch of flies then they rise as consistently as any trout. But most of the time they are busy well below the surface and so weighted nymph fishing usually results in a bigger catch rate because the fly gets down to where the fish are feeding. The biggest single technological advance that has improved my grayling fishing in recent years is the tungsten bead. A tungsten bead gets the fly down to the fish faster and more effectively than any other weighting method.

Grayling don't grow as big as trout and so if I am specifically targeting grayling I use lighter tackle. Generally, I use a 7 ft 6 in 3 weight rod for the bigger streams and 6 ft 2 weight rod for the small streams, carriers and when wading. All rods are full flex to allow for more delicate fly presentation and for power absorption when playing a fish. I use a 5 ft braided leader as a butt section to which I attach a tippet that varies in length depending on the requirements of particular casts, but which is usually between 6 and 7 ft, giving an overall leader length of about 12 ft. I match leader length and tippet diameter to the fly size not the fish size. A 5X tippet has a higher breaking strain than the weight of the British record grayling.

I love to fish for grayling and do it as often as I can. Perhaps the best way of getting across to you what so fascinates me about grayling fishing is to take you along with me on a few trips to some of my favorite streams. Let me hurriedly add that the following stories are about times when things went more or less right. There have been plenty of other times when things did not go right at all, but I am sure you are not interested in stories where the only thing that happens is an emotionally overwrought angler flailing away fishless into the fading light.

First Time

This is a story of my first visit to a beautiful stretch of the River Bourne on a summer's day a few seasons back. This tale incidentally also reveals some of the important 'do's' and 'don'ts' when approaching a river for the first time.

On the day in question, the weather was overcast, with a high cloud base and no sign of rain. It was early afternoon and the light was good. The water was gin clear and about two and a half feet deep. I could see the river bed clearly, so seeing fish would be relatively easy. Perfect, except they could see me too. Proof of this was demonstrated immediately, as I spooked two trout within the first twenty yards of starting to move upstream from the beginning of the beat. Both fish shot upstream. I slowed down my approach and promptly spooked another two trout, probably the same ones, back downstream. I then saw a grayling glide into a small pool sheltered by the overhanging branches of an alder tree. The flow of the water had scoured out this hole which was fed by a fast riffle about a foot deep. Peering carefully I could make out the shapes of five grayling and two trout in the hole and immediately dropped to my knees. Given the restrictions caused by bank-side vegetation, overhanging branches and the position of the fish, a cross body cast was required. This meant I had to edge forward a couple of feet. As I did this one of the trout rocketed away, the other started nervously fluttering from side to side, but two of the grayling lay motionless and the remaining three continued swaying gently within the confines of the hole. As I flicked the line into a back-cast, the last remaining trout shot away, the two motionless grayling remained motionless and the three other grayling became agitated; I was sure they had all seen me. Unfortunately, the back-cast foul hooked a barbed wire fence behind me. To recover my fly meant parading in full view. I used 'ostrich logic', reasoning that if I could not see them they could not see me, turned my back on the fish and retrieved my fly. Shuffling back on my knees I could clearly see – no fish! I stood up, wound in my line and continued upstream scanning the water. Around the next bend the main current tracks from right to left creating another hole about two feet wide, two and a half feet deep and six feet long in the shape of a giant banana. Food comes down with the main current which slowly disperses through the pool. Fish can be on either side of the main flow, conserving energy, but with a good view of what is coming to them and with enough time to inspect potential food items in a leisurely way. The fish are also able to drift into the deeper parts of the pool upon any sign of danger. I could see no rises, no fish movement, no shadows, no weeds and no reflections that looked fish-shaped or like parts of a fish. I must have spooked them all long ago, I thought. Stepping forward carefully from the bank and wading forward into the deeper water at the back end of the pool, two grayling and one trout, all about a pound in size, shot off upstream. I made a mental note of where that hole is!

The next stretch has a high bank with branches and thick foliage on both sides for about five hundred yards. Small depressions pocket the riverbed throughout, but these contain only small fingerlings. I now had the choice of either climbing out and going forward on the bank or continuing to wade. I decided to carry on wading. I soon managed to round up and herd all the fingerlings before me through the whole five hundred yards, apart from maybe ten percent that scuttled back past me in a panic. I fear the spooked fish spooked more fish and the fact that I accelerated my progress in eagerness to complete this section did not help. Upon reflection, I probably should have climbed out and walked along well back from the bank until I came to more hopeful looking water.

Eventually, I came to a better stretch about thirty yards from an abstraction pipe where I noticed three grayling lying under some overhanging trees in a depression about fifteen feet ahead of me. I decided a straight overhead cast would give me the best chance of an accurate presentation. I felt I could probably get the fly to drift past on the left, within two feet or so of the fish. Tying on a size 16 Peasant Tail Nymph (PTN), I carefully cast. The fly drifted past without so much as a side glance from the fish. To get a more accurate cast, I went down on my knees in the water, edged a little closer and cast left to right, stopping the rod at two o'clock with a short flick of the wrist. The nymph landed five feet above the fish and rapidly sank to the bottom. I retrieved excess line hurriedly and pointed the rod tip towards where I thought the fly was, thereafter retrieving figure-of-eight style to match the flow of the stream and keeping the line as straight as possible. The trick is not to tighten so much that the fly moves from its line of drift, which on this occasion would bring the fly down slightly to the left of the fish. A grayling moved from its position, to the left and back again, roughly where I thought the fly was. All I needed to do was to lift with the same gentle force as used when performing an 'induced take'. The line tightened and the rod went into a pleasing arc, the grayling thrashing left to right, its body contorting in and out of a crescent moon shape before shooting off upstream. With the reel drag set at zero, the line played out for ten feet or so, with the rod bouncing down with each effort the fish made against the current. Unhooking my landing net and opening it with a strong flick, I laid it in front of me in the water. I now retrieved line, bringing the fish towards me through the pool. This increased the agitation of the remaining two grayling, which had been darting randomly within the confines of the pool during the fight, occasionally coming to an abrupt stop, facing upstream, and then darting off again. I landed and released the fish and it streaked off downstream.

Without moving my position, I looked for the other grayling. They were still there, but surely by now they knew all about me. I cast anyway. As the PTN drifted towards them, the closest grayling moved sideways to allow the fly to pass and then returned to its original position. Every time I cast it did the same thing. Ha! It knew the fly was an object to be avoided! I changed from a PTN to pheasant tail bodied 'F' Fly, trying to deceive them by using a dry fly. No response whatsoever, so I changed to a size 16 tungsten bead Red Spot

Nymph. The fly rapidly descended to the river bed, I could feel it trundling downstream and a grayling moved slowly to the right then back again. I wasn't sure where my fly was but gently lifted the rod anyway, and connected! As the second fish thumped against the pressure of the rod, the third fish had finally had enough and scooted off upstream.

Continuing upstream and continuing to scare fish because I couldn't see them, I came to a part of the stream that was fairly straight for about twenty-five yards. The trees and foliage met overhead in several places, causing blackout spots on the water surface and making it difficult to see the riverbed. Was that a rise? A bubble the size of a ten pence piece floated down and popped ten feet from me. I stripped off some line and made a few false casts. The rod, with a full flex action, gave me larger line loops in the cast than I felt comfortable with in these confined conditions. Moving my hand to the top of the rod handle effectively reduced the rod length by about a foot, which helped. Keeping the rod in the horizontal plane, I cast to a spot approximately four feet above where I first saw the bubble. As the fly was sinking I removed as much slack as possible and tried to match the water speed. Nothing happened for the first three casts, but on the fourth cast two large grayling swam into view, looked at me and unhurriedly continued downstream. I had probably lined them with my casts. About ten feet further on and in the centre of the stream, I came upon a depression in the riverbed. This must have been where those two grayling had been holed up. I again cast to where I thought the rise had been. Immediately a large grayling sauntered past, heading downstream. Moving about six feet upstream whilst scanning the riverbed around me, I noticed a hole to the right, near the far bank, probably where the large grayling had been positioned. The act of casting had alerted all three fish, not enough to panic them, but sufficient to cause them to move on. I took another step forward and saw several shadows dart upstream from about fifteen feet ahead of me – another missed opportunity. I completed wading through the section, looked back to survey the scene and reminded myself to write down the position of those holes, then turned back upstream knowing that I wouldn't.

By now the sun was a little way off the horizon – not much light left. For the next two hundred yards the stream looked very shallow, only about a foot deep, with some depressions here and there up to two feet deep or so. Fingerlings were darting about and would probably alert other fish as they swam past. I concluded it was easier to wade on rather than circumvent this stretch, risking detection for convenience and consoling myself with the thought that this section would be treated as an orientation exercise. I tanked through at speed as time was short until about twenty yards from the end where I could see a right angled bend overshadowed by trees. The trees on both banks had extended and intertwined their branches over the river like an arch in a bridge. Looking through this archway, the low bank disappeared to the left and the fields and sky were clearly visible. The current flowed left to right, quite fast compared to the rest of the river, bouncing off the right bank, changing direction by ninety degrees and reducing speed by half, creating a relatively slow pool. I could see some dark shadows fluttering around the shallow pool exit. Creeping as stealthily as I could, I hugged the left bank, getting closer to my chosen casting point which was about twelve feet back from the pool's tail. A trout and a grayling each around a pound glided out of view and under the far bank opposite. Now the light was bad and I could only see into the shallows immediately in front of me. I slowly knelt down in the shallow water and looked around me. An overhead cast was impossible; a side cast from this position would line the deep part of the pool, so best to start at the back of the shallow tail. I shifted position carefully to the middle of the stream and cast to the right hand side under the trees, taking the slack out of the line as the fly sank and letting the current control the path of the fly. On the second cast the line stopped momentarily, I lifted, connected, stopped the fish from going upstream into the pool, and finally landed a graying nearly 14 inches long.

Casting again to roughly the same spot, the line stopped again, I lifted, the rod bent but stayed firm and stable. I had snagged the bottom. Slow increasing pressure released it. The next few casts also snagged the bottom, so I changed from a tungsten bead fly to a lighter (three turns of medium lead wire) PTN. I cast again, the tippet seemed to sink faster than it had done previously; I lifted, hooked and landed another grayling, 13 inches this time. Many casts later, during a retrieve, a rise appeared in the middle of the deep water. I immediately changed to an 'F' Fly, cast a further ten times or so, but got no response. Maybe it was a onecer. I figured a better drift angle was required, which meant going back to my original position. Any fish left in the area were probably alarmed by now, having been cast to so many times, so I tried not to show my profile against the skyline any more than was absolutely necessary. It would mean shuffling on my knees, not good for my waders, but the best option in the circumstances. Eventually I got back into position, stripped some line off the reel and replaced the 'F' Fly with a copper-coloured tungsten bead PTN. Pinching the fly between my thumb and forefinger and facing the hook bend towards the rod handle, I let about five feet of fly line hang from the rod tip to the water. To begin the cast I brought the rod slowly towards me in the horizontal plane and this caused the main line to double-up. Before the fly line, leader and tippet could straighten, I flicked the rod away sharply and let go of the fly. The fly plopped into the water about halfway across the stream. With the first part of the cast completed, I stripped fly line out to the distance I wanted to cast, loaded the rod by casting forward in the horizontal plane with enough force to pick the fly up out of the water and send it forward. Before the fly landed, I executed a single back-cast and then shot the line forward again towards the far bank, two feet above where the main current entered the pool. The fly line landed quietly on the deep pool's surface and I instantly tried to take as much slack out of the line as I could to ensure I was in direct contact with the fly for as long as possible. The drift was uneventful, although I couldn't fault it technically. I cast again and again; nothing. What I needed to do was to cast further upstream to allow more time for the fly to sink. Aerializing as much line as I dared, I chopped the rod forward, but got the rod angle and power transfer all wrong so that the rod failed to load on the back cast resulting in only about ten percent of the power being transferred to the fly. I instantly know when this happens because there is a momentary lack of feeling in the rod as the line goes slack and a few seconds later the fly travels past in slow motion. This is commonly known as a 'crap cast', with the fly moving slowly by in a 'trebuchet trajectory' also known as a 'lob'. This particular cast caused the fly to nestle in the branches overhead. I reeled in the slack and pulled very slowly and gently to see if the fly would release itself. No. I thrashed wildly trying the opposite strategy. No. Nothing for it, I would have to stand up, wind the line in to the top of the tip ring and shake vigorously. It's surprising how often this works with barbless hooks. The rod tip ring acts as a disgorger and the shaking finds the position under tension that will release the hook. A word of caution – rod tip sections have been broken using this technique. Standing up effectively ended the day's fishing. I made my way up to the edge of the deep pool and attempted the rod tip technique with no success. Into the middle of the pool I went, pulled down the branch holding the fly and released it. Looking down, my heart skipped a beat; there must have been fifteen or even twenty grayling, all in the region of one and a half to two pounds, darting around me. Reflecting on the day's events during my drive home, I concluded some may have been larger. A couple of weeks later, I reckoned they were larger still.

Bushy Dry Fly

Trying to ensure that grayling (or any fish) are unaware of your presence doesn't end with a stealthy approach. The act of casting and the fly entering the water are equally important. On occasions your best concealment and your most accurate and delicate presentation still causes a grayling shoal to panic. I have observed this panic when any or all of the following actions are performed: at the start of the back-cast; when the line, leader or tippet lands on the water; and when the fly makes an audible plop or splash. Initially the fish scatter, but even if they don't disappear from view they will doggedly refuse all that is put before them, by either moving out of the way of the drift of the fly or by ignoring it altogether. One day on the Wylye I found an unusual solution to this problem more by luck than judgment.

About fifty yards from the end of the beat, the river splits into two, one side going through a village, the other around the outside. The two streams then converge. The water on the left hand side of this convergence runs faster than that on the right. There are good banks of weed throughout and an average water depth of about two feet. Where the two parts of the stream meet, a V is formed and within this V the slack water is clear of weed. Alder bushes line the banks of the inner part of the V and overhang the water. A lot of grayling inhabit this area and they can easily be seen. They are regularly fished for and they know all about fishermen. They seem to recognize artificial flies, casts and the effect of the line landing on the water. They can be very difficult. I only have permission to fish the right-hand bank, which is three feet higher than the water level. I used to stand upright on this bank which makes back casting easy, gives good all round visibility and normally the barbed wire fence behind doesn't come into play. Early season I could catch a few fish here casting upright from the bank, but nowhere near the numbers I could see swimming about. This is probably because I stood out against the horizon. I now keep as low a profile as I can. The tallest I get is kneeling down, but the most comfortable is to sit on the bank with my legs dangling over the edge unless casting to the nearside right-hand bank when I gain purchase with my left foot by digging it into the face of the bank below me and then kneel on my right knee. Making a conscious effort to stay low has significantly increased my catch rate of both fish and barbed wire fences.

On the day in question I started fishing in earnest at the confluence by casting to each of the fish closest to me, then working my way across the middle and ending by casting to the far bank. Progress upstream was made by crawling along the bank a couple of yards at a time and then repeating this casting procedure – nearest fish first, far bank last. For about half an hour I tried various plans of attack; weighted and un-weighted PTNs, Comparaduns, black and green 'F' Flies, black and green Baetis Nymphs and so on; all to no effect. As each cast hit the water some fish would shuttle two or three feet to one side and then return to their original position, some would lie doggo and not react at all, others would avoid the fly by doing a complete circle before returning to their original position and some just moved away to another part of the confluence. The most perplexing thing was that I could see them feeding, mainly during the times I was changing my fly. These fish seemed to know when it was safe to eat.

Delicacy was called for, so I scaled down to a 6X tippet. A grayling was taking duns off the surface about two feet from the alder bushes in the middle of the widest part of the V formation. A dry fly was needed. I tried to concentrate on getting the fly as close to the alder bushes as possible, ignoring any impact that lining the fish might have. I performed a couple of false casts to approximate the distance and then sent my size 16 Adams Irresistible sailing through the air. The fly line landed gently, the braided butt section of the leader landed about four feet behind the grayling and the fly landed in the alder bushes about three feet above the water, trailing the fine tippet section behind it. Just leave it and let nature take its course, I thought. The current pulled the line towards me, causing the tippet lying on the water to straighten. When it was completely straight, it lifted off the water surface, going higher and higher into the air to form a rough triangle of line, water and bush. The force imparted by the line became greater than the force holding the fly in the bush, causing it to tumble and bumble from leaf to leaf, finally dropping ever so gently onto the water.

Immediately the grayling accelerated forward in a beeline interception and engulfed the fly. It was an easy matter to bring the fish downstream straight into the net – blank saved!

Since this first success I have repeated this technique in similar situations with some success. The fly has to be a well hackled, bushy dry fly with the hook point somewhat masked. This reduces the risk of hooking the foliage (and unfortunately, also the fish). The vegetation must have broad-type leaves, not brambles, thorns or thistles. The mindset needed to attempt this strategy is 'do or die', but doing it does seem to give greater confidence in taking casting risks in other situations. Expect fly loss.

Barton Carrier

Catching a fish on the first cast of the day can be the reward for careful planning, correct observation, accuracy of presentation and stealth of approach, or it can be pure luck. Whatever the reason, if I pull this off, then from that point on, I fish with more confidence. When I was first introduced to the Lower Beat of the Itchen, the carrier path was pointed out to me as a good way of getting to the start of the beat without disturbing three hundred yards of the main river. This path runs alongside a carrier stream which, although much smaller than the main river, is considered a beat in its own right and is predictably called the Carrier Beat. At the start of the Carrier Beat there is a small groyne which, over time, has created a small depression in the stream bed. A little further upstream is a second one, much older, with less pronounced features, but a food trap nevertheless. I was there one day in mid-November, on a dark, overcast day with very little wind. The water was tinged with colour and visibility was only about two feet. I arrived at eleven o'clock in the morning and nothing was rising. Having tied on a size 16 PTN with a copper-coloured tungsten bead, I flicked the fly plus a few feet of line onto the water in front of me and stripped three yards of line from the reel in preparation for casting. I picked up the line from the water, slowly accelerating upward for the first back cast and bang, I was in! With all the emphasis on stealth and concealment that surrounds chalk stream fly fishing, you would think this would be impossible, but surprisingly it happens quite often. Lifting the rod high over my head to avoid a clump of weeds, I walked downstream for five or six yards and played, landed and released a 10-inch grayling. It was a lucky start, but it confirmed my choice of fly and made me feel confident. Back in position, I cast about nine feet upstream. As the line and leader floated down, the leader tip dipped under water. I lifted and held another fish gyrating on the end of the line. To ensure the least disturbance to the shoal, I again walked downstream to net and release the fish and then quietly returned to the same spot. Four casts produced four more fish. After the fifth cast, the line floated down uninterrupted. What was I doing wrong? I cast a foot further up and pow, another fish! The next three casts produced nothing so I let the fly sink for longer, only taking up the slack line when the leader was just a foot in front of me. I felt a sort of grating through the line and thought I must be dragging bottom, so I lifted the rod high over my head in an attempt to remove my fly from the snag. Over went the tip and I was in again. The next few casts were fruitless. I reacted to what I thought were bites, but ended up with nothing. Time for a change, I thought. On went a size 16 black Baetis Nymph followed by a short cast. The line stopped momentarily during the drift and a short quick lift ended in a 13-inch grayling. How often does a change in fly get a result, particularly when fishing a feeding shoal? I continued to catch another seven fish with this fly and then changed to a Gold Bead Hare's Ear Nymph. I walked a couple of steps upstream and proceeded to catch another four. Near the end of the old groyne area, I finally changed to a Red Spot Nymph and finished the session with three more.

Twenty-three grayling in one and a half hours, the majority around 10 inches with an exceptional couple at 13 and 14 inches, over a distance of nine yards! How rare is that?

Bubble

I was on the Avon, on a premium beat, nymph fishing for trout in July. The water was four to five feet deep, slightly discoloured, with only about two to three feet visibility. It was late afternoon and a few medium olives were hatching. I was not expecting any fish bigger than two pounds, so I was using my 6 ft, full flex, 2 weight rod and a size 16 copper tungsten PTN. I was fishing to a shadow lying in the centre of the river about four yards upstream. I heard a loud plop and couldn't help looking up in the direction I thought it came from. I always do this and it's not a good idea, especially when nymph fishing, because it breaks your concentration. When you look back and try to find your fly you can't see it and have to rely on watching the leader for indications of a take. On most occasions when this happens, I prematurely abort the drift. A quick scan along the far bank and I saw a bubble the size of a two pence piece floating past a clump of grass overhanging the far bank. Mark that! I heard it again, looked up, same place, so I quickly retrieved my line, changed the tippet from 6X fluorocarbon to 6X standard mono, tied on a size16 olive 'F' Fly, greased two thirds of the tippet and prepared to cast. During the time I was tackling up, the fish rose again. I didn't need that; it just got me more worked-up. I false cast until I had roughly fifteen yards of line in the air. This amount of line, I calculated, would allow the fly to land two feet above the clump of grass and six inches from the bank. It did. Brilliant! The fly drifted, one foot, two feet, up came the fish and took the fly. I lifted and it was caught and landed with complete and utter control – textbook. I didn't measure this grayling but estimated it at one and a half pounds and returned it very quickly and unharmed. Perfect!

WAEF (When All Else Fails)

There are times when fishing for grayling is relatively easy; the fish are feeding, you are in the right place, at the right time, with the right fly and with the right calm, controlled and focused frame of mind necessary for casting accuracy. And then there are times when it's not easy – the 'dog days' of August come to mind. By August the fish have become 'educated', it is bright, it is hot, the water is crystal clear and there are no flies hatching. Stealth is paramount. Trying something different may work.

I was nicely in position and could see that the river ahead had been pinched in by a large tree growing right out of the bank surrounded by brambles that hang down onto the water. The tree and the brambles created an effect much like a small hatch pool with the current accelerating through the narrow middle, but with slack water along the nearside bank and a little eddy against the far bank. Over time the brambles had collected debris floating downriver and this had created a small raft of weed and other flotsam on top of the slack water. Under this raft lay a 10-inch trout and another trout about the same size had taken up position close to the opposite bank. About two feet behind each of these small trout and further in towards the centre of the stream, two grayling lay on the edge of the main current. All four fish were about six inches from the bottom. The furthermost grayling dipped its head to the right and back again. Was he feeding? I tied on a size16 copper tungsten bead PTN and cast out into the centre of the stream. The right-hand trout shot upstream, the left-hand trout disappeared under the weed raft and the two grayling flinched, but remained where they were. The next few casts produced no reaction at all, nothing, not a sniff. Understandable, I thought. The PTN is my most successful fly and is probably everybody else's favorite too. They must have seen hundreds lately. I took my time, watching, thinking about what to try next. The furthermost fish dipped to the right again. I tied on a Red Spot Nymph, cast and promptly landed the fly right in the middle of the brambles. Brilliant! Now what? It was definitely a lost fly. I couldn't wind up the line and stretch forward and waggle the rod tip because the 6 ft rod was 15 ft short of where the fly was. If I struck rapidly, whether the fly came out or not, I would scare the fish. If I crawled forward to get close, I would scare the fish. The best I could do was to point the rod directly at the fly and pull the line, gently at first, but with increasing force, hoping that the fly would come free before the tippet broke. The tippet broke.

Whilst preparing a new tippet, I noticed the nearest grayling move two feet to the left, look at the river bed, spit out some bits and then glide to the right again. Maybe caddis, I thought. I had no specific caddis imitations with me, but a size 14 Gold Head Gold Ribbed Hare's Ear nymph would be close enough! I replaced the leader with a floating braided 4X leader to which I attached a 4X fluorocarbon tippet and tied on the fly. My cast caused the nymph to hit the water right in the middle of the narrowest section of the stream with an audible 'plop'. Both grayling instantly shot upstream. They really couldn't get out of there quickly enough. Ah well! Best thing for me to do now was to sit down and eat my sandwiches. I backed away from the bank edge and sat down looking at the river. While chewing away, it suddenly came to me how lake-like the slack water created by the tree and brambles actually was. There was a current certainly, but a lethargically, painfully slow current, no faster than the currents created by the wind on a stillwater. The 'When All Else Fails' (WAEF) fly originally created by Steve Hare came to mind. This fly was used by Bill Sibbons as a stillwater stalking fly. It has a body of lead wire tightly wound round a nymph hook which is then superglued and a tuft of short-cropped white deer hair is tied in near the eye for visibility. I tie mine in sizes 16 and 18.

I reasoned that these grayling had been bombarded all year long with all sorts of conventional river patterns. Perhaps if I could get an unfamiliar stillwater pattern down to them without them noticing me, then maybe, just maybe, I might have a chance. I crawled back to the bank edge. Would you believe it! The two grayling were back. I tied on a WAEF and slid into position. I flicked the back cast higher than normal and instead of my usual final forward punch, I stopped the rod at twelve o'clock causing the fly to accelerate past the leader and tippet and enter the water first. The fly cleanly punctured the surface film and descended to the bottom – no splash, no audible plop. The grayling showed no visible reaction. Gently does it now, I thought, and allowed the almost non-existent current to take up the slack in the hope that the resulting pressure on the line would trundle the fly downstream. Oh, how painfully slow it was, how agonizingly slow. I couldn't stand the torment any longer and decided to give matters a helping hand. With my left hand I pulled about six inches of line in. The fly jumped up about three inches from the bottom and came to a standstill a foot further downstream. The closest grayling showed some interest and glided over for a look at the fly, but its mouth didn't open. I tugged on the line again, harder this time, trying to perform an induced take without using the rod tip. Up came the fly, up came the grayling's head and it followed the fly downstream for about a foot before turning back. I lifted the rod to vertical, punched forward as if to roll cast but before completion, changed to a high back cast and then flicked the fly back into the water. This time, the cast was a little shorter and about a foot to the right. I lost sight the fly. The closest grayling moved to the left, stopped and opened its mouth. I lifted as if by rote and he began careering around the pool closely followed by his companion. The hooked fish came downstream towards me and the other, following, saw me and scooted out of sight. After some commotion on the surface, I managed to land and release him quickly – which all goes to show that even worldly wise fish can fall for something a little different now and then.

Solitary Fish

There are big grayling in all rivers where the species occurs, but 'big' is a relative term depending on the average size of the grayling in a particular river. The biggest grayling in the chalk streams that I fish are to be found in the Itchen. The problem is finding them consistently.

Early one October I was fishing a beat of the Itchen when I encountered a real monster in the context of that river. I was fishing a section that has wooden casting platforms built out from the bank because a dense reed bed grows out into the water for eight or ten feet and casting would otherwise be impossible. The platforms reduce the width of the river to about twelve yards and a giant hedge of rhododendron bushes covers the opposite bank. The depth is about five feet and streamer weed surrounds a hole that looks like a diagonal Bonio biscuit. I was looking into the clear water trying to spot fish when this huge grayling came into focus, holding position in the stream in the company of three large trout. I cast to these fish and managed to hook one of the big trout, but the grayling just faded away into the darkness of the far bank.

From then on, each time I fished that beat I looked for the big grayling and if I didn't see it, I wouldn't fish the platform stretch at all, even if there were smaller grayling present. My hope was that if I left the water alone and returned later in the afternoon or evening I might see it and be in with a chance. Then the day came when I finally saw it again. This time it was holding station in the top part of the pool. Pulling line off my reel, I walked out onto the platform. The fish immediately glided out of sight. Having learned my lesson, the next time I saw it I slowly dropped to my knees and shuffled to the end of the platform, keeping as low as possible. The fish was stationed very deep in the water, almost touching the riverbed, so I would have to cast into the weeds above its position to have any chance of the fly sinking to the correct depth in time. First cast the fly landed mid-pool – the fish remained stationary. Second cast, the fly landed just short of the weeds. Third cast, the fly landed in the weeds as planned, but as the line travelled downstream the leader passed close to the fish and it glided into the shadows of the far bank. I was annoyed with myself. Why hadn't I performed some practice casts behind the fish, to get an idea of the correct distance?

Two weeks later I was back again. The light was very good for late afternoon at this time of year. There were no leaves on the trees and virtually no wind, allowing for a perfectly reflected silhouette of the opposite bank and an unobstructed view of the river bed through the clear water. I was straining my neck to catch a glimpse of any recognizable fish shape. Yep, there he was, a solitary fish outline, dark, about three quarters across the river and a foot or so from the surface. I pulled the leader and line through the top ring, bent my torso to the horizontal position, gripped the fly (a size 14 black Baetis Nymph with black tungsten bead) in my left hand, turned my head to the right, stared fixedly at the dark shape and walked forward slowly raising my knees and placing my feet carefully. This is known as the 'tyrannosaurus stalk', especially if performed in thigh waders. Arriving at the platform, I went down on my knees and crept to the end. Sitting on my calves, I tethered the fly in the chicken wire non-slip covering of the platform while I opened my landing net in hopeful preparation. From this position I was completely in the open, the reeds had died down by this time and there were no trees or bushes behind me; easy. My first cast was three quarters across the river and well below the fish. Leaving the line in the water, I stripped off another ten feet of fly line to allow for the extra distance then made three false casts to change direction and punched forward to completion. The fly landed slightly to the left and about two feet above the fish. The grayling moved to the left, drifted slightly downstream, then turned back upstream. I lifted and held, the rod arched over and the grayling shot into the weeds. I just hung on, keeping the rod high and applying as much pressure as I dared. There wasn't really much cause for concern because I was using a 4X tippet with a breaking strain of 6lb which easily prevented the fish from going deep into the weeds. I wound up more line and increased the pressure. Slowly the fish came out of the weeds and downstream into the open belly of the pool. It stayed there for a while, then started coming towards me. I wound, it came quickly, I wound quicker, it came quicker still, I wound as quickly as I could, it went past me downstream ending up about ten feet away and close to the bank. I gave it side strain and its dorsal fin came into play, kiting the fish from right to left and back again. Would the hook hold? I increased pressure, slowly pumping the fish upstream until it was directly in front of me. I slid the landing net into the water and the grayling lunged to the bottom. I held firm, it completed a full circle deep down then came to the surface thrashing and splashing. I lifted the rod higher, its head came out of the water and then turned on its side. I slid the net under it.

Wetting my hands first, I measured him. Both his length and girth were 19 inches exactly. It took some time to revive him lying on my stomach at the end of the platform holding him with outstretched arms facing upstream into the current. After what seemed to be at least five minutes (but which was probably only two or three) he stopped tilting to the side and was able to stay upright on his own before gliding forward, down and away to the far bank.

This, my biggest grayling ever, would have weighed about 3lb (extrapolated from his dimensions using the fish weight calculators available on the internet and from the Grayling Society). I have never seen him again, although I always look for him. I have found another monster though, even bigger I think. Where is that, you ask? Couldn't say, I'm sure.

Chapter Ten

Chalk Stream Fly Fishing for Coarse Fish

Dominic Longley

Why fly fish for coarse fish on chalk streams?

When coarse fishermen find themselves walking beside the upper reaches of chalk streams, what's on their minds as they contemplate a trout, poised between tresses of water buttercup, or a shoal of grayling concealing themselves beneath the ruffled surface of a small hatch pool? I guess that most picture themselves crouching in the bank-side herbage, gently swinging out a float and a size 16 hook baited with a single maggot or a piece of bread-flake.

So what of the fly fisherman's train of thought when the boot is on the other foot? They are just as likely to be passing by parts of the river where chub, barbel, dace and roach occupy weed-fringed glides and pike, perch and bream reside in deep pools. Does the fly fisherman feel an instinctive yearning to put a carefully chosen fly in front of those unfamiliar species? Do they have faith that fly fishing would not only be enjoyable and productive, but also, in certain circumstances, more effective than the various popular forms of bait fishing? They certainly ought to, for there is no logical reason why the fly fishing ethos should not be applied to all British fish species that can feasibly be taken on fly, so long as the practitioners enjoy it and are stimulated by the venture. This fish-list stretches way beyond salmon, brown trout and grayling, so regardless of any questions of taste, preference or tradition, there is a substantial stock of satisfaction, fun, adventure, insight and learning to be had amongst these non-salmonid, non-thymallid fish.

The last decade has seen considerable development in fly fishing for coarse fish by a relatively small number of pioneers and much progress has been made in identifying the most rewarding locations and techniques. One thing is for sure – these adaptable anglers, through perseverance and problem solving, have enjoyed some very satisfying fishing and have developed a broader understanding of the geography and ecology of their home rivers. Another certainty is that, despite the impressive dedication and progress that these fly-fishers-for-coarse-fish have made, there remains a wealth of challenges, both technical and creative, yet to be addressed.

Of course, the brown trout populations of most chalk streams include a migratory component (sea trout) and most Southern English chalk streams also support Atlantic salmon, so variations of fly fishing are likely to have been practised on both upper and lower reaches for centuries, with both sets of anglers having some experience of catching non-salmonid species from time to time. Avon salmon rods tend to land significant numbers of pike, whilst chub and even barbel are also taken from time to time. But there has generally been an ideological constraint that has checked the development of fly fishing for coarse fish as a progressive branch of angling in its own right. Thankfully, these multi-faceted rivers have a habit of producing free-thinking innovators who see opportunity where others see entrenched ideological and physical boundaries. Chalk streams support some of the most diverse fish communities in Britain and offer an unparalleled range of angling opportunities within close proximity. Given this degree of opportunity, it's inevitable that a small proportion of the angling community has decided that they would like to sample all the delicious treats at the banquet of places, species, seasons and methods. These anglers fall into the 'glass half full' camp and they also tend to speak highly of sea fishing. Inevitably, this multi-culturalist angling mindset blurs boundaries; barbel fanatics take up salmon rods, salmon rods have a crack at winter grayling, grayling specialists get to grips with using centre-pins to long-trot for roach and, finally, it occurs to people to start trying to cast flies for all the fish species that might, conceivably, offer good and varied sport on the fly.

The waters

If you decide to pursue non-salmonid species with the fly, where will your endeavours take you? In many cases, it will be to the middle reaches of your home fisheries where a range of coarse species is likely to co-habit with the stars of the show; brown trout, salmon and grayling. However, there is likely to be a distinct downstream drift from where you usually fish. One of the most valuable rewards on offer to the downstream-migrating fly fisherman is a universally sought-after commodity amongst anglers, solitude, for although the number of anglers may not decrease, the landscape expands, providing wider vistas and a great deal more elbow room.

If you are an incorrigible brown trout aficionado, the journey downstream will be a lesson in the river continuum theory, as certain new characteristics become evident; the broadening of the river channel, its floodplain and its valley; the more extensive sweep of the meanders and their more pronounced, serpentine loops. The pools at the zeniths of these loops will be deeper, darker and slower and the gravel shoals thrown up from them by the winter floodwaters can be vast. The increased diversity in the submerged and marginal vegetation is striking, reflecting the greater range of water velocities and bed materials encountered in the different parts of the meander. There is more silt around; deep deposits on the inside of bends and trapped by reed beds fringing the channel. Areas resembling ponds, silty and lily-covered, occur as spurs away from the main flow, often overhung by patches of impenetrable wet woodland; alder and willow carr.

Chalk streams are often cited as being low energy rivers, which is true, but only relatively so; it is not unusual to feel the banks of the lower Hampshire Avon, Frome or Test quake as winter floodwaters thunder through, taking vast quantities of flotsam and thousands of tonnes of suspended sediment with them whilst peeling clay boulders and strips of turf from the banks. Although this pales in comparison with a major upland river in the full glory of a winter spate, the power of the winter chalk stream is evident throughout the year in its undercut banks, submerged clay boulders and deeply scoured holes – always beware walking on the edge of a bank on the outside of a bend or when wading upstream of a fallen tree (feeling the ground give way in either scenario is quite alarming and potentially serious).

Exploring these magnificent lower reaches of the typical chalk stream makes it clear why the brown trout, supremely adaptable as it is, no longer commands the monopoly it does farther upstream and has to compete with an extraordinary array of other fish species. There is simply such a plethora of habitats available that a variety of forms, life histories and survival strategies has evolved to exploit them (the difference between a pike and bream is comparable to that between a dugong and a leopard seal).

The principle that describes the distribution of fish species in an upstream/downstream order throughout a river catchment is usually termed 'zonation' and typically starts with the 'trout zone' in the headwaters and ends with the 'bream zone' at the downstream extent adjoining the tidal limit, with barbel, grayling and other zones between the two, depending on the particular version of the hypothesis. For anglers, the value of this concept doesn't lie in the memorisation of the various notional zones (it's a continuum and actual boundaries rarely exist, unless we built them), but in appreciating the factors that cause fish species to thrive in certain latitudes of river systems and to lose their competitive edge in others. More importantly, the angler should strive to appreciate (and this is a life's work) how and where these principles are reflected in the fish communities in *their* rivers, from source to sea. Why? Because this appreciation of the fish species and their environments is the basis for contriving informed and effective means of fly fishing.

The scarcity of coarse fish species in the upper reaches and headwaters of chalk streams is almost universally *not* the result of diligent removal programmes by clubs and keepers, but a reflection of fish species thriving in the environments to which they are best adapted. Most keepers who have attempted to eradicate unwanted species will generally report the same long-term effect: you can't keep a good species down. Like a glowing ember placed in oxygen, a small number of breeding fish missed by the removal programme, or that subsequently move into vacant habitat to which they are naturally adapted, is sure to result in swift repopulation, often at a far greater rate than if they had to compete with others of their own species.

Basic principles

In my view, fly fishing for non-salmonid species per se is *not* a case of trying to fit a square peg into a round hole just for the sake of doing something different. It is not like doing your ironing on a mountain top or at the bottom of the sea (barrels of fun maybe, but it won't get you better-pressed shirts). The same principles that make fly fishing for traditional quarry so satisfying and effective hold true for other fish species as well and to my mind, these revolve around the tried and tested tenets of 'observation, imitation and presentation'.

The stomach contents of non-salmonid chalk stream fish species (that grow large enough to fish for) reveals that the bulk of their diets consist of aquatic and terrestrial invertebrates and include most of those species preyed upon by trout and grayling. In fact, the variety of invertebrates will be greater, with the result that those not typically eaten by trout and grayling may provide fertile ground for imitation. If you include typical vertebrate prey items as well, then there is even more scope for innovation and creatures such as elvers, lamprey larvae, juvenile crayfish, slugs, earthworms, caterpillars, froglets, small shrews and voles and a host of others provide an exciting and novel challenge for the fly-tier.

In fly fishing for coarse fish, good watercraft is fundamentally important. Nothing proposed in this chapter will ultimately be of any value unless the angler grasps this. If, up until now, you have spent much of your fishing time pursuing stocked, essentially domesticated, trout, then you must appreciate that when you go hunting for coarse fish, you are setting your sights on wild things (and all the more worthy for it). If you do not go to great pains to lower your voice, reduce the vibration of your footfalls and conceal yourself using all available cover, even if that means kneeling on your arthritic knees, you are doomed to failure.

Kit

The fly-fisher-for-coarse-fish operates in territory where, for the majority of situations, no standardised approach has yet been, or may ever be, agreed. The exception to this is pike fly fishing, which is fundamentally different from any other branch and which has really seized the imagination of many UK anglers in recent years. Otherwise, the watchword is adaptability. A skim through any catalogue of fly-fishing gear these days reveals what are essentially fairly complete continuums of rod lengths, weights and actions and the same is true for lines and reels. Of course, the situation with flies, as ever, is that not only is it virtually impossible to conceive of any kind of fly without discovering that it is both easily and cheaply available, ready tied, but that, provided you have a vice and a pair of steady hands, you are truly limited only by your imagination and access to raw materials.

So, you're thinking of fishing for an unfamiliar species in unfamiliar waters – should you a) work from a list of equipment for that species prescribed by someone else, or b) consider the questions raised by your particular fishing scenario and piece together a logical response in terms of gear? I would argue that if you do not produce your own response by careful consideration of the question, then maybe you would be better off sticking to stocked trout. This is why there are no equipment lists in this chapter, but merely some words of advice aimed at clarifying the conundrums posed by the various species and their habitats and providing some indication as to where the answers might lie. Wherever I have first or second hand experience of reliable flies, or an idea for a fly as a sensible starting point, I'll point it out. As a result, the paragraphs on kit for each species are somewhat anecdotal and are certainly not intended to be prescriptive. You may come up with much better solutions for your particular water and probably will.

The fish:

Dace

Leuciscus leuciscu (British rod caught record: 1lb 5oz)

Form, habitat, feeding & breeding

Although a variety of smaller cyprinid species are often referred to as 'silver fish', it is for dace that this is the most accurate description; no other species can match it for the cleanliness of its lines and the silvery sheen and flawlessness of its scales (the scientific name is derived from the Latin prefix *leuc*, meaning white). This is a slender, elegant fish – a totem of the middle and lower reaches of the natural, unpolluted chalk stream and undoubtedly a worthy fishing quarry on light gear. In fact, as a species, the dace is so attuned to the habitat of the unmodified chalk stream and so dependent on clean, well oxygenated water, that it serves as a good indicator of overall river health. There has been considerable discussion about whether or not anecdotal observation of a decline in dace populations in British rivers is a genuine cause for concern. Suffice it to say that anglers on the middle reaches of the Hampshire Avon are unequivocal in their claim that the population is significantly reduced in comparison with the decades preceding industrial scale aquaculture and agricultural intensification.

Regardless of the purported decline, the species remains relatively ubiquitous in the lower reaches of most English chalk streams and is certainly abundant in a great many fisheries, especially those less affected by impoundments such as weirs and flow control structures (the absence of these features usually means there will be gravel riffles on which dace can spawn).

The dace's streamlined form is an adaptation to swift, shallow glides and life over clean gravels, although high winter flows tend to see them retreat to deeper, slower waters. Like grayling and barbel, a shoal of dace can melt into near invisibility against the gravel of a glide or riffle by virtue of their uniform colouration, ability to hold station with very little movement and the remarkable reflective qualities of their pearlescent scales. As a result, this species is a master of daytime concealment. Spotting dace in the daytime can be an art in itself; polarised glasses and patience are essential and it is often necessary to stare long and hard at gravel runs seemingly devoid of fish before the shoal finally comes into focus. Towards dusk, detection can be a much easier task as rising fish continually dimple the surface with their delicate takes. Dace have a pronounced tendency to move into shallower waters as the light fades – in full daylight they would be extremely vulnerable to predatory fish and birds in these areas, but as dusk develops, the feeding opportunities in these exposed expanses are too good to miss. As a result, the fly-fisher-for-dace must often cast into little more than six inches of crystal clear water, completely devoid of cover, to a fish whose presence is only betrayed by its subtle rise.

Possibly the best opportunities for observing dace at close quarters are in the side streams and tributaries, where quite dense shoals often congregate in smooth glides. These shoals often include a few roach and juvenile chub of similar size, which provides a good exercise in fish identification; small chub have blackish tails, a broad head and distinct white lips, whilst roach have red fins, red eyes and a deeper, more diamond-shaped body than the other two. At a distance, dace are identifiable by their streamlined form and overall lack of colouration, whilst at close quarters the best diagnostic feature is the concave trailing edge to their anal fin; on a chub this is convex.

Dace are gravel spawners and they prepare for reproduction by shoaling on riffles as early as January, around which time small tubercles (small, whitish, wart-like structures) appear on their heads, as they do on many cyprinids. As a result, spawning fish are often vulnerable to capture some weeks before the coarse fishing season closes on the 16th of March. It is at this time of year that the fish's remarkable ability to remain hidden on exposed gravel shoals, without a scrap of cover, is most appreciable. As happens in winter grayling fishing, sometimes the first indication of a take is that the nymph suddenly disappears from sight as it is enveloped by a mouth belonging to a hitherto unseen fish.

Like all chalk stream fish, the main part of the dace diet consists of invertebrates. Dace become preoccupied with taking flies at the surface to a greater extent than any other non-salmonid species and this behaviour becomes more prevalent with rising air temperature. In fact, the feeding habits of dace are probably more similar to those of brown trout than to any other chalk stream fish species; in addition to taking flies from the surface, dace will forage for shrimp, molluscs and larvae on the riverbed and will intercept emerging nymphs in the water column. Prey items tend to be small, often minute – a point well worth bearing in mind when tying or selecting flies.

As their quicksilver livery suggests, dace take surface flies at lightning speed and have a distinct habit of drowning them, that is, splashing at them to submerge them before deciding to ingest them or not. This causes the common occurrence of striking into what looked like a decisive take, only to meet no resistance. Although the pessimist might find this a frustration that downgrades the species, in the view of many it is simply another layer of challenge. Experience reveals that better fly selection and presentation, as well as a sharply focused approach to striking and line control solves the problem – suspicion of the fly is reduced and immediate physical contact with the hook is the result.

Fly fishing for dace

The best approach to take when setting out to fly fish for dace (especially bigger fish) is to consider them an excellent quarry upon which to hone your skills; they are shy, selective of their prey and very quick.

It would be pointless to commence describing suitable equipment without strongly emphasising the need for effective watercraft – at least as much effort is required from the angler in concealing his presence as is put into actually fishing. Along with minnows, bullhead and the young of other shoaling coarse species, dace are a staple for the river's piscivorous predators, especially herons, pike and, increasingly, cormorants. As a result, they are eternally vigilant for bank-side movement, shadows and vibrations, so before selecting your tackle remember that you will be in for some degree of kneeling, crouching and casting whilst seated. Thigh waders are excellent for this but only chest or trouser waders will be sure to keep you completely dry and protected from unfortunate experiences. A saving grace of the species is that while they are distressed by movement, they appear to have little memory of stationary objects positioned near them. Therefore, it is not unusual to find dace returning to their stations in the shallows and rising freely, in crystal clear water, within a few feet of the wading angler, as long as he or she remains as still and quiet as possible.

Equipment

Given the dace's small size, speed and very discerning approach to taking surface flies, tackle must be delicate. It is also essential that the angler chooses gear that can be handled dextrously and confidently. Line and fly drag is a particular concern in the reaches occupied by dace – water velocity will tend to be quite high and there will be an assortment of emergent vegetation liable to catch the line and drag the fly. Dace might require anything from a long, well-executed cast to a simple lowering, or flicking, of the fly and leader from the rod tip. Just as importantly, they are great fighters on light rods and it would be a crime to prejudice the full enjoyment of this by being over-gunned. Therefore, consider your casting style and ability and the distances you anticipate needing to cast and go from there. Based on these vague, contradictory criteria, I can only recommend a lightish rod, having a strength and action you feel particularly comfortable and confident with – for me, this is a slim, fast-action 8 ft 6 in 5 weight, but anything light and long should be suitable.

I have one fly that is my steadfast fall-back option for dace: a black sedge on a size 14 hook, which is not only my most successful rise-inducer, but is also visible deeper into the dusk than any other fly, which has often been a crucial virtue. I've found virtually all small mayfly patterns, especially parachute types, to be effective, as are black gnats and ants. Fly choice will be utterly redundant unless leaders and tippets are light and close to invisible – which must come as a familiar refrain to wild trout anglers.

Chub

Squalius cephalus (British rod caught record: 9lb 5oz)

Form, habitat, feeding & breeding

Whereas elegant, fine-lined dace grow into elegant, fine-lined adults, pretty, juvenile chub grow into big, tough brutes. The scientific name translates, approximately, as 'rough, scaly big-head'. Consequently, the juvenile and adult forms of the species are quite distinct as angling quarries. For the first few years of their lives, chublets are sleek, quick, shoal fish, with pewter-tinged scales, distinctive black-edged tails and a broad, white-lipped mouth. Other than the differing anal fin profile (concave in dace, convex in chub), two other clear features that differentiate similarly sized chub and dace are the distinct charcoal hues of the scales on the chub's back and the prominent upper lip (whereas dace have a slight snout protruding above the mouth).

Small chub tend to occupy peripheral habitats; side-streams, tributaries, backwaters and sheltered marginal areas, probably as a means of predator avoidance at their most vulnerable size. They have neither the speed nor the clear-water camouflage of dace, so have developed a different survival strategy; small chub are found a remarkable distance up the many streams that flow into the Hampshire Avon from the New Forest plateau and are notable for the low numbers recorded in fish population surveys conducted on the main river.

Juvenile chub feed quite similarly to dace, taking small invertebrates of all kinds from the bed, mid-water and at the surface, making them an enjoyable target for the fly fisherman. However, once chub reach a couple of pounds or so, their behaviour begins to change – they are now less vulnerable to predators (although they remain very wary as they are still on the menu for otters, determined herons and large pike) and they begin to display the catholic approach to feeding for which they are so noted. In particular, a piscivorous tendency becomes apparent and the chub turns its attention to small fish of any species and virtually any terrestrial creature small enough to be engulfed by that huge mouth is fair game if it falls in. The creatures that may be taken are on a sliding scale according to the size of the chub, but large slugs, small bank voles, fledglings and frogs are all frequently taken by chub that are mouthy enough for the job. As well as the overhead cover provided, this is another reason that large chub usually reside close to overhanging trees or bushes. The boldness of this predatory behaviour shouldn't be underestimated – chub are regularly caught on whole mackerel and herring-sized lures deployed for large pike.

The chub's great strength is that it is an opportunistic all-rounder and this is reflected in the range of plant matter that also becomes a part of its diet as the fish increases in size – many kinds of berries are eaten, having fallen in from bank side bushes, and chub can sometimes be observed grazing on a variety of submerged plants, even long pieces of reed, which are chewed by the pharyngeal, or throat teeth.

Chub can be remarkably long lived and fish of around twenty years old have been identified by scale reading. Large fish become distinctly battle-scarred and it is unusual to find a scale-perfect fish much above 5lb. In addition and in contrast to the jewel-like juveniles, old-timer chub often take on a slightly saggy, loose-skinned appearance.

Fly fishing for chub

This species offers two quite distinct opportunities for great fly fishing sport; targeting the smaller fish with light tackle and beefing up to go after the bigger beasts. Small chub can be aggressive snatchers of both dry flies and nymphs, yet are remarkably discerning avoiders of any hint of artificiality. I recently enjoyed a spell casting tiny, sinking beetle imitations to a shoal of 6-inch chub that were occupying the submerged foliage of a fallen willow and it was like being marked on a piece of coursework – I was constantly being sent away to make small but essential improvements until my submission was finally accepted, after which I landed several and had a much better idea of the standard required at that and similar swims. To begin with, the pattern, hook size, hook colour and strength of leader all appear to have been show-stoppers. Fly fishing for small chub is a similar prospect to fly fishing for dace, except that the pursuit of chub is more likely to take place in slacker, marginal waters, as well as the main channel. Another possible exception worth bearing in mind is that because of chub's more aggressive approach to feeding, they are not always put off by a dragging fly, so if chub are your quarry, hang in with a dragging fly and don't be surprised to see a small bow-wave tearing towards it.

Big chub, too, range across a wide spectrum of water velocities and the species as a whole does well in lakes and ponds – it is not uncommon for stillwater coarse fisheries to stock chub these days and some huge specimens have been taken from completely slack river backwaters. Therefore, when seeking out large chub on a chalk stream, you are likely to bump into outsize specimens in an insignificant side stream or carrier, as well as beneath an overhanging tree on the main river, although in all circumstances, a prerequisite is the availability of cover for the fish within a short distance.

Fly fishing for big chub provides opportunities for a wide range of approaches, although each will only be effective in the right season and weather – like most coarse fish, chub will tend to feed when temperature is rising relative to the recent average, regardless of the time of year. Prime conditions reflect the chub's most likely preoccupations: "Am I likely to be seen by a predator and is there a good chance that a big, juicy morsel may drop right onto my nose from a bank-side bush?" It follows and this is certainly borne out by experience, that dull, overcast but warm and humid (often thundery) conditions see large chub throw caution to the wind (relatively speaking) and become quite competitive in their efforts to be the first to seize anything splashing onto the surface, whether or not it subsequently floats.

In these conditions, the fly fisherman would do well to bear in mind the traditional big-chub coarse fishing technique of plopping a huge slug right on top of the fish – the response needs to be seen to be believed! The fish displays a momentary shock before either turning to inspect the object before grabbing it (if alone), or grabbing it without hesitation (if in competition with others). Consequently, chunky slug, moth, worm, cricket, froglet or caterpillar patterns are ideal for such circumstances, but these will be worthless without excellent concealment and observational skills on the part of the angler. Remember that it is the resounding 'plop' that triggers the take, because it indicates the immediate vulnerability of the unfortunate creature.

Following the same logic, a terrestrial creature that has just fallen into a river is likely to struggle and even swim for it and, given that chalk stream floodplains are usually teeming with tiny frogs by late spring, chub are likely to encounter small, kicking, tasty and nutritious creatures at the surface on a regular basis. This introduces one of the most exciting methods for taking large chub on the fly; popping. A fly popper usually consists of a simple feather body and/or wings, but with the addition of a small cylinder of foam or balsa close to the hook's eye, the blunt face of which is angled so that a sharp pull on the line causes the fly to pop and splash in an imitation of a struggling creature. This can be a particularly exciting method because of the unexpected and explosive nature of the takes. Even more thrilling, on occasion, is the sight of a powerful bow wave caused by a big chub accelerating towards its quarry from quite a distance. Tweaking a popper, or any kind of floating fly, gives the added advantage that you can fish to chub lurking deep under overhanging cover, provided that you have a clear cast to the water immediately upstream.

It has to be emphasised that any kind of surface fishing for large chub is almost a complete waste of time in clear, bright conditions and windy conditions also seem to discourage them.

Big chub rarely settle into a rise to hatching flies, with the exception of prolific mayfly hatches when the morsels are worthy of the chub's great maw. However, they may be induced to rise to most types of large, bushy dry fly and it seems to be size (and therefore energy content), rather than preference for a specific pattern, that seals the deal. Remember that chub are evolved opportunists and a key aspect of their feeding strategy is to grab first and ask questions later.

Equipment

Although adult chub can be mighty fish, you should not be intimidated by their power when choosing your equipment: they tend to charge upstream vigorously two or three times before diving into the nearest vegetation. So, although you certainly need a little power, some flex and no less than a three-pound tippet to check those weed-bound runs, the main consideration is accurate and effective presentation, often to quite distant fish, skulking on the periphery of overhanging bushes.

The chub is probably the only British river fish that will take any kind of fly under the right circumstances, including salmon, sea trout and pike flies and the entire range of dries, wets and nymphs. If you're after small chub, rising to a hatch, then dace tactics apply nicely and will probably result in bolder, more forgiving takes. If it's a lunking great adult chub you are after and they're taking on the surface, try the bushiest, most moth-like pattern you can muster. When trying to incite a sub-surface response, flashy sea trout patterns are excellent, especially those imitating wounded minnows or small silver fish. However, nothing will work unless the climatic conditions induce excitability and reckless feeding in the chub, in which case they are pretty unselective, especially if there's a chance one of their neighbours may get the grub first.

Pike *Esox lucius (British rod caught record: 46lb 13oz)*

Form, habitat, feeding & breeding

Pike are the overwhelming champions of piscivorous behaviour amongst British fish – the species occupies such a clearly defined and unchallenged niche in fish communities that it is not surprising it inspires both devotion and loathing amongst anglers. However, loathers must keep in mind that it is the diseased and injured that are always most susceptible to elimination and that pike are voracious cannibals (the most reliable and diligent culler of small pike is a large, territorial adult).

Devotees are captivated, above all, by the awe-inspiring convergence of beautiful form and efficient function: the gin-trap jaw with its enigmatic suggestion of a grin, the armoured skull, swept-back fins and cryptic green and white mottling are all evolutionary adaptations to improve the creature's effectiveness as an ambush artist. For me, the feature that most encapsulates this synergy is the very slight arching of the spine, just forward of the closely grouped dorsal, anal and caudal fins. Together these fins provide explosive thrust, firing the jaws out of cover in a sudden lunge at the target. Simultaneously, the arched spine extends, providing a moment's increase in reach, like a praying mantis striking at a butterfly. Of course, the extra centimetre or two increases the chance that the hundreds of tiny, backward-pointing teeth will find purchase in the victim's flesh.

Ambush artists must remain unseen so, like perch, pike are indelibly associated with submerged vegetation and shadows. They complement their habit of concealment with a predisposition for stillness, hovering motionless like a submerged branch (when I scan the river whilst pike fishing, it swells my confidence to think that, lying still amongst the weeds and shadows, there are numerous deadly green traps, just waiting to be sprung). Juvenile pike behave the same way, only in the shallower backwaters and marginal slacks – juvenile pike are, in my opinion, among the most beautiful river fish in the British Isles. They are living jewels, perfect facsimiles of their parents, with the exception of a vivid orange spot on top of the head that fades within a year or so. Breeding adults venture into these slack, marginal areas to court and lay their adhesive eggs on submerged vegetation in March, so that the young are ready to take advantage of the abundance of prey fish fry later in spring. Cannibalism is a particular trait of young pike in their first year and it results in a tiny proportion of the brood achieving very rapid growth at the expense of the rest which are simply gobbled up.

There are three vital principles that the angler must be aware of regarding pike feeding behaviour. Firstly, they perform a distinct ecological function in eliminating injured, diseased or malformed fish and so are strongly predisposed to taking fish that appear to have a problem. As a result, there is probably no object more certain to be hit hard by a pike than a lively roach or dace being reeled towards the landing net by a coarse angler. Secondly, for a surprising proportion of the time, pike are not inclined to feed at all; at any time of year, you will experience days when you seem to get a take in every likely looking swim, but also days when you would swear the river didn't contain a single pike. Lastly, popular tales of pike taking ducklings, grebes, frogs, grass snakes, rats and water voles are all generally true, but are based on very infrequent occurrences; the species is a fish specialist through and through. In five seasons of catching large chub on surface popper lures on the Hampshire Avon, I have never once had a take or even a follow from a pike.

Fly fishing for pike

Along with saltwater fly fishing, this is the branch of fly fishing that has attracted the most interest and seen the most development in recent years – the array of flies and fly-tying materials available from an amazing number of burgeoning internet businesses has to be seen to be believed. There is a simple reason for this; fly fishing for pike is fantastic fun and very productive. And here's the killer factor: it is, in most circumstances, a far more effective technique than any of the traditional coarse methods, with the possible and controversial exception of live baiting.

The first time I witnessed pike fly fishing was with a friend on the Hampshire Avon near Fordingbridge, on a sharp winter's morning. I had no faith in the method whatsoever and not even any respect for it – I cynically thought it a perfect example of trying to create a hybrid approach for the sake of it and was certain that my lures and deadbaits would demonstrate what an ill-conceived, even presumptuous, concoction it was. The day played out like a neat scientific experiment; we were roaming along the bank and my polite companion allowed me to cast into each swim first. In each, I carefully sank-and-drew my dead sprat and when I got bored with that, gave most of my spoons, spinners and rubber shads an outing, all to no effect. How on earth, then, did my companion take pike from the first three swims immediately after I had vacated them? The flies in his box looked ridiculous; rudimentary and completely lacking in subtlety of imitation. For goodness sake, he was fishing a fly line with a steel trace!

In the fourth swim, I put on my polarised glasses, laid down my rod and watched intently as the flimsy four-inch fly was delivered to a spot twenty feet or so from the steep, willow-rooted bank at our feet. As the slow-sinking fly was worked gently back towards us through the bluish winter water, all was revealed. The laughable orange and black tassel with toy stick-on eyes pulsed, paused and flexed with such convincing suppleness that I instantly recognised it as a pike-enticer far superior to my clumsy, stiff offerings. As it came within a few feet of a lily bed, a green torpedo shot out and seized it aggressively – virtually a foregone conclusion.

Shimmering supple fibres, preposterously large eyes and close to neutral buoyancy give a good pike fly a very appreciable edge over all other kinds of lure. Combine this with the fine control afforded by a fly rod and you have a new branch of fly fishing that will undoubtedly go from strength to strength, bringing a great deal of enjoyment and winter sport to a great many anglers.

An important word on pike handling: pike are possibly the British fish species most susceptible to poor handling and the most important aspect of this is oxygen deprivation – handle pike as you would a salmon; unhook them in the net if at all possible (much easier with a large single de-barbed hook) and make sure they are fully revived by holding them head up into the current. If you need to place them on the bank to unhook them, do so quickly and efficiently and use an unhooking mat. If unhooking is problematic and is going to take time, or if you're going to set up a photograph, hold the fish in your landing net for a while to re-oxygenate the blood and dissipate lactic acid. Big pike are more prone to keeling over as a result of poor or protracted handling than small ones.

Equipment:

Equipment for pike fly fishing has been quite rigorously developed, to the extent that this section can be relatively prescriptive. The list includes a few unfamiliar items for the typical fly fisherman, but these are absolutely indispensable, as explained below.

Regardless of how or where you are fly fishing for pike, there is a reasonable chance that you will become connected to an intimidatingly large fish, possessing speed, endurance and a great deal of raw power. Equip yourself with a rod of somewhere between 8 and 11 weight (I would say 9 weight is the best all round pike rod), but bear in mind that casting a pike setup is quite energetic and physically demanding, so you must be happy with the way the rod casts or you'll be in for a long day of arm ache and frustration.

All pike require a pretty spacious landing net and you do not want to foolishly shove a titchy trout net at a pike that could probably swallow it in one gulp. Soft mesh nets designed for salmon or large sea trout and which come with a carrying sling are ideal. Small, roll-up unhooking mats can be carried by a roving angler without any inconvenience and if your fish dwarfs the mat, then use it to protect the eye and the side of the head from contact with the ground.

A wire leader is absolutely essential because pike teeth are so numerous and pointed (rather than sharp-edged) that no type of monofilament or braid can withstand being raked across so many tooth-points more than a couple of times before parting. Bear in mind that the teeth are coated with a very effective anticoagulant, so even a minor nick to a finger may bleed profusely for an annoyingly long while, whilst a proper laceration will require bandaging and an early end to the session. Therefore, good quality long-nosed forceps must be kept accessible at all times and I'd also recommend keeping a gardening glove to hand.

It is highly debatable what role colour plays in pike flies. Like all other flies, the principal attribute of pike flies is the way in which the essential form and movement of the imitated organism are portrayed. The most important elements are generally accepted to be: slight negative buoyancy, suppleness, use of flashy or reflective materials, large eyes and the way the fly responds to line-stripping. The standard pike fly format is a single suitably robust hook of around size 4/0, with a dense bunch of fibres set into a cone or triangle of resin (in which the eyes are also set) immediately behind the hook's eye. The fibres are swept back, almost parallel to one another and taper to a point 6 to 8 inches from their origin, giving the fly the general form of a small roach, dace, chub or perch, whilst ensuring that the hook point is not obscured. Using modern synthetic materials sparingly on the hook can give better movement and a degree of translucency in the water. In home tied flies, the resin cone is often made using a compound that sets immediately upon exposure to UV rays emitted by a small, purpose-designed lamp or torch. Variation between flies is generally in their colour and in the combination of fibrous materials used, which can result in subtle differences, sometimes quite profound, in the fly's appearance and movement when stripped back to the rod.

Perch *Perca fluviatilis (British rod caught record: 5lb 15oz)*

Form, habitat, feeding & breeding

Perch are surely among the handsomest of British river fish and certainly the most robust. To those with sea fishing experience, perch will probably appear similar to sea bass, also a member of the order *Perciformes*, with the most notable features being the thick, rough scales, spiny dorsal fin and pointed gill covers. Like bass, the perch is excellent to eat and has a relatively simple skeleton composed of stout bones, making filleting an easy task for those inclined to consume their catch. Perch colouration varies according to the clarity of the water in which they live, with turbid lake dwellers often being a pale yellow and chalk stream fish having the most vivid orange fins, olive green back and the dark, vertical bars so emblematic of the species. The eyes and protrusible mouth are large, for this is a predator that hunts by sight, occasionally in shoals in open water, but more typically from the cover of reed or weed beds. It is obvious that they are coloured specifically to hide against a backdrop of vertical green stems. Beds of any kind of submerged weed close to the river margins might harbour perch, especially where the flow is either static or is a slow glide and the depth exceeds a metre or so (the species is not built for speed and thrives in lakes and ponds). But the classic perch hangout is the emergent reed bed; Norfolk reed, greater reed mace, reed canary grass and reed sweet grass often form dense bank-side stands in the lower reaches of chalk streams, especially fringing deep pools, and this is where to look for perch. Where such reed beds also contain large woody debris – sunken branches and fallen trees –

the habitat could be considered ideal. Mature perch gather to spawn in such environments in spring and their eggs are laid in ribbons of sticky mucus on woody debris and submerged vegetation. An old trick of keepers and fishery managers wishing to deplete perch populations was to place bundles of branches in the margins just prior to optimum spawning temperatures and then whip these out to dry as soon as they were covered in perch spawn.

Perch predominantly feed on aquatic invertebrates and are especially reliant on midge larvae and pupae, but they are very opportunistic and will seize most suitably sized creatures that present themselves, both aquatic and terrestrial. Even smallish perch may take minnows and juvenile fish, but larger perch become piscivorous to such an extent that they will take surprisingly large fish and sometimes attack outsized baits and lures intended for pike. Probably more than any other British fish (including pike), perch respond to movement (pike can be very olfactory hunters at times) and for coarse fishers, wriggly items such as lobworms, maggots and minnows, as well as spinners, are the tools of the trade.

Fly fishing for perch

Specifically targeting chalk stream perch with the fly is certainly a worthwhile and rewarding pursuit, but one which will demand patience and excellent knowledge of the reach being fished. Consequently, I would only recommend it for those with some experience of the chalk stream coarse fish reaches and with a few chub, dace and possibly pike, already under their belts. As is the case with trout and roach, perch can be caught virtually to order and in large numbers at hundreds of densely stocked stillwater fisheries, but the wild, chalk stream version, especially at specimen size, is an utterly different prospect – something to revere and which will not come easily.

The main challenge in catching perch on the fly in chalk streams is to locate them, and although it is worth casting speculatively in the vicinity of suitable holding features, good fish are few and far between. Therefore, I would strongly recommend that the first phase of any chalk stream perch campaign should be to choose a reasonably clear day, arm yourself with your favourite polarised glasses and stare intently into every weed-bordered main channel pool, hatch pool, side stream confluence and backwater that is accessible to you, until you are lucky enough to discern those jungle stripes amongst the greenery. Like many well-camouflaged animals, perch are prepared to rest confidently in quite clear view as long as they remain reasonably immobile, whilst less cryptically-coloured fish simply hide away entirely. Once you've seen a few perch and you are familiar with the species' key features, its not difficult to get your eye in and to spy the fish in their green lairs; on many occasions, I've spotted a solitary orange fin, wafting gently, or a single, dark-scaled bar amongst a tangle of stems, only for the whole fish to gradually come into focus some moments later. Spotting a chalk stream perch is always a special moment, even if you have no intention of casting for it – their bristling form, sharp colouration and mysterious habitat enhances any river.

Equipment:

Although perch are tough fighters, they do not possess great speed or power, so unless you've stumbled across a colony of record breakers, a 5 weight rod would be ideal. Lines and leaders should be selected with the purpose of sight fishing with relatively fast sinking nymphs or lures firmly in mind.

The perch's aggressive and predatory nature means that as long as the water temperature is not too low, they are likely to seize any kind of fly that is correctly sized, well-placed, moves constantly and convincingly and resembles any of the wide range of dietary items that are likely to fall, drift or swim into the fish's field of vision. The most effective fly patterns for chalk stream perch are likely to be chironimid (larvae & pupae), damsel and mayfly nymph imitations for smaller fish and modern worm patterns, fry patterns (such as Clousers or small, reflective bass flies) and scaled-down pike flies for larger ones. However, it's highly likely that perch will be taken from time to time when fishing with any kind of submerged fly for virtually any other chalk stream species in the lower reaches when your fly wanders close to a dense bed of submerged vegetation.

Roach

Rutilus rutilus (British rod caught record: 4lb 4oz)

Form, habitat, feeding & breeding

The roach is probably the most ubiquitous and most frequently caught of all British fish species; it is abundant in virtually all lowland rivers, canals, lakes and pools. But this 'everyman's' fish has an ace up its sleeve; whilst small and medium sized roach are generally held in modest regard, once they attain weights approaching two pounds they shoot to the top of the rankings and start to get taken very seriously indeed. Two-pounders from a river are especially revered and those from chalk streams are the stuff of dreams. Given this exponential rise in status, how could one possibly aim higher than to land a wild, two pound roach from a chalk stream? How about by taking one on a fly?

Where large shoals of small roach are encountered, be it in a river or still water, there are times when the catch rate is limited only by the speed with which the bait-fisher can unhook, re-bait and recast. The bait is seized by another ravenous member of the shoal even before the float settles. These fish are barely given a second glance by anglers who would become quite emotional if they were to land a fish pushing the magical 2lb mark and this despite the two being physically identical in every respect, other than stature. As is the case in most acquisitive pursuits, demand in angling is inversely proportional to supply.

Roach are undoubtedly lovely fish, despite being the archetypal 'standard' coarse species. The body is flattened in the vertical plane and is covered in bright, silver scales. The head is smallish, with a delicate mouth and the eyes and fins vary from bright red in fish from clear waters, to a dull yellowish in those dwelling in more turbid habitats. Roach are often confused with rudd (which have upturned mouths, a yellowish eye, orange-tinged fins and brassier scale coloration) but you are unlikely to encounter rudd on chalk streams unless you fish close to the outlet of a coarse fishing lake.

Roach are very adaptable and successful opportunistic generalists; their ubiquity demonstrates their ability to exploit an impressive diversity of habitats, from upland lakes and tarns to eutrophic lowland canals and chalk streams. They will feed on virtually any form of invertebrate small enough to ingest, as well as plankton such as daphnia, fish eggs and fry, and will turn to plant material, including filamentous algae (green 'silkweed') and other weeds when necessary.

In lakes, pools, canals and impounded rivers roach can thrive to such an extent that the habitat becomes degraded, usually resulting in poor fish growth and a 'stunted' population. However, in natural, unmodified rivers the more complex habitat, flood events, predation and competition with other more specifically adapted species serves to constrain the roach to relatively modest population levels. The unrelenting selective pressures of this environment results in fitter, wilder fish than their stillwater cousins. Of course, in chalk streams, clarity serves as another prime cause of mortality for shoaling, bite-sized fish like roach because cormorants, otters, herons and pike are able to sight feed so much more effectively. As a result, daytime feeding patterns of chalk stream roach are probably more affected by light levels than any other species. As long as temperature is not a significant factor, the waning sun in the hour or so before dusk or a slight increase in turbidity following rainfall are the two most reliable triggers for roach to commence feeding. I have put a nymph through a pool on a chalk stream carrier over and over again on a reasonably bright winter's afternoon, concluding that the pool was entirely unoccupied, only to take a fish on every other cast within minutes of the sun dipping below the tree line on the valley rim. Where had they been? Well, roach are phytophils in a broader sense than simply that they spawn on plants (willow moss, *Fontinalis,* is their preferred medium). Submerged weed provides essential cover and the thread-like tresses of water crowfoot or the ribbon-like leaves of arrowhead, bur-reed or club rush are all likely to harbour roach wishing to remain undetected.

It is worth stressing at this point that whereas salmonids can usually be induced to feed if the offering is sufficiently attractive and the fish is absolutely undisturbed, coarse fish of most species, and especially roach, have a very distinct 'standby' mode if light levels, temperature or some other factor is sub-optimal and no amount of cajoling or inducement will elicit a response other than the fish getting fed up and seeking solace elsewhere.

Fly fishing for roach and recommended equipment

Taking roach on the fly is less a question of delivering an alluring deception than of simply being there when feeding commences. The species' liberal culinary philosophy means that fly size and the depth at which they are feeding are probably the main considerations; even a near-record sized roach has a small, delicate and weakly-muscled mouth, so flies must be small. Roach are as well-adapted to surface feeding as they are to feeding in mid-water and on the bed, so the entire range of suitably sized dry-flies, buzzers and nymphs may be appropriate on occasion. In addition, bread-flake imitators are popular and effective for roach, with simple cotton-wool flies taking good fish from reaches where duck-feeding occurs or fishing with bread is practised by coarse anglers.

Roach are tenacious, jagging fighters and are excellent fun to play, but they will not test rod or line overly, so fish as light as you dare – a new British record roach could easily be subdued on a 5 weight rod.

Carp

Cyprinus carpio (British rod caught record: 65lb 14oz)

Form, habitat, feeding & breeding

Carp are sturdy, thick-set fish, with a fleshy, protrusible mouth which has two barbels (feelers used for locating food items) on either side. They tend to be high-backed and broad across the shoulders and compared to all other British fish, are heavy for their length. This build gives them the first of the two key attributes so valued by carp anglers; their quite awesome power. The initial run of a hooked carp is only comparable to that of a salmon, large sea trout or barbel (amongst our river fish) and was likened by 'BB' to being yanked out of bed by a grapnel from an aeroplane.

The second attribute is that they are extremely canny – to the extent that they are almost never hooked cheaply. It can be guaranteed without hesitation that anyone who has set his sights on catching a decent river carp, by any method, will be driven to distraction at some point. This virtue may be linked to the fact that carp, like roach, are such accomplished generalists. They have evolved to take advantage of a wide range of food sources and habitats and are as likely to be found foraging for shrimp and caddis larvae on the gravel bed of a chalk stream pool as tail-up, filtering bloodworm from the deep silt of an ancient estate lake – this makes them very hard to predict.

Strictly speaking, the carp is a non-native species to Britain, its natural range being from Eastern Europe and eastward across Asia. However, possibly the ultimate expression of how thoroughly it has naturalised in this country is that well-established colonies of carp exist in the lower reaches of most chalk streams. These fish are the 'king' carp; common (fully scaled), mirror (partially scaled) or leather (virtually scale-less) varieties, first bred for culinary purposes and now much more commonly for stocking into stillwater carp fisheries.

It has often been claimed that the Romans introduced carp to the British Isles, but the earliest texts referring to their presence here indicate that they were probably imported around the fourteenth century. Their import and distribution was certainly based on their value as a fast-growing and easily farmed source of fish protein and not for angling purposes. Whilst carp farming for food is still hugely important on the Continent, the species has now become such a favourite angling quarry in the UK that specimen fish can attain remarkable monetary value and are often treated with reverence. In fact, it's not unusual these days to come across quite heartfelt obituaries in the daily papers when a particularly well-known and pet-named individual is found floating in the margins of its home lake. This situation has led to something of a clash of ideologies between immigrant Eastern European and British carp anglers because the former are from a culture where carp are deeply ingrained into the culinary tradition and the idea of releasing them once caught is thought to verge on lunacy.

The first carp to be brought to Britain and which were so widely farmed in the stew ponds of monasteries and manor houses are now known as wild carp or "wildies" – a much leaner, fuller scaled form that rarely exceeds 10lbs – colonies of these fish remain in some older lakes and pools, but I have not heard of them occurring in rivers. In order to appreciate the widespread distribution of carp, take a good look at an OS map and note the number of historic fish ponds, hammer ponds and other kinds of artificial pools, virtually all of which would have been designed or put to use for the cultivation of Friday fish flesh. Given that the species has been so widespread in the British Isles for the best part of six hundred years, there was very little chance that they would not find their way into most river systems through either deliberate or accidental release.

The definitive factor that has led to British rivers supporting only quite modest colonies of river-carp, whilst river systems in Australia and North America experience near plague proportions, is water temperature. In order for their ovaries to develop completely and for successful spawning and egg development, carp must reside in water at close to 20° Celsius for some weeks – something that rarely occurs in British rivers. I think it feasible that chalk stream carp occasionally breed in long, warm summers where the adults frequent weedy ditch systems or backwaters, but it is likely that that the majority of carp encountered by the chalk stream angler find their way into the river from stillwater pools and ponds on the floodplain, most commonly during floods or as the result of lack of effective screening or failure of pool outlet structures.

Once in the river, carp tend to inhabit weedy, slow flowing areas such as deep pools and slacks – wherever you find thriving stands of yellow water lily (*Nuphar lutea)* either floating or submerged (and known to anglers as 'cabbages'), you are likely to find river carp. However, river carp are quite different to their stillwater cousins because the physical demands of the unceasing current (and the absence of carp anglers feeding them kilos of bait), makes them lean, muscular and powerful. I have often seen large river carp foraging on gravel glides alongside barbel and they are most commonly captured when they take baits intended for barbel.

Fly fishing for carp

The concept of fly fishing for carp marks a transition from the fly fisherman's 'bread and butter' species, such as dace and chub, to those that require a much greater degree of perseverance, skill and bloody-mindedness. Carp are difficult fish to catch in most circumstances, so if you set yourself the goal of catching one from a chalk stream on the fly, you have a mountain to climb. You will be extremely fortunate to stumble across an opportunity to cast a fly to a feeding river carp. Instead, you will have to conspire in earnest to make this happen. My advice is: first, identify a place occupied by a colony of carp and then spend as much time as you possibly can observing them and their habitat through the days and the seasons. You will probably find that they feed in a number of different ways and places; sucking snails' eggs from the underside of lilies, sifting through the silt in ditches and side channels and scouring clean gravel runs for shrimp and other invertebrates. You may note that they do not appear to take flies from the surface, even when these are extremely abundant and are a worthwhile and easy meal, such as during a good mayfly hatch. Consider offering some loose food items to see how the carp respond, which is likely to inform your choice of fly pattern. Throughout this period of preparation you will undoubtedly become keenly aware of just how timid and conscious of their surroundings carp are. You are also likely to become familiar with individual fish and their habits.

Equipment

Fly patterns for carp fall into two principal categories: benthic invertebrate imitators and bread imitators, both floating and sinking. A wide range of the first kind seems to be effective, especially Czech or other weighted nymphs of various kinds, but not necessarily fished in the typical style. The great challenge is to present the fly within the quarry's field of vision without spooking it and to move the fly effectively to induce a take. In order to do this, the fly is usually reasonably heavy or weighted with split shot. Lobworm imitators made of various kinds of supple fly materials and presented in this fashion are also effective.

Rods and leaders for carp must be very robust – no less than an 8 weight in my view – and I can guarantee that the fish's first run will take your breath away and either give you perpetual faith in the strength of your rod, or else expose its weak points instantly. Speaking of which, one of the best pieces of angling advice ever given to me is, after tackling up, to carefully place my hook onto a wire fence, or a plastic loop on a heavy tackle bag and to then apply the kind of pressure to the rod that I would expect from the biggest fish I might hook that day – having passed that test, you can rest easy that you won't discover a weak point at the worst possible moment.

A generous and sturdy landing net is essential for carp, as is an unhooking mat.

Barbel

Barbus barbus (British rod caught record: 21lb 1oz)

Form, habitat, feeding & breeding

The barbel is the king of the chalk stream coarse fish community and is more highly prized by coarse anglers than any other species. Apart from the fact that it is a relentless and powerful fighter and a beautiful creature by any standards, the barbel's enigmatic quality is mostly a result of its ability to materialise into clear view on shallow gravel runs, only to then drift lazily under its water-crowfoot canopy and resume its usual state of invisibility. To the avid fish-watcher, the barbel is the most exciting prospect: thumpingly muscular, yet barely a vapour.

Even someone seeing a drawing of a barbel in a book would be able to discern that this is a fish evolved for life close to the riverbed. The lower surface of the body is rather flattened, whilst the back curves gracefully over the shoulders and tapers into an elongated tail-wrist, with the caudal fin itself quite deeply forked, like a salmon's. The dorsal fin is tall, triangular and proud. It is the head, though, that reveals in which direction the barbel directs most of its attention – it is wedge-shaped, with a large, fleshy mouth on its underside and four thick barbules on the upper lip. The relatively oversized fins tend to be pinkish and the belly white, whilst the back and sides are a light tan or bronze, which is ideal concealment against the mottled dun of the riverbed gravel.

As the head and body shape suggest, the vast bulk of the barbel's diet comes from the riverbed: shrimps, larvae, molluscs and small fish are the key prey items. However, snorkelling amongst shoals of barbel on the Hampshire Avon has taught me that the morphological adaptations that make it resemble an inveterate bottom-dweller are in fact more likely to be geared towards reducing overall energy expenditure rather than simply equipping the fish for feeding solely amongst the benthos. I have frequently swum with a shoal of fifteen or so individuals and have never yet seen one make contact with the riverbed. Instead, they tend to hold station at least six inches above it, often more. The reason this is significant to the angler is that it shows that barbel are well accustomed to intercepting drifting food items in the mid-water. In fact, many serious coarse-fishing barbel hunters swear that, when conditions are right, float fishing with the bait drifted some inches off of the bed is the most effective method.

The driving force behind the barbel's evolution of these energy-saving adaptations is to allow it to occupy and exploit the food resources of the swiftest glides, which are too fast-paced to allow most other coarse species to spend any significant time there. However, when observing barbel at close range (which is far more conveniently done with a good pair of polarised glasses than by snorkelling) one is struck by the harmony between the fish's form and movement and that of the beds of submerged waterweed, especially water crowfoot (*Ranunculus sp.*) which are such an integral feature of barbel habitat. There is a surprising amount of clear space and an astounding reduction in water velocity beneath such trailing weed, so between sorties onto the open gravel (where invertebrates are most abundant), even the largest barbel can slip into a perfectly shaped pocket of cover by just drifting a few feet sideways. In winter, increasing flow combines with decreasing temperature resulting in many fish, including barbel, adopting a state of relative dormancy and retiring to the deeper slacks and pools, only feeding when water temperature rises, usually as milder, wet weather pushes in from the south west.

Like chub and dace, barbel are lithophils; stone-spawners. They gather in shoals on extensive gravel riffles in early summer, often intermingling with spawning chub, and lay their adhesive eggs into shallow depressions in the gravel. The run-up to spawning can be spectacular for the observer, with 10-15lb females tearing around in the shallows pursued by numerous, ardent males. This is by far your best chance in the whole year to see barbel out in the open in clear, shallow water and relatively impervious to disturbance. I have a favourite bridge over the middle Hampshire Avon where, as the river warms up in May, I lean on the railing for hours in the evening watching barbel and chub courting and spawning on the riffle directly below, as they are likely to have done for centuries.

More than most coarse species, barbel are stressed by the exertion of spawning and often remain out of sorts well into the early part of the coarse season (which runs from June 16th to March 14th), especially if spring arrives late. Under these circumstances they should be left alone to recover for a few weeks.

Fly fishing for barbel

Barbel are a genuine challenge even when all rod and line fishing methods are available. To set out for them with a box of flies when most serious coarse fishermen wouldn't venture forth without maggots, hemp, pellets or boilies measured by the *gallon,* is a brave crusade. However, fly fishing for barbel has the potential to be uniquely exciting and if you succeed, will allow you to grapple with one of the hardest and most tenacious fighting fish in British freshwaters.

The odds of taking a barbel on a dry fly are so long as to be not worth discussing. Instead, it is the careful working of a weighted natural food imitator downstream along weed-fringed gravel glides, that presents the best opportunity. A popular barbel fishing method amongst coarse fishermen is the 'rolling meat' approach, where a large, lightly weighted cube of luncheon meat is delicately manoeuvred downstream along a likely gravel run adjacent to weedy cover. Although scent is likely to play a significant part in this particular deception, barbel are keenly sighted and frequently take items on the basis of movement alone (minnows, bullhead and, occasionally, salmon flies being good examples). The basic fly-fishing principles apply: the aim is to present an attractive, freely drifting morsel right onto the barbel's dinner table, especially where you see that one or more fish are looking impatient and are ready to order.

Equipment

The Czech nymph method is a good source of flies and technique, although the cast will have to be adapted to the particular lie, as the relative positions of the angler and barbel are likely to be more restrictive than in the usual nymphing scenario. However, the design of benthic flies for barbel (and carp) that go beyond the conventional Czech format is certainly an area ripe for experimentation. I have also seen some lobworm patterns that look like they would be deadly for barbel, chub and carp.

A rod with some backbone in the butt section is necessary (an 8 weight or heavier would be my choice) because there is a strong chance that your fish will force its way into weed beds and will need persistent pressure to convince it to re-emerge. A large landing net is mandatory and an unhooking mat is highly recommended. Barbel usually exhaust themselves utterly in the fight and are prone to building up a dangerous oxygen deficit, so a period of recovery in the landing net prior to photographing, weighing and release is a very sensible idea.

Bream, Tench and others

Aside from those described already, there are a few other species of coarse fish that the fly-fisherman might happen across, but which are probably too testing to pursue on fly in their own right.

Common bream, *Abramis brama,* is, like the carp, a different sort of fish when encountered in swift chalk streams than in its more usual habitat of lakes and pools. In stillwaters, bream shoals behave like dairy herds; slowly and meticulously grazing the silt-plains of the lake bed, never moving at anything other than a snail's pace and often with all fish oriented in the same direction. In chalk streams the relentless current tones and conditions the fish into leaner, stronger and more vividly coloured specimens, which retain their strong inclination to shoal, usually in the deeper pools and slower glides. They are often to be seen (more easily with polarising glasses) suspended, motionless in mid-water in the narrow gaps between streamers of water crowfoot. Amongst coarse fish, this species is the master of energy efficient swimming and I find their form reminiscent of tropical discus or angel fish, or even the permit of the mangrove flats. However, impatient specimen hunters after barbel or chub disparagingly refer to them as 'dustbin lids' and this does convey with a degree of accuracy the manner of their fight when hooked, which is about as far removed from a permit as you could imagine. However, if you hook a lively one in summer and it turns side-on to the current, you may be surprised how lively they can be. Their other moniker is 'snotter' or 'snotty', against which I cannot argue because they leave a horrendous and smelly mess of slime in landing nets. Common bream have a tendency to roll gracefully on the surface on warm, still evenings, giving away the position of the shoal and usually indicating that feeding has commenced in earnest. Beware though that although active at the surface, they will be feeding only on the bed, so don't waste any time under the delusion that the rolling fish may take a dry fly.

All told, I strongly recommend trying for a chalk stream bream if the chance presents itself. The species is so utterly different from all other British fish that there is value in landing one, if for no other reason than to appreciate it at close quarters. Bream are often seen searching for shrimp and larvae side-by-side with barbel and chub on clean gravel runs, so the heavy nymph or imitation bait techniques employed for those species are also the best approach for bream.

Whereas bream are bona fide chalk stream natives, tench are only truly at home in still waters and sluggish, lowland rivers. Those that one comes across in chalk streams are likely to have originated from pools and lakes in the floodplain. Consequently, you are only likely to spot tench in the very slowest, weediest parts of chalk streams, especially backwaters and ditch mouths.

Tench are even more notable than bream for how different they are from other coarse species and this distinctiveness is quite remarkable. The fish's scales are so minute and embedded in its skin that the creature is silky smooth in its entirety; there are no hard structures such as spines or spikes to interrupt this slipperiness, which is further emphasised by the gentle curvature of every part of the body and fins. Small tench are often fondly referred to as 'bars of soap' and they are just as hard to hold on to. The tench's lustrous sheen has been likened to well-worked fine green leather and this wonderful hue is complimented by a small, reddish eye.

Tench are slow and deliberate benthic feeders and although I have frequently seen six or seven pounders coming and going from a small, weedy ditch into the main flow of the Avon, I have never seen them feed other than within the confines of the ditch or at its mouth. Carp, bream, perch, pike, chub and trout have all been taken on fly close to this ditch mouth, but never tench. On several occasions I have found myself poised almost directly above small groups of quite large tench feeding where the silty, leafy debris from the ditch meets the clean gravel at the edge of the Avon's flow. I have never yet been able to get my nymph to them before they sense me and slide effortlessly out and down into the forest of 'cabbages' that are so prevalent on this particular bend. If I could get the nymph to the perfect place, I certainly fancy my chances of a take and I know from coarse fishing experience that these fish fight stubbornly for every inch of line. What this species lacks in exterior armament, it makes up for in sheer muscle.

Eels have undergone a radical rebranding amongst anglers and conservationists following the discovery that the number of glass eels arriving to populate European rivers has decreased to an alarmingly low level compared to only a few decades ago. This has prompted an unprecedented interest in eel research, as embarrassingly little is known of its overall population dynamics (and its precise life cycle is famously shrouded in uncertainty). A clear message from the research is that, contrary to previous received wisdom, eels are not the denizens of muddy backwaters – they are actually highly sensitive to pollution and have very high standards when it comes to habitat quality. When snorkelling in the Hampshire Avon or the Piddle in Dorset, I know to look out for eels on the clean gravel where they will be foraging amongst the stones for invertebrates, often alongside barbel, dace, trout and salmon parr. If not here, they will be found beneath the cover of the fringing mass of water cress and brooklime close to the bank, which is where otters spend most of their time foraging for them.

Eels are fascinating to watch because their body shape is so unexpectedly well suited to dealing with this exacting habitat – the creature's key adaptation being to keep the entire body in the friction zone close to the bed where water velocity is a fraction of that just a few inches higher in the water column. It's a joy to swim with a decent-sized eel right out on the gravel, especially as they feed voraciously when I use my hand to dig amongst the stones, throwing up a cloud of sediment and displaced invertebrates (salmon and trout parr also find this irresistible).

It is certainly feasible to take a chalk stream eel on fly. I've never done so, but have tried and come close. Unlike tench, and probably counter-intuitively for most anglers, the best chance of taking eel on fly will not come in the slack margins or backwaters, but when a decent sized fish is observed foraging on a clean gravel run, in a foot or two of water. This is not an unusual occurrence, especially at dawn and dusk, during misty, low light conditions and particularly when there are fish eggs or larvae amongst the stones. Eels will take virtually all forms of invertebrate and small fish but they are quite lethargic feeders, so the key consideration for the fly fisherman is to manoeuvre a convincing pattern, quite slowly, into the eel's field of vision and hard on the bed. They are not a fun fish to handle and unhook, but do give a solid fight, plus they are the only British fish fitted with reverse gear, so playing one feels quite unlike anything else.

Finally, having provided what I hope is a thorough and informative overview of the coarse fly fishing world, I'm now liable to blow any credibility by stating that my last species can be great fun to catch on fly; the minnow. Minnows are ubiquitous in chalk streams and are as fascinating as any other British fish species in both appearance and ecological significance. The real highlight is to watch a shoal spawning on a shallow gravel riffle, the males in their incredibly vivid breeding livery of orange and crimson with white-flecked pectoral fins and both sexes thrashing vigorously as the eggs are shed. If one can suspend one's comprehension of scale, the event is as spectacular as watching salmon spawning in a highland headwater. This principle also applies to minnow fishing.

To get the most out of minnow fishing one must be the kind of angler who recognises that using smaller, lighter gear to catch the same sized fish is a far easier way of feeling as if you've caught a bigger fish than actually catching one. I subscribe to this approach wholeheartedly, but I admit I'm pushing the premise to the extremes with minnows. Minnows, rather, are for those occasions when your fishing has been so unsuccessful that you are prepared to fall back on the easiest of quarries in order to bring some form of fish life to the bank, even if your net remains dry – or when you've done so well that you're inclined to while away a sunny half hour indulging in the surreal, complete diversion that is drifting a tiny fly through a shoal of minnows.

Accordingly, I can wholly recommend the timeless, innocent pursuit of relocating a minnow shoal, one by one, from the river into a large glass jar or small beach bucket, especially when fishing with a youngster or disillusioned novice. As they are so numerous (especially in summer), feeding is intensely competitive and minnows will attack anything remotely resembling a food item. As a result, it would be disingenuous to suggest fly patterns. Even a shiny bare hook is likely to be as deadly as anything you might strain your eyes to tie onto a tiny hook.

Chapter Eleven

River Management

Andreas Topintzis

One morning during my first year working with the Salisbury and District Angling Club there came a knock on the office door followed by a frowning face: "There is weed floating down on beat seven," reported a disgruntled-looking angler in a serious tone of voice. I looked back at the angler. He must have read the question mark on my face and so continued "… but it's mayfly time!" Welcome to the chapter on managing rivers and perhaps more importantly, on managing anglers' expectations.

As earlier chapters have made clear, chalk streams are essentially a man-made environment and have been historically managed for a multitude of purposes, game fishing being only one of them. In fact, from conversations I have had with landowners over the years, it is clear that in a number of cases game fishing comes in a distant third behind farming and sport shooting from an income generation point of view. Naturally, being a poor cousin commercially severely limits what can viably be done to create the best possible fishing, and often angling interests must give way to other land management concerns. Piscatorial management encompasses a number of distinct activities, such as weed management, bank and fringe management, stocking, predator control, beat systems, fishing rules and so on. Each of these topics could fill a book in itself, but in this chapter I hope to give you an overview of what is involved behind the scenes, so to speak, in creating a successful day's fishing on an idyllic chalk stream.

If I was asked to select the most important fundamental factor that ensures the quality of our sport, I would say without hesitation that it is healthy water flows. Our chalk streams are fed by aquifers. I often picture these as huge underground barrels that gradually fill with water as the rain droplets slowly percolate, drop-by-drop, through the ground. They fill up during the late autumn and winter months and start releasing the water in early spring through the winterbournes, small streams that flow only when the water table is high enough. The amount of rain, as well as its frequency and type, are all important factors in the natural process of replenishing the aquifers. Continuous light rain ensures that each drop gradually penetrates the ground and finds its way to the aquifers. Sudden torrential rain mainly produces run-off and most of it rushes down into the sea and is lost. Naturally, some years are drier than others, but the long term trend is worrying.

Healthy water flows and good spells of sunshine result in good growth of 'ranunculus' weed, an essential ingredient of healthy chalk streams. Ranunculus is seen as a sustainable water level control mechanism. Its stem contains mostly water and a large heap of cut weed on the river bank can be reduced to almost nothing in just a few days through evaporation. There is a direct relationship between water levels and the presence of weed. A healthy blanket of weed will retain good water levels. The river level may drop significantly during a heavy weed cut, but historically weed-cutting has been practised on chalk-streams for a very long time using a variety of tools such as hand scythes, chains and weed-boats. Why cut the weed? There are a few good reasons. Too much weed may contribute to flood risks, especially where the river is shallow and passes through a flood plain. When it comes to fly fishing, weed management ensures that anglers have areas where they can cast with a realistic chance of targeting, playing and landing a fish. If a river becomes entirely blanketed by weed, then fly fishing becomes impossible. A balance must be achieved. Weed management practices vary depending on the overall strategy of particular fishing clubs, syndicates and private riparian owners. On one side of the spectrum there are the corporate-type venues, where often relatively new and inexperienced anglers take part as guests in corporate hospitality events paid for by corporate customers. Some, but not all, of these fisheries are heavily managed, both in terms of weed cutting and bank vegetation. Easy angler access and trouble-free casting are seen as essential levers to ensure that customer satisfaction is achieved and a repeat booking is made. On the other hand there are angling clubs and small syndicates which manage weed lightly, in full recognition of its importance to invertebrates and fish and in anticipation of more challenging angling suitable for more skillful and experienced anglers. This distinction between corporate stretches, wild fisheries and those in-between, drives the strategies and day-to-day practices of the different organizations involved in river management and reflects their different priorities.

Weed management along the full length of a river with multiple riparian owners can be a complicated task. Agreed weed-cut dates ensure that the resulting weed rafts can be managed in the most efficient way. Weed cut dates are well defined periods when river keepers can attack the weed on their waters and also ensure that their stretch is clear for safe passage of weed rafts from other fisheries upstream. Communication and coordination between river keepers and clubs is absolutely essential. As you can imagine, there are many places where rafts of weed floating down the river can get caught up, for example in hatches, tree branches and shallow bays. A fallen tree branch in the river can hold back hundreds of yards of weed, as raft upon raft piles up. There is a fallacy among anglers when it comes to weed-cut dates. Anglers expect that after the end of a weed-cut period there will not be a trace of cut weed floating anywhere on the river. In practice this may be impossible. Keepers and managers do their best, but resources do not allow for every bit of weed to be freed from every obstruction on every fishery. At the end of its journey, the weed is collected in weed-booms, extracted and transported to suitable waste management sites, but it takes some time to make its way downstream. In view of the importance of ranunculus weed in maintaining a healthy balance in the chalk stream ecosystem, there is an encouraging trend towards more sympathetic weed management. Many fisheries now avoid overcutting designed simply to make it easier for anglers and anglers are coming to recognize that limited weed means limited food and cover for the fish, limited retention of water and a featureless, almost lifeless, stretch. Creative and restrained weed cutting can produce interesting and challenging fisheries. Anglers learn how to cast effectively into the holes and channels in the weed where the fish take up feeding positions and learn how to free a hooked fish that has lodged itself in a weed bed. The result is that anglers become more skillful, fish are healthier and the river is more attractive

There is a close link between weed and swans. Swans simply love grazing on ranunculus weed and often one can observe a large group of them enjoying a fast food veggie burger as they pick the weed from floating rafts. Large congregations of swans and reduced water flows may result in a serious thinning of the weed beds because the birds can comfortably uproot the weed without much effort. Swans pair for life and well-known nesting sites can be mapped on each stretch of river. The nests are heavily defended by the resident swans and all intruders, which from time to time may include anglers, are chased away. Swans are protected birds and the only means of achieving some form of population control is by oiling, or removing, some of the eggs laid by the females every spring. Removing or oiling a few eggs under licence keeps the population fairly static. Swans are curious birds and will often come over to investigate what the angler is up to. This frustrates some anglers because they get in the way and disrupt the water. Personally, I appreciate their beauty and accept them as part and parcel of the idyllic chalk-stream scenery. I am happy to just watch them and wait until they move on before continuing with my casting. The fish do not seem to mind them much either.

River bank and fringe management is also about achieving a balance. On one hand angler expectations must be met and on the other, a healthy environment for the invertebrates, fish and other riverine species must be provided. Think of a bank where the grass is cut very low, almost as if it were a golf course. The vegetation along the edge of the bank is fringed to below knee-height. Back from the bank edge the vegetation has been heavily trimmed. There is ample space to cast because there are no trees or bushes either in front of or behind the angler. Comfortable benches are distributed along the bank where one can sit and have a picnic and observe the water in a leisurely way. This is an example of an over-managed fishery, catering for anglers who expect that no physical obstacles of any sort should get in the way of a relaxing and comfortable day's fishing. But, does this achieve the right balance between angling and the environment? When river flies start hatching, they first and foremost seek a place to rest and dry their wings whilst going though the transformation process from duns (freshly hatched insects) to spinners (mature insects). A healthy fringe, consisting of long sedge grasses and other water plants becomes a point of instant attraction and accommodation for flies. The flies also land on various other plants, bushes and trees on the banks and remain in the near vicinity until concluding their short lives by mating and depositing their eggs in the water. A long fringe and sufficient bank vegetation therefore helps the invertebrates considerably, for how are they to manage without it? It also provides cover for the fish. It is not surprising to see large trout sheltering under the overhanging branches of a willow that has been left to stretch its arms over the water. If temperatures are set to rise globally in the long run, trees will become a lot more important in managing the microclimate of a particular river stretch in the future. They are already important and provide much needed shade, which helps to cool the water and at the same time offers a welcome respite to the fish. Fish do not like sunny conditions and they will be seen hiding in places offering some shade. The best fish lies are often right under a low-hanging tree branch, or under some tree roots protruding in the river.

A healthy variety of different tree and plant species also aesthetically enhances the overall landscape and contributes significantly to the scenery for which the chalk streams are famous. A straight piece of river with uniform flow, regimented bank fringes, level ground, low grass and a very wide bank devoid of bushes and trees might be easy to fish, but it cannot compare on any other level to a meandering stretch adorned with different trees and bushes, some of them overhanging the river, and a naturally luxuriant fringe growth. In the latter case, of course, there will be some obstacles to be negotiated by the fly fisherman in a test of his skills. It could be an overhanging branch, or a fallen tree, or a part of the river where reeds have encroached. It may be that here and there the obstacles cannot be overcome. However, isn't there a need to have some places that the fish can use as a refuge to rest and avoid us anglers constantly bombarding them with various offerings? In fact, there is a growing segment of the angling community who appreciate catching wild fish in extremely challenging stretches of water, where the banks and the river have been left in a very natural state. These anglers prefer catching a 9-inch wild trout with an extra difficult cast to catching a 4lb stocked fish with a straightforward overhead cast delivered whilst sitting on a comfortable bench. Faced with the question of bank and fringe management, a fishery has to prioritize and choose the best course of action to achieve its short term objective of providing satisfying fishing for its members without seriously risking its longer term ecological future.

The fly fisherman is not the only predator attracted by chalk streams. Naturally, Mr. and Mrs. Pike also reside in the chalk streams and their youngsters, jack-pikes, can be quite boisterous and have ravenous appetites. Yes, pike will take trout, grayling and other coarse fish, but they also target their own species. Their role in the chalk stream ecosystem is better understood these days. In earlier times it was likely that every single pike would be removed from game waters and would not live to see another day. Today pike are selectively taken from the water and some large females are left to perform a population control function through eating smaller pike. Studies have shown that up to 20% of the pike diet may consist of other pike. Removing all large pike from a stretch of water may result in an explosion of small pike with a heavier biomass than that of a few large fish and consequently a greater impact on other species and on the ecosystem as a whole. Small pike, being fast and energetic, are likely to chase and take more prey than their parents and will optimistically attack fast, healthy fish of other species more often in the hope they might get lucky. Bigger pike, being slower and stealthier in their hunting techniques, are quite content with mediocre meals consisting of easier prey such as injured or diseased fish. Pike are usually removed by electro-fishing techniques and these days are usually transported to coarse fisheries and released where they are appreciated by both coarse anglers and by fly anglers who specialize in pike fishing. Pike on the fly has seen growing interest in recent years and can be an enjoyable activity during the winter months when other fly fishing activities, apart from grayling fishing, have ceased.

Terrestrial predators are not to be underestimated either and certainly need to be managed. Mink are not a native species. They were brought from America years ago for the purposes of fur-farming. There is a European species, now endangered, but it did not occur in the United Kingdom. Mink farms were established in the United Kingdom in the 1920s and by the 1950s there were four hundred farms. Over the years, escapees from these fur-farms established the first feral mink populations in the wild. Then, in the 1990s, numerous mink were released into the wild by animal rights activists, exacerbating the problem. Mink will take game birds and game fish, but it is their extremely detrimental effect on water voles that forced a decision in 2001 to strategically control their numbers. Control is achieved through specialized traps and humane dispatching.

Another terrestrial predator, seen as both 'friend' and 'foe', is the otter. The otter is one of the nation's favourite animals and has been very much part and parcel of the chalk stream habitat over the centuries. Having been persecuted to the brink of extinction, otters were reintroduced into the wild in 1983 in an effort to boost their numbers. Otters prey on trout and other chalk stream fish and will naturally take their toll in the chalk stream environment, but it is primarily their devastating impact on commercial carp fisheries that has made many anglers and fishery owners regard them as an enemy. Carp fishing has been a fast growing segment of the angling market and a big carp costs thousands of pounds to replace. Well-stocked lakes are extremely attractive to otters and they will often target the biggest and slowest carp, particularly in the winter when fish become sluggish. What infuriates carp anglers and fishery owners alike is that an otter will drag a prize fish onto the bank and then only consume about a pound of soft flesh, usually from just under the gills, and then leave the fish to be gradually consumed by revisiting otters, rats and other scavengers. An inaccurate but understandable human reaction to these events is to believe that otters are senseless, wasteful killers and this creates feelings of animosity towards these beautiful creatures. Otters are very playful animals and will often chase fish and play with their tails and fins causing damage. Pictures of this damage are often used as examples of 'bad otter' behavior. Angler opinion is divided, but it would be fair to say that game anglers are predominantly sympathetic towards otters whereas the coarse angling fraternity is less tolerant. However, if the number of otters increases and we start seeing evidence of highly prized specimen river fish being targeted, attitudes may harden in the future. Whatever individual feelings may be, otters are legally protected and the only way a fishery can exercise some form of control is by erecting specialized otter fencing. This is a very expensive means of protection on lakes and would certainly be highly impractical and prohibitively expensive on rivers.

Another problematic terrestrial predator is the unauthorized homo-sapiens, otherwise known as a poacher. Poaching may range from isolated incidents where local teenagers get hold of an inexpensive spinning rod and a few maggots and attempt to catch a few fish, to systematic theft of fish by adults for commercial gain. Casual poaching by kids who just want to go fishing is tacitly tolerated by most fishing bailiffs as long as the problem does not become too widespread or too large-scale. A number of fishing clubs offer some water to the local youth to fish for free. If I were a betting man I would say that a lot of us, reborn today as respectable fly-fishermen, may have done just this sort of thing in the past. I have met children and teenagers poaching on the club's water. Each incident presents an opportunity to recruit a new junior club member. It is also an opportunity to highlight that the young offender needs a rod licence to legally do his fishing. Systematic poaching where adults are involved and the fish are sold for monetary benefit is a different matter. A strong, well-trained bailiff team is needed to patrol the rivers and apprehend poachers. Systematic poaching involves trespassing through someone's land without permission, fishing without permission and without a rod licence, most likely using illegal fishing methods such as night lines, nets etc. Poachers can be pretty ruthless and intimidating. It is not a good idea to try and apprehend a group of poachers unassisted. Best practice is to call the police, or rural crime teams that may have been established locally. Fisheries may wish to prosecute the offenders, but it will depend on the policy and finances of the fishery. It is rather unfortunate, but trespassing is very low on the priority list of offences that the magistrates' courts deal with. Although illegal fishing is clearly breaking the law, if a fishery loses two or three fish, costing £10 to £15, it may take the pragmatic approach of not pressing for prosecution of the offenders, purely in view of the legal costs and the overall time and money that would have to be spent to recover the very small cost of losing a few fish that can easily be replaced, especially if they are stocked.

Last but not least, there are winged predators that take their toll, ranging from small kingfishers to egrets, herons, cormorants and lately, goosanders. Kingfishers and herons have always been present on chalk streams. Egrets used to be rare, but have been increasing in numbers. However, the most important predator of all in terms of overall numbers, ferocity and scale of damage is the cormorant. Depletion of fish stocks in the sea and the presence of disused gravel pits near the shore have encouraged these birds to move inland, particularly in the winter. Flocks of birds are seen every winter heading upstream to fill their boots with both game and coarse fish before returning to their roosting places. Fisheries may apply for shooting licences, but the bag limits are very small – three cormorants per season per fishery. Constant patrolling and scare tactics, plus the use of floating shelter islands on lakes, are being extensively used for cormorant control. Floating islands are contraptions that can be easily built by someone with basic DIY skills. The top part is made with flat rectangular, or square, pieces of wood. Wire baskets are attached to the wood, which form the under-part. The wood keeps the contraption afloat and the baskets attached underneath provide the fish with shelter from predators. The last few years have also seen an increase in goosanders. This is a sea-duck species that is a particularly effective predator because it hunts in groups in a very methodical way. On some spate rivers, like the Wye in Wales, they are becoming a real menace and they have recently been seen moving further upstream on chalk streams.

A very important aspect of river management is fish stocking practices. The important question is 'why stock?' There are occasions when stocking is unavoidably necessary. It could be that a pollution incident has killed many fish. It may be that there is intense fishing pressure on a particular stretch of water and a lot of fish are kept for the table. Stocks must be replenished if angling is to continue. The question is easier to answer on lakes because they are mostly closed eco-systems and their stock holding capacity is relatively straightforward to calculate. A quantity of fish goes in and anglers record their catches. Once the quantity of stocked fish drops to a pre-defined level, re-stocking takes place. Things are different on rivers. Section 30 of the Salmon and Freshwater Fisheries Act (1975) regulates the stocking of inland waters. The Act requires written consent for the introduction of fish or ova into controlled waters, which essentially means all rivers and lakes. The Act itself doesn't specify the size of fish to be stocked, but gives the Environment Agency's local consenting officer discretion to ensure that stocking is appropriate for the receiving water and complies with general Environment Agency policy. In practice, this usually means that lakes can be stocked with rainbow trout and other trout species, but a river, in almost all cases, must be stocked with brown trout of a stipulated size (usually about thirteen inches or one pound) to ensure that the river's ecosystem is able to support the biomass of introduced fish. There are some exceptions where consent has been given for the stocking of rainbow trout in rivers and this practice continues in some places. Scientists and various piscatorial organizations have long maintained that the distinct genetic differences of wild trout need to be protected. Historical stocking with 'diploid' (fertile) trout over the years has created the risk of interbreeding and disruption of the genetic identity of local strains of wild trout. This has led to the Environment Agency 'National Trout and Grayling Fisheries Strategy'. The strategy stipulates that after 2015, no consents will be given for stocking 'diploid' trout obtained from fish farms. Only 'triploid' (infertile) trout will be allowed. The delay in implementation of the policy is to allow fisheries time to change their practices. Equally, fish farms need time to ensure there is sufficient production of triploids. Triploids versus diploids is still a hot topic of conversation, with some parties arguing that triploids eat the ova of spawning wild trout during the winter and are inferior in quality when compared to diploids. There is a lot of anecdotal evidence and continuing discussion, but nothing conclusive. The best guidance is to use the 'precautionary principle' and stock triploids just to be on the safe side.

After deciding that stocking is required and defining the supply source, type, number and size of fish to be stocked, a fishery manager still has important decisions to make. Timing the first stocking of the season is difficult. Depending on the fishery, the trout season may open sometime in April, or in early May. The dilemma is whether to stock before the opening date to allow the fish time to get used to their new environment, or after the opening date when the river conditions are easier for the fresh arrivals. The most common practice is to stock fish from mid-April onwards, just a short time before the mayfly season. Freshly stocked fish have a lot of adjustments to make to their new environment. They have to get used to different temperatures and oxygen levels, deal with the river currents and learn what to eat. Initially, they do not spread out and occupy individual lies in the river, but stick-together and mill around in the deepest pools, seemingly bound by a group instinct developed in artificial hatchery ponds. Whilst their wild cousins are up on the surface hammering the first hatches of large dark olives and grannom, they will stay in the deep trying to figure out what is edible and what is not through trial-and-error. Things change when the mayflies start hatching. This is when stocked trout seem to appear miraculously out of no-where and start surface feeding. Fish that are stocked later in the season seem to adjust more quickly to the river conditions.

Various fisheries have attempted to 'mark' their stocked fish in order to understand their movements and overwintering survival rates. The one fact that has been established without any doubt is that there are considerable losses of stocked fish during winter. Reports indicate that only about 5% of stocked fish survive to see the next season. There are many factors affecting survival of fish over the winter months. High flows may result in fish being pushed downstream, especially when flash floods create very strong currents. It is believed that triploid trout overwinter better because they do not spawn and thus remain in much better condition by not expending the significant energy involved in spawning. Stocked diploids on the other hand have been observed spawning as early as late autumn and certainly much earlier than their wild cousins, who usually start spawning around Christmas and on through January. The role of natural predators is a key factor affecting fish populations during the winter months and should not be underestimated. With the absence of regular fishermen on the banks and a reduction in activity by bailiffs, fish predators have a much easier time. When the temperatures fall below freezing and the lakes are only suitable for ice skating, large flocks of cormorants raid the rivers. Their effect is devastating, particularly if the water is low, as it has been in the last two years. Whilst the cormorants target the smaller fish, larger predators target the big specimen fish. One can only assume that stocked fish are easier prey than wild fish that have learnt to fend for themselves from an early stage, because it is mainly the stocked fish that suffer.

This raises questions of cost and benefit in managing the stocking of a fishery. The financials are largely driven by the profile of the end customer. If a fishery is offering day tickets that cost hundreds of pounds, it can justify spending generous amounts of money on stocking. Fish losses are treated like stock losses would be in any other business. The emphasis is on keeping the customers happy so that they return and buy more expensive day tickets. Sometimes over-zealous stocking is practised to keep the customer happy, especially if the customer is a novice and unaccustomed to the intricacies of wild trout fishing. On the other side of the spectrum are well-maintained wild fisheries which provide a healthy habitat that has been lightly managed in sympathy with natural processes. These can also be economically successful and satisfy the wild trout aficionados who are willing to pay high prices to catch a small wild brown rather than an oversized stockie.

Managing the anglers can be almost as difficult as managing the fish. The majority of chalk streams are privately owned and the riparian rights of a fishery may well have a very long history indeed. Riparian rights are the rights that an owner of a river bank has to the use of the water in the river, and this includes angling. An owner is entitled to deal in these rights and may even sell them to someone else entirely. Thus an owner can lease out or sell a fishery on his land to a syndicate, a club, a commercial outfit or even to a single individual. A great many owners of chalk stream river banks have entered into agreements like this. There are very limited pieces of water where public fishing is allowed and careful reconnaissance is needed if one is to find these free spots. Most chalk stream anglers get access to chalk streams by being members of syndicates or clubs or by purchasing day tickets for a specific fishery where these are available.

Regardless of whether a fishery is controlled by a syndicate, a club or a commercial concern, the norm is that the river is divided into beats, i.e. smaller segments of the river where a rod is allowed to fish, either both banks of the river, or only one bank. The terminology 'double bank', 'true left bank' and 'true right bank' is used to describe how these beats function. A true left bank is the one on the left, as one looks downstream. The purpose of a beat system is to give individual anglers (plus, perhaps, their guests) exclusive use of a defined section of the water for a pre-determined length of time. In syndicates, access to beats is often given exclusively to a 'full rod', or a 'half rod', for a significant annual fee. A full rod is an angler who is allowed to fish the water on a specific day, every week of the season. A half rod, on the other hand, has access to the water on a specified day every other week. Normally the rods are allowed to invite fishing, or non-fishing, guests. However, there may be cases where no guests are allowed. This is driven by the riparian agreements in place, which sometimes prohibit guests in order to limit the numbers of people wandering around and picnicking on what is otherwise a working farm or estate. Clubs also employ a beat system, usually on a first-come-first-served basis, but by contrast, some also allow general access to longer stretches of river. In this instance club members share the water, adhering to the accepted chalk stream etiquette where an angler starts at the bottom of the stretch and moves in an upstream direction. Commercial fisheries rent out entire fisheries on a daily basis, usually to corporate customers or sell day tickets to individual anglers permitting access to specified beats on a specified day.

The most successful model for running a fishery is one where fishing pressure is not detrimental to either the fish or the sport. Busy fisheries result in very elusive fish, especially if catch and release is practiced. They can also discourage many anglers from visiting them. Imagine a conveyor belt of anglers queuing at the downstream end of a river stretch, waiting for the next angler to move upstream while he spends substantial time stalking a fish. Fishing is meant to be a relaxing activity, although not necessarily a solitary one. It is part and parcel of the experience to have a chat on the bank and exchange tips and flies with fellow anglers. However, allowing too many rods on the river bank has risks and it is not uncommon for overcrowding to bring out the worst behavior in some anglers. Mayfly time is possibly the worst time to be out, due to its popularity. Etiquette can sometimes be forgotten with inappropriate wading, downstream casts and some anglers pushing in front of fellow anglers who are patiently stalking rising fish. I have met anglers who avoid the mayfly time like the plague, preferring the tougher fishing conditions of early spring and late summer. This is the main reason why clubs put restrictions on the number of anglers allowed on a stretch and in some cases only allow certain beats to be fished every other day to alleviate pressure. Chalk stream etiquette has developed to allow for a challenging sport that at the same time gives the fish a fair chance. Upstream casting has been adopted because it is an effective way of approaching fish without being noticed. Why do clubs insist on upstream single dry fly only? It seems illogical not to allow nymphing in the early part of the season when the fish are clearly hugging the river bed busily taking ephemeroptera nymphs. The answer is quite simple – to minimize fishing pressure and make the sport more challenging. As a famous quote goes "there's more to fishing than catching fish".

Chalk stream fishing has always been a valuable commodity. The most exclusive stretches of water on historically famous chalk streams fetch very demanding prices. Tickets for a guided day can be worth hundreds of pounds and club or syndicate membership can cost thousands, far beyond the reach of the average earner. On the other side of the spectrum there are syndicates and clubs offering lower cost memberships, but the resulting waiting lists can test the angler's patience to the limit.

As mentioned above, access to the water is determined by riparian titles that can go back for centuries. Sometimes a single mile of water will involve multiple owners and multiple agreements. It is no wonder then that there is a considerable degree of difficulty involved in reaching agreement on day-to-day keepering standards, let alone more ambitious and expensive habitat improvement projects. I suppose the question is: why worry so much about habitat? The simple answer is that unless we do so there will be no fishing left, as we know it, in generations to come. As chalk streams are man-made systems, it could be argued that no one really has the moral high ground in terms of how lightly or how heavily fisheries ought to be managed. One thing is for sure though, we cannot afford to close our eyes and neglect what is happening around us. The main issue facing chalk streams is diminishing water levels and slower water flows through a combination of insufficient rainfall and increased abstraction. As the water recedes in a river, deposits of silt accumulate along the margins. This results in terrestrial plants like reeds and watercress colonizing the river margins and the banks gradually becoming inaccessible. Attempts to control the reeds and watercress by mechanical means can only be a temporary measure. A longer term solution is to assist the flows with various techniques. Removing structures, for example hatches, sluices, bridges and so on, can increase the river flow, but before doing this the compound effect of the proposed removal, both above and below the structure, needs to be comprehensively modeled and fully understood. Another popular method is to narrow the river channel by building berms. Berms are essentially bank extensions backfilled with soil and their purpose is to narrow the width of the river. Berms can be built on both banks so that the selective narrowing of the river deflects the water from bank to bank in a zigzag fashion. The resulting accelerated flows scour and clean the gravels, which in turn provide better quality habitat for invertebrates and an improved environment for salmonid spawning. Other techniques are also effective, such as using large woody debris. These are significant sized trees, or large branches, that are felled in the water and pinned down. The flow of water through the branches gradually creates pools, back eddies and other flow features which provide better habitat. Water deflectors such as logs, boulders and so on can also create welcome features that improve conditions for both fish and other organisms.

It would wrong to think that habitat improvement works will restore the chalk streams to their former glory. River trusts, angling clubs, wildlife organizations and numerous volunteers are desperately playing catch-up with vanishing rivers and the overall degradation of riverine ecosystems. It often feels that habitat improvement works are mere string and tape solutions, a papering over of the cracks in a wall that is crumbling before our eyes. The true solution is structural and until the value of conserving, properly managing and paying higher costs for water is understood and accepted by the general public, water companies will continue abstracting water from the aquifers to fill an insatiable and often wasteful demand for a cheap commodity that was once abundantly available but which is now becoming scarce. The justification "we never used to pay for it" is not a tenable way forward. One way or another, we will all pay for it in the end. I just hope that, as a society, we decide to pay for water and use it more wisely, rather than presiding over the irredeemable destruction of a unique and extremely valuable resource.

Chapter Twelve

The Future of the Chalk Streams

Theo Pike

When I started fishing the chalk streams around Salisbury and Winchester in the early 1990s, the south of England was simmering in a four-year drought.

From 1988 to 1992, lack of rainfall set new records. The seven months between March and September 1990 were the driest spring and summer since 1767, and the chalk and greensand water tables stayed stuck at their lowest ever level for a solid twelve months. Long stretches of volatile rivers like the Chess and Misbourne apparently dried up completely: at Stapleford on the Wylye, trout and grayling floated belly-up in the silty margins, unable to suck enough oxygen from the sluggish currents even when I waded in and held them facing upstream.

After the winter of 1991/92, when many aquifers received less than ten per cent of the recharge necessary to bring them back to health, I couldn't stand it either. I packed my rods away, suspended my membership of the Salisbury and District Angling Club, and spent several summers sculling on the tidal Thames. By the time I came back to chalk stream fly fishing from competitive rowing, encouraged by several catastrophic collapses of Mogden sewage treatment works which filled the Tideway with shoals of dead bream and rampant E coli, the rains had apparently returned. But that drought, already twenty years ago, looks less like a climatic aberration than a shot across our bows: a warning of what could come to the chalk streams. What will the next twenty, forty, sixty years bring to these globally-precious rivers and the iconic, pollution-sensitive fish we love to catch from them?

Never make predictions, it's said – especially not about the future. But without tempting fate too far, I think we can afford to tease out a few trends for the chalk streams which are more likely to be right than wrong. And their lowest common denominator is climate change.

Most serious commentators now agree that the early effects of climate change are already noticeable, even in the UK where our climate is known to vary widely. Across Europe, the average temperature has increased by almost 1° C in the past hundred years, and spring now arrives a week earlier than it did in the 1970s. This long-term warming has also been reflected in our rivers, with southern English chalk streams, the upper Rhone, and mountain streams in the Swiss and Austrian Alps all registering increased temperatures of up to 1° C since 1980.

Despite clusters of dry winters between 1988 and 2002, and again between 2004 and 2006, the pattern of annual rainfall in England and Wales has reversed the nineteenth-century trend towards dry winters and cold, wet summers, the conditions that wrecked many years' mayfly hatches for Victorian fly-fishers. Today, winter rainfall is already ten percent above the nineteenth-century average, and summer rainfall ten percent below. In thirty years' time, if this trend continues to match the majority of climate change predictions, low summer flows in many rain-fed southern and eastern rivers could be fifty or even eighty percent down on what they are today.

In an earlier chapter of this book, Malcolm Anderson has written of the unique geology of chalk streams, and how their aquifers are most effectively recharged by long periods of steady winter rain when trees and plants are dormant and leafless, and water can soak straight into the ground. So you'd be forgiven for thinking that perennial chalk rivers should be well-insulated in a future which maps hotter, drier summers and warmer, wetter winters to chalk and greensand aquifers. But that's without the added randomness of climate change and the extreme weather events predicted by most scientists: brief, violent downpours, for instance, running off soil baked hard by intense heat and drought. Nor does it take account of the detail of human interference and how systematically we've already imposed our own patterns of civilisation on the natural cycles of rainfall, aquifers and rivers. In the flashier freestone catchments of the north and west, lack of rainfall can become obvious within weeks, if not days or even hours, as the rivers sink down into their stones. In the chalk country, the public perception of clear, constantly-flowing rivers, endlessly refreshed by unseen, infinite aquifers, has proved dangerously deceptive – a tacit invitation to exploit an apparently endless resource without any thought for the consequences.

As soon as you sink a borehole into a chalk aquifer and start pumping water out, you create what scientists call an inverted cone of depression. Water levels fall in this area of the aquifer, and hydrological pressure decreases in the veins of flint that feed water to local rivers, pushing their spring-heads further and further down-catchment or even cutting them off completely. These effects can be swift and dramatic: immediately after the London, Brighton and South Coast Railway borehole began abstracting from the Wandle's aquifer on the North Downs near Carshalton in 1906, the springs dropped to half flow and the general level of the river fell by a foot in just two days.

To compensate for over-abstracting chalk stream aquifers for public water supply, many water companies have installed stream-support systems which boost flows when they fall too far, often by pumping augmentation water from even deeper boreholes. Most summers, that's what happens on the upper Wylye, and there are similar emergency systems in place for the Itchen's Candover Brook and the little River Shep near Cambridge. On the Wandle, the 1970s brought the unique approach of re-abstracting water from the river several miles below the headwaters, before re-circulating it back to flow through concrete-lined ornamental ponds in Carshalton, and back down the river again. Then, less than fifteen yards below the re-abstraction point, the river's total flow increases by more than five hundred per cent when it's joined by the constant gush of treated effluent from Beddington sewage treatment works: a strangely back-flipped way of making sure a river stays flowing when over-abstraction would have wiped it off the map a hundred years ago.

If nothing else, stream support keeps the idea of a river temporarily alive. But such sticking-plaster solutions are dangerous if they help us deceive ourselves about the scale of over-abstraction, or stop us addressing it sooner than we should. Worse, they do nothing to cure our chalk streams' chronic underlying problem in the long term: as a society, we all use far too much water, and we fail to value it properly.

Under current climatic conditions, South East England already gets less rainfall per head of population than Saudi Arabia or the Sudan. Yet every one of us still uses around 148 litres of water each day: an average which rises even higher in some areas of the Chilterns, where the most prolific daily usage in Europe topped out at 176 litres per person in 2010, leaving the Chess without enough water to meet its environmental needs for sixty-five per cent of the year. With government predictions suggesting that the population of England and Wales will grow by six million by 2021, the total demand for water looks set to rise steadily, and most noticeably in summer months when rainfall is expected to decrease. By the end of the 2020s, more than one and a half million new homes will have been constructed in the south-east, almost all dependent on chalk stream aquifers for their public water supply. (No matter how many new homes are built, or how much extra stress this places on the surrounding environment, local water companies are obliged by statute to provide them with water and sewerage services.) And then there's the water companies' own statistic that for every litre of expensively-purified water consumed, flushed down lavatories or sprayed onto cars and gardens, almost a litre and a half has to be taken out of the environment.

So it's lucky for us as anglers that the problem hasn't just been left to the water companies and the environmental regulators to solve. England has eighty percent of the world's chalk streams, and their habitats and the range of species they support are globally rare enough to have caught the attention of some of the world's most effective environmental campaigners. In 2009, WWF-UK brought its international freshwater conservation expertise to bear on the issues of smarter water management with the Rivers on the Edge initiative: a campaign to highlight the damage caused by over-abstraction on the Itchen, the Kennet, and two little tributaries of the upper Lee, the Beane and Mimram. This campaign had two target audiences: firstly the general public, who could make an immediate difference by using less water, and secondly the politicians who were just about to fix the regulatory framework for water policy, years into the future, under measures including water company business planning, the government's Water Resource Management Plans, and River Basin Management Plans for delivery of the European Water Framework Directive.

By studying the Itchen and its problems in particular, and then presenting them as a vivid case study, WWF-UK provided an extra thinking resource for government. In 2011, its conclusions about future water policy were published under the banner of the Itchen Initiative: a hard-hitting document laying out sixty tightly-argued pages of recommendations for meaningful catchment abstraction management.

Underneath all the policy detail, the whole water wisdom issue is really quite simple, the report's authors Tom LeQuesne and Rose Timlett told me during its launch in London in early 2011. *Once you realise that under the current mechanism for ending over-abstraction, it could take between three centuries and two millennia to reach sustainable levels of abstraction across England and Wales, everything else starts falling into place. The water regulator OFWAT needs to allow water companies to practice better demand management in areas where water is available on paper, but where in fact rivers are running dry because of over-abstraction. This will help water companies move away from capital-intensive new projects, which at the moment they find easier to justify than effective demand management. And finally, the majority of water customers don't know how much water they use, or pay for it realistically, even at times of peak demand when water is scarce. In some cases, the true cost of providing the water to run a sprinkler for an hour in a dry year could be as much as £50. So universal metering and fair pricing for water, as long as it doesn't cause real social hardship, is really the only way forward.*

Given the right sense of urgency, this sort of cultural shift could happen very quickly. Within months of the Itchen Initiative's launch, Defra's White Paper on the Environment made the first commitment by any government to reform the abstraction licensing regime, much of which has remained unchanged since the 1960s or even earlier. Saving our chalk streams by re-valuing clean water at its real environmental cost could be as simple as passing a few well-worded laws.

In general terms, as the editor of this anthology once pointed out to me, the British legal system isn't ideally geared to measure our enjoyment of a clean, healthy environment. Pollution usually happens because, for the polluter, it's cheaper than the alternative, whether that means proper disposal of waste or simply putting the right safeguards in place to prevent environmental damage as a result of doing business.

For campaigners against pollution, the real challenge lies in following the money and forcing the true cost of polluting to vest where it originated – usually with the entity or person who was trying to avoid the cost of acting responsibly in the first place. As we'll see in a moment, this is still a moral and logical outcome which the UK's legal system seems perversely designed to prevent. But there are tantalising signs that the landscape could be changing.

At Bradford Crown Court in January 2008, Judge Jonathan Durham Hall QC presided over a relatively routine criminal prosecution: a case brought by the Environment Agency against Adam Khan and his company Dr Clean (UK). When Adam Khan's business failed in December 2007, he was left with a pallet of five-litre containers of washing-up liquid in his industrial unit near the banks of the River Holme in Huddersfield. He instructed one of his employees to arrange for the unit to be cleared, and unknown persons duly agreed to remove the pallet, but negligently spilled large amounts of washing-up liquid in the unit's yard whilst loading it into their lorry without supervision. This detergent ran into the river, killing at least 755 trout, grayling and other fish, many of a pound or more, over a mile and a half of the Holme and the mainstem of the River Colne. The Environment Agency's appraisal concluded that this pollution incident was the worst in West Yorkshire for fifteen years, with ecological impact so serious that trout populations would be unable to recover naturally.

Khan argued in mitigation that he had entered an early guilty plea, and that his company was a small failed enterprise, but this implied suggestion held little water for Judge Durham Hall. In passing sentence, the judge ruled that Khan had a duty to protect against pollution and that his attitude had been cavalier. He had failed to take advice and neglected to put measures in place to prevent a serious breach of water resources legislation and a major environmental catastrophe. Most importantly, Judge Durham Hall identified the fact that Khan's failures had stemmed from a financial motive: the desire to save himself and his company from the costs of proper disposal of the detergent. So the judge felt justified in imposing a fine of £50,000 on Khan plus £1 for his now-defunct business: a suitable and sensible deterrent financial penalty to demonstrate to local people that he took their outrage at the incident seriously.

As a Crown Court judgement, Judge Durham Hall's decision carries no weight of precedent to force other courts to follow his lead in future cases – his decision would need to be confirmed by the Court of Appeal or the Supreme Court to achieve that – but it does amount to an early recognition of the underlying financial reasons for negligent environmental damage, and attempts to make the punishment fit the crime with a fine of a size that could have crippled the company responsible had it not already ceased trading.

Another indication comes from my own home water in South London. In September 2007, contractors cleaning tertiary screens at Thames Water's Beddington sewage treatment works mistakenly released 1,600 litres of sodium hypochlorite into the Wandle, bleaching five kilometres of urban chalk stream and killing more than seven thousand fish. Spurred by the Angling Trust, the water company admitted liability at once, and put up funds for a river restoration project worth £500,000 over five years. A fine of £125,000 was imposed at Croydon Crown Court in January 2009, but this was later reduced to £50,000 by the Court of Appeal, with clear acknowledgement from Mr Justice Sweeney that Thames Water's efforts to repair the damage in partnership with local stakeholders had been exceptional. At this writing, the Living Wandle project remains the single biggest commitment by any UK polluter to cleaning up its mess: a brave and progressive response which earned Thames Water a great deal of opprobrium within the water industry, but which we can all afford to hope will set a precedent for future voluntary reparations by polluters with an eye to their corporate social and environmental responsibilities.

On the other hand, it's disappointing that Mr Justice Sweeney's ruling also condemned the original penalty as *manifestly excessive*, and we can probably read this as a sign that the judiciary has some way to go before starting to recognise the true cost of environmental damage. Within a framework of pre-set guidelines, fines tend to be imposed according to the skill of the barristers' arguments, or how well the judge understands the implication of his judgement, rather than any hard valuation of the damage done. As a result, *pace* Judge Durham Hall, most fines are far too low to deter repeat offending, and in any case the cost of restoring the environment to its pre-pollution condition would usually far exceed the amount of the fine: a situation which reduces the court's judgement to a slap on the wrist for breaking the law rather than proportionate punishment for destroying the environment that the law was conceived to protect.

In fact, more than a decade after getting involved in river restoration, I still find it hard to believe that the UK's legal and regulatory regime provides business with little real incentive to stop polluting, while the mechanisms of government are actually profiting financially from the continuous destruction of our environment. Between 2000 and 2010 alone, according to Environment Agency figures, the Agency brought prosecutions for 2,416 water-related pollution incidents in England and Wales. But with the possible exception of very limited 'fish kill funds' in Wales, not a penny of the resulting fines was ever re-circulated through the system to restore the 'controlled waters' that suffered damage in the first place. Instead, the Treasury received a steady low-level drip-feed of unrestricted funds totalling just under £15 million, creating a model of licensed environmental destruction that wouldn't look out of place in a banana republic:

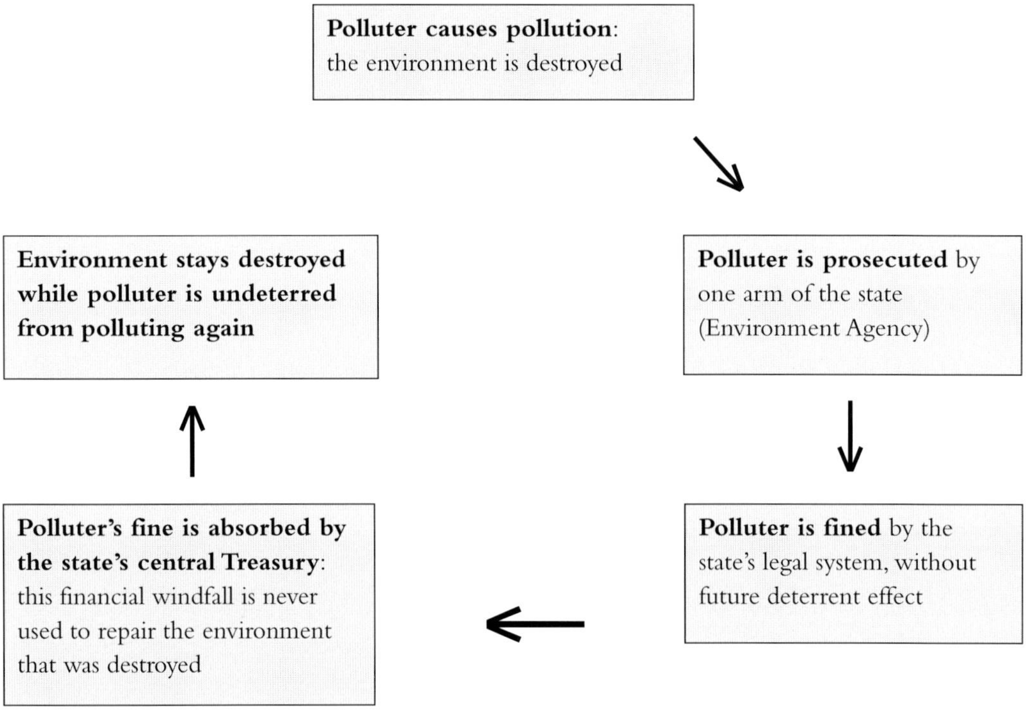

Without any suggestion of deliberate intent or collusion, legal and bureaucratic drift has left our law of environmental restitution looking suspiciously like an ass. Whilst researching this chapter, I found a number of contributing patterns falling into place: less-than-zealous pollution investigations when day-to-day working relationships may have been more important than strict enforcement; court guidelines that peg fines to a level where they're regularly derided by anglers and the general public as tokenistic and no more than part of the cost of doing business; even magistrates with business backgrounds who may be sympathetic to corporate interests and imperatives when it comes to reducing fines still further in response to eloquent lawyers' pleas for mitigation.

But as James Babb once asked sardonically about a completely different kind of relationship, *who'd even think of screwing up something like that?*

In the end, failing fearless reforms to sentencing guidelines and the creation of catchment restoration funds liberally watered with business-bankrupting fines and scrutinised by local environmental interests, we may come to rely upon other pressures to protect our rivers. And like WWF-UK's paradigm-breaking effect on over-abstraction and the water industry, some of these may well originate beyond or even above the UK's own powers.

One such level of supranational impartiality has already arrived in the form of the European Union. Uninfluenced by the texture of local business relationships, EU lawmakers are interested only in harmonisation across the Member States, and have the power to back their laws with crippling financial penalties. At the same time, the whole European project is underpinned by the principle of subsidiarity: the delegation of decision-making powers to the lowest possible competent level, creating a two-pronged approach which may be the most effective safeguard for our rivers' long-term health.

From the top-down legislative angle, the most important development so far has probably been the dryly-named 'Directive 2000/60/EC of the European Parliament and of the Council of 23 October 2000 establishing a framework for Community action in the field of water policy'. More commonly known as the Water Framework Directive (WFD), it requires all European Member States to ensure that their rivers and lakes meet a standard defined as Good Ecological Status by 2015, 2021 or 2027. Only heavily modified water bodies are exempt from this requirement and even these must reach the level of Good Ecological Potential by the same dates.

In contrast to many previous assessment methodologies, WFD breaks new territory by examining the water environment as a whole, integrating water quantity, quality and physical habitat with relevant ecological indices. Fish are seen as key indicators of ecosystem health, so there's heavy emphasis on fish passage and river connectivity to allow them to migrate freely throughout whole river basins to complete their life-cycles. Since WFD is designed to be delivered via River Basin Management Plans in consultation with local partners, it automatically incorporates the idea of whole-catchment management. Perhaps best of all for the chalk streams, WFD looks at interactions between ground and surface waters: if there's not enough water in an aquifer to maintain the ecological status of the rivers and wetlands it feeds, it will fail its 'groundwater quantitative' status, with very real legal implications.

As a result of WFD and the earlier Habitats Directive which established Special Areas of Conservation (SACs) throughout the UK and Europe, the benefits are already being felt on the chalk streams. For instance, one of the most ambitious river restoration projects I've seen so far has taken place on the Lambourn in Newbury, where Natural England and the Environment Agency spent at least £900,000 to restore the river's habitats to 'recovering' status between 2006 and 2010.

In October 2010, a few months after the wet work had finished, I fished up the Lambourn's public footpath from the Newbury Manor Hotel to the recreation ground at Shaw, the site of a major battle during the English Civil War. Every thirty yards, the Environment Agency had sutured dragons' teeth structures into the banks to re-meander the river's straight-dredged channel: in some cases, whole tree trunks were held in place with stakes and brushwood mattresses. The dark tunnel of trees over the river had been thinned and recycled into flow deflectors, making room to cast even a ten-foot rod and allowing tentative new beds of ranunculus to take root in the shafts of light that now slanted through the canopy on that autumn afternoon. Deep sediment beds full of mayfly nymphs were already forming behind the mattresses, and wild grayling danced in the clear currents over four thousand tonnes of gravel which had been introduced with excavators to restore the riverbed exposed by modifying two previously-impassable weirs in the gardens of the hotel.

Unlike the upper Lambourn's famously lock-jawed specimens, these urban grayling kept hitting my little weighted nymphs until it was too dark to see the end of the fly line, and I finally reeled up with the profound impression of fishing a river that's literally been reconstructed from the gravel up. Perhaps not all chalk streams are so amenable to restoration, and river-mending on this scale can be extremely expensive, but the Lambourn's success story could offer a very plausible blueprint for the future of our chalk streams and for our own sport too.

In his 1998 article 'Planet of Weed's, David Quammen reluctantly predicted *the age after biogeography [when] virtually everything will live virtually everywhere, though the list of species that constitute 'everything' will be small.*

This is a dystopian vision, but an unsettlingly realistic one – and one with ominous relevance to the chalk streams. Beyond the common-sense benefits of wise water use, and the urgent requirements of supranational legislation like the Water Framework Directive, we'll need to ask ourselves more and more frequently in the coming years: what counts as an indigenous species, what is its value or threat to our rivers' health and resilience, and what are we prepared to do to save or eradicate it?

Biosecurity issues are far from new, but the environmental community has recently achieved significantly better understanding of invasive non-native species (INNS) and their possible ecological and economic impacts. In part, this has been driven by harsh experience: the march of Himalayan balsam, Japanese knotweed and American signal crayfish along rivers the length of the UK, for instance, or the ecosystem-wide destruction caused by our own much-loved chalk stream native, purple loosestrife, as it reached North America in ships' bilges before spreading out to dominate hundreds of square miles of wetlands on the eastern seaboard and the Great Lakes.

It's also an issue of critical mass. In our increasingly interconnected world, species are able to move to new areas more quickly, and we're noticing them more. As David Quammen points out, our modern plethora of INNS *tend to thrive in human-dominated terrain because in crucial ways they resemble Homo sapiens… they reproduce quickly, disperse widely when given a chance, tolerate a broad range of habitat conditions, take hold in strange places, succeed especially in disturbed ecosystems, and resist eradication once they're established.* Crucially, they often flourish because no suitable predator has evolved alongside them in their new environment and the population bottlenecks that controlled their numbers on home turf can no longer keep them in check. Once the genie is out of that bottle, there's often no putting it back.

In fact, many species now regarded as invasive took their first steps to world domination thanks to Victorian-era plantsmen, gardeners and other proponents of 'acclimatisation'. Nothing pleased those early explorers more than to bring new plants and animals home from abroad, or to take native British species abroad with them to help them feel at home. Enthusiastic Acclimatisation Societies took starlings to America, rabbits to Australia and mustelids to New Zealand, with disastrous consequences, while brown, rainbow and brook trout were also dispersed far beyond their native ranges. (There's a strange, contradictory savour in catching a stream-bred rainbow or brookie beneath a fringe of Himalayan balsam in the Austrian Alps, but it's a hint of how strictly we may have to monitor our value systems if we really do want to avoid our fate on Quammen's Planet of Weeds.)

Near the headwaters of the Wandle, Alfred Smee was a typically active Victorian pisciculturalist, introducing as many different species as possible to the river during the 1860s. Through his contacts at the French commissioners' fish-farm at Huningue he got hold of stocks of char, salmon and 'salmon trout by thousands' for his riverside hatchery: he also procured adult grayling, tench and burbot, none of which seemed to survive and breed. But such experiments were widespread and frequently more successful. Self-sustaining populations of rainbow trout persisted in the Chess and Lambourn within living memory, and it's an anomalous point of pride for Derbyshire anglers and riverkeepers, uncompromisingly purist in every other sense, that non-native Shasta-strain rainbows continue to spawn and provide them with spectacular sport in the limestone spring fed Derbyshire Wye.

Every generation thinks it knows best, but in fishery management at least we can claim to be guided by better science than our ancestors'. In our own time, genetic fingerprinting is helping us to understand the real effects of past stocking programmes on individual rivers' own strains of trout and grayling, sometimes with startling results. For instance, despite studies showing that stocked diploid trout are more than capable of spawning with wild fish if they survive their first few months in the river – and the fact that most rivers in the UK have probably received at least one infusion of Scottish Loch Leven-strain brown trout – a recent investigation of sixty Wylye trout has revealed that they were virtually all truly wild native fish, with very little hatchery-gene introgression from an extensive incubator-box stocking programme.

But a little forethought never hurt anyone and the precautionary principle of the Environment Agency's National Trout and Grayling Strategy, which forbids stocking diploid fish from 2015 onwards, is something that should be welcomed by any thinking angler.

Only last season, on one particular stretch of the Hampshire Avon, I found myself catching a beautiful strain of wild brown trout with extravagant, dark spotting right through the rays of their tails: a phenotype I've only ever seen in rainbows and never in brown trout anywhere but this part of the river. Is this a meaningless skin-deep mutation, or could it be the outward and visible sign of an inward and spiritual grace that gives those trout a special advantage in this area of the Avon, perhaps even representing a hardier adaptation equipped to resist low flows and everything else that climate change will throw at them? We may never know for certain – but why subject those trout to any more genetic risk than necessary, even if that means putting a stop to stocking with non-native strains and recalibrating our expectations of authenticity on the chalk streams?

To see just how easily our mindsets can change, look no further than our attitude to grayling. Recent genetic sequencing by the Grayling Research Trust shows that all the UK's grayling are derived from just four main groupings, but enthusiastic Victorians like Alfred Smee distributed these to almost every river in the land. Over time, the Kennet was stocked from the Derbyshire Derwent, the Frome's grayling came from the Dove, and native Avon fish made their way to the Test and possibly the Itchen. (Until very recently, according the Grayling Research Trust, the Environment Agency's fish farm at Calverton has been stocking Test-strain fish into the Aire, Wharf and Dove, so this redistribution still continues.)

In that early heyday of grayling fishing, separate northern and southern fly-fishing traditions developed, each with its own suite of flies. But attitudes hardened after the Second World War: chalk stream fisheries turned increasingly trout-centric, and grayling came to be regarded as vermin, to be culled by almost any method. Frank Sawyer invented his deadly Killer Bugs and wire and herl nymphs for precisely this purpose, and you can still meet fisheries managers who remember netting and electro-fishing chalk stream grayling by the tonne before spreading them on the fields or dumping them in riverside pits. By the 1980s, this holocaust had nearly succeeded in its aim. Conservation assessments concluded that grayling as a species was endangered in the UK and threatened in Europe by overkill, habitat destruction and habitat fragmentation: all issues identified by David Quammen as factors that can easily combine to cause extinction.

Today, almost in parallel with gamefishers' general conversion to catch and release, our attitudes have come full circle, and most discerning anglers now see grayling on a sporting par with trout. But the hard questions may still be as valid as ever. Those genetic investigations tell us that grayling are genuinely native and adapted to the Avon and Wylye – no wonder Frank Sawyer found it so difficult to eradicate them – but what about non-native Derwent-strain grayling in the Kennet? Arguments about angels on pinheads have nothing on grayling in chalk streams. It's a discussion that could carry on for years.

By definition, most INNS take time and money to remove once they've turned invasive and made their successful break for freedom. According to the National Ecosystem Assessment of 2011, the economic cost of invaders like giant hogweed, Japanese knotweed, Himalayan balsam and American signal crayfish is £1.7bn annually in the UK. But in an age of global austerity, some of those problems have grown too big for government to tackle. *We're not going to take the high-risk strategy of trying to eradicate Himalayan balsam nationwide*, admitted a Defra representative at Britain's national INNS and biosecurity conference just days after the National Ecosystem Assessment was published, *but if you want to prevent its impacts affecting your interests on a local level, go for it!*

Put simply: when the emanations of the state are in full retreat from the things they know they should be doing for our rivers, it's probably time for us as anglers to take on some of those challenges ourselves, and there's evidence that we're already quite capable of achieving this level of environmental stewardship. North-west of the chalk streams in Monmouthshire, the Monnow Rivers Association is well on its way to clearing Himalayan balsam from the Monnow's whole mainstem and tributaries: the first time this feat will have been achieved on a whole-catchment scale. By working downstream from the headwaters, following up initial spraying on each site with hand-pulling by volunteers, and revisiting each site three or four times to make sure no more plants are able to germinate, flower and set seed, the Going Native project looks set to reach the confluence with the Wye by 2012, a year ahead of schedule. Hundreds of volunteers have been involved, from organisations as diverse as Keep Wales Tidy and the Brecon Beacons National Parks, educating many non-fishing members of the public to think about the value of native biodiversity.

There's an intriguing coda to the futurology of native and non-native species on the chalk streams. For many years, the elusive cocktail of effects known as chalk stream malaise has been blamed for eroding insect life to the extent that many experienced fly-fishers now don't bother waiting for the evening rise that they know will no longer materialise.

By 2002, the time had come for action, and as Cyril Bennett has eloquently described in his earlier chapter, the idea of reintroducing lost species of river flies has slowly been gaining traction from his pioneering mayfly work on the Wey and the Derbyshire Wye, and blue-winged olive ranching with the Salisbury and District Angling Club on the Avon. If reintroductions run alongside monitoring programmes, habitat enhancements and other efforts to reverse the problems that caused the localised extinctions in the first place, it seems entirely reasonable to try to restore species we've lost before the effects of their disappearance cascade even further through the ecosystem.

A few hard-core observational scientists may not entirely approve, but as John Gierach once put it, leaving any river to look after itself is *like leaving your wallet on the bar while you go to the bathroom: it might be there when you get back, but if it's not, it's your own damn fault.*

Water wisdom, the legal landscape, native and non-native species... the threads we've pulled so far in this chapter all seem to run in the same direction. Look at them closely and they imply one thing: the need for a paradigm shift of thinking not just among anglers, but in society at large.

Basic principles of ecology tell that any population, human included, can only grow as far as it can absorb the necessary resources from its surrounding area. Beyond that point, when urban growth and its demands destroy the very resources that sustain them, the whole top-heavy structure is likely to collapse catastrophically: a form of self-regulation which explains why so many medieval English villages were deserted when rural populations failed to renew the fertility of their soils by practising sensible crop rotation.

Since rivers tend to aggregate the factors in their landscape, the chalk streams' own struggle for survival could be an accurate prediction of the problems that will soon challenge us as a society if we fail to come to better terms with the environment that supports our everyday life. Even using less water or pulling errant stands of Himalayan balsam is no longer enough. What we need is a new approach to valuing the benefits of a healthy, balanced ecosystem: a framework that aligns self-interest with conservation and ensures that we're leaving a healthy natural environment for generations to come. If we manage that balancing act, it almost goes without saying, the future of chalk stream fishing is secure.

As we've almost come to expect in matters relating to river restoration, America has already shown us the way in this practical marriage of social needs, economic imperatives and environmental benefits, under the fast-developing international theory known as ecosystem services. At the end of the last century, the Catskill mountain reservoirs which supply New York's residents with a billion gallons of clean water every day were threatened with contamination by fertilisers and urban development. New York's Department of Environmental Protection realised in 2003 that it faced an epoch-making decision: either pay $8 billion to build the water purification facilities necessary to make polluted water drinkable again, and commit to paying up to $400 million each year to operate those facilities, or work with the environment to deliver the same effects through natural processes.

Wisely, the latter course was chosen. Instead of building treatment works, New York invested more than $6 billion in projects to improve water quality and protect the Catskill / Delaware catchments from pollution: purchasing environmentally sensitive properties, reducing agricultural pollution and nitrogen discharges from sewage treatment works, and controlling runoff. Thanks to intelligent land management costing just $200 million per year – half the price of equivalent end-of-pipe solutions – eight million New Yorkers now drink water piped straight off their rivers' catchment. There's no need for expensive additional treatment with granular activated carbon, and the rivers are healthier too.

By broadening the argument from punishing environmental destruction under the *polluter pays* principle, to a system of positive reinforcement and financial incentivisation in which the *provider is paid* for the real value of their service, New York created a trailblazing case study for investing in the ecosystem services that underpin the city's daily life, and where appropriate paying for them. This isn't just an economic argument: it also offers the opportunity for ecosystems to be repaired, and rationalises the benefits of improving their resilience to future threats such as climate change. The ecosystems services approach provides a tool – for everyone from government to judges to water companies to river restorationists – to acknowledge the benefits that healthy ecosystems provide, and move towards putting the right value on a functioning planet.

The lesson hasn't gone unnoticed. In the UK, between 2005 and 2010, United Utilities' Sustainable Catchment Management Project was designed to investigate how restoring upland blanket bog on the moors above Manchester could help to reduce runoff and sediment loading, improve water colour and cut the costs of water treatment. (As side benefits, the status of Special Sites of Scientific Interest were also improved, and sequestered carbon loss from the degrading peatlands was reduced by the equivalent of nine Ford Focus cars driving 20,000 kilometres per year.) In Devon and Cornwall, South West Water and the Westcountry Rivers Trust have also translated the New York experience into a catchment restoration programme called Upstream Thinking, based on the principle of paying farmers for the economically-valuable clean water, restored rivers and other natural benefits that well-managed farmland can generate. In 2011, the UK's National Ecosystem Assessment valued the UK's inland wetlands at £1.5 billion for the clean water that they help to produce, while pollinating insects are worth £430 million to the national economy, and even the health benefits of living close to green space can be costed at £300 per person per year.

So how could we apply the idea of payment for ecosystem services to the chalk streams? Very easily, according to ecological practitioners like Mark Everard and Alex Inman, who have been thinking around this subject for years. On the River Glaven in Norfolk, for instance, a recent chalk stream restoration scheme was designed to benefit sea trout by improving connectivity within the river as well as reconnecting dredged sections with their surrounding floodplain. The project won the Wild Trout Trust's prestigious Conservation Award in 2007, but the positive outcomes weren't restricted to sea trout alone. By Mark Everard's calculations, the economic return on investment for the project came out at a staggering 325:1, including a wide range of benefits from his variation on the standard Millennium Ecosystem Services menu:

Provisioning ecosystem services
Fresh water, food, fibre and fuel
genetic resources, natural medicines,
Higher Level Stewardship payments

Regulatory ecosystem services
Regulation of climate, air and
water quality, flood risk, erosion,
pollination, pests and diseases

Cultural ecosystem services
Cultural heritage, recreation,
(including fishing, eco-tourism),
aesthetic and spiritual value,
literary and artistic inspiration

Supporting ecosystem services
Soil formation, primary production,
nutrient cycling, water recycling,
photosynthesis, habitat production

Predictably enough in the chalk stream areas whose most immediate natural capital is water, the water companies are making most of the running – for now. On the aquifers around Salisbury and Dorchester, Wessex Water is already pursuing an active policy of pesticide and nitrate reduction. As a result, no additional treatment plants are needed where catchment management has been implemented, and the rivers stand to gain from reduced levels of contamination that could kill invertebrate communities on the one hand, and contribute to eutrophication and algal blooms on the other. In this scenario, everybody wins.

Seen from this angle, it's no stretch of the imagination to envisage payment for ecosystem services as the future for the chalk streams, and by extension as the basis of a new social valuation system for our whole environment. Naturally, a wider range of markets will need to be developed to achieve that level of adoption and sustainability. According to Alex Inman, *the trick will be valuing all the potential services correctly, deciding what restoration work needs to be done, and then paying for it by selling different services to different customers. Some people will value the attenuation of flood water that's provided by a healthy chalk stream system: others may want to focus on wetlands and how they harbour different species of rare birds. Businesses will have other views again: breweries need clean water, while supermarkets are slowly coming round to the realisation that their growers and suppliers are often impacting the environment quite negatively. But what's really nice about the ecosystem services approach is that it looks at all the potential trade-offs, positive and negative, and helps us structure a debate within society about what sort of environment we want, and what ecosystem services we really want to value.*

As I'm writing this, many of south-east England's chalk streams are back on their bones again, suffering from the driest spring on record. But the Avon's early-season algal bloom has cleared, the Wandle's water-recirculation system is keeping the river alive until the government gets round to reviewing those abstraction licences, and we have plenty of room for hope.

With the swift development of the ecosystems services approach, the growth of third sector Rivers Trusts, the Riverfly Partnership and other volunteer networks to help us take ownership of our local environment, and article 14 of the Water Framework Directive which positively requires Member States *to encourage the active involvement of interested parties*, there have never been more opportunities for chalk stream fishermen to get involved in debating our rivers' destiny, and restoring them to health.

In the words of the political commentator Philip Johnston, in an essay on public sector reform in 2011, *community spirit isn't necessarily altruistic: it can also be an aggregation of self-interest.* It's an observation that perfectly fits our future role as stewards of the chalk stream environment.

After all – if not now, when? And if not us, who?

ACKNOWLEDGEMENTS

A huge number of people have contributed their help in very many different ways to the process of bringing this anthology into existence. In particular, the contributors, the editor and the publisher extend their thanks to the following:

John Constantine, Barrie Cook, Hans Weilenmann, Roy Christie, Ulf Hagstrom, Gerard Grace, Steve Wilkinson, John Horsfall, Bella Davies, Andy Thomas, Rose Timlett, Tom Le Quesne, Alex Inman, Mark Everard, Nick Johansen, Andrew Herd, The Medlar Press Limited, Debra Chalmers, Andrew Chalmers, Troubador Publishing Ltd.

INDEX

Abstraction, of water from chalk streams, 12-13, 15, 16, 44, 172, 182, 183, 185-187
Adams, 93, 134
Aelian (Aelianus), Claudius, 53, 67
Aire, River, 194
Alder fly, 41, 42, 43, 93, 94,
Alkalinity, of water in chalk streams, 15
Amesbury, 45
Angler's Curse, 34, 42, 43
Anglers Monitoring Initiative (AMI), 45, 51
Angling Trust, 9
Ants, 97, 102,
Aphids, 97
Aquifers, chalk, viii, 2-3, 15, 172, 185, 198
Autumn dun, 33, 42, 43
Avon, River (Hampshire/Wiltshire), 33, 34, 45, 49, 80, 83, 86, 136, 142, 143, 194, 199
Avon Special Emerger, 65, 68
Babb, James, 190
Baetis, 29-31, 42, 43
Baetis Nymph, 134, 139
Barbel, 165 - 168
Bare Hook Nymph, 126
Barker, T, 54
Beetles, 97, 102
Beer, Stream, 4
Berms, 182
Berner, Dame Juliana, 25
Betters, Frans, 64
Black gnat, 41, 84, 94,
Black flies, 40
Black Sedge, 37, 43
Blaisdell, Harold, xviii,
Blue-winged olive, 16, 20, 34 , 42 ,43, 45, 49-50, 52, 97, 98
Blue-winged Olive Variant, 34
Bourne, River, 4
Bream, 168-169
Brown Sedge, 37, 43
Brown Silverhorn, 37, 43
Buzzers, 40, 42, 43, 92, 93, 94-95, 126
Caddis, 35-38, 42, 43, 97, 100
Caenis, 26, 34, 42, 43
Calcium carbonate, 2
Caperer, 36, 43
Carp, 162 - 164
Casting, 88-90, 110 - 117
Catch & release, xvi
CDC Dun, 73
CDC & Elk, 72, 76, 94, 100
CDC flies, 66, 72, 76, 93, 94, 95, 98, 100, 105
Chess, River, 184, 193
Cholomondely-Pennel, H, 56
Christie, Roy, 64-65, 68
Chub, 149 - 152
Cinnamon sedge, 36, 43
Clarke, Brian, 63, 84
Climate change, 12, 184 - 185
Coarse fishing, xii
Codes of behaviour, on chalk streams, 18
Concealment, 19, 88, 95, 144
Comparadun, 134
Copperjohn, 125
Cormorants, 178
Cotton, Charles, 54
Crane flies, 40, 43, 100, 102
Crayfish, 47
Cul de Canard (CDC), 66, 68
Czech Nymph, 125, 167
Dace, 145 - 148
Daddy Longlegs, 40, 43, 72, 91,
Damselflies, 98
De-greasing, of leader, 105
Derwent, River, 194
Diapause, 46, 47, 50
Diploid trout, 179, 193
Dove, River, 194
Dragonflies, 98
Drag, 110 - 117
Dry fly only rule, x-xiii,
Duffer, 7, 80
Durham Hall, Judge Jonathan Q C, 188
Edwards, Oliver, 69, 86
Eels, 169 - 170
Electro-fishing, xvi, 9, 24, 194
Emerger, 82, 83
Environment Agency, 9, 11, 45, 178, 189, 191
Ephemera danica, 26, 42, 43, 80-91
Etiquette, 181
Ethics, 18
European Union, 191
European Water Framework Directive, 187
Evening rise, 98
Everard, Mark, 197
"F"-Fly, 66, 69, 91, 130, 134, 136

Fitzherbert, J, 6
Floatation, of fly line, 83, 105
Fluorocarbon, 85, 107
Fly boards, 46, 48
Fratnik, Marjan, 66
Frome, River, 143, 194
Funneldun, 63, 66, 68
Gammarus, 41
Geirach, John, 195
G & H Sedge, 63
Ginger Quill, 99
Goddard, John, 29, 69, 84
Gold Ribbed Hare's Ear Nymph (G.R.H. E), 75, 93, 96, 98, 124, 136, 137
Goosanders, 178
Grannom, 37, 42, 43, 51, 93-94, 179
Grayling, xv, 99-100, 127-140, 194
Grayling Research Trust, 194
Greenwell's Glory, 93
Grey Goose Nymph, 61
Grey Wulff, 86
Griffith's Gnat, 95
Habitat, improvement of, 13, 182 - 183
Hagstrom, Ulf, 77 -78
Halford, Frederick, xi, 3, 6, 8, 25, 56-58, 67, 71, 102
Hall, H S, 56
Hammond, John, 56
Hare, Steve, 138
Hatch, meaning of word, 81
Hatch pools, 17, 98
Hawthorne fly, 41, 42, 43, 70, 93, 102
Haystack, 64, 68
Henry, Cliff, 63
Herd, Andrew, x, 54, 55
Herons, 178
Hills, J W, 56, 80
History, of chalk stream fly fishing, x-xiii
Humpy, 99
Imago, 26-27
Induced take, method, 123-124
Inman, Alex, 197
Institute of Fisheries Management, 9
Iron blue dun, 30, 42, 43
Itchen, River, 81, 135, 186, 187
Iwi emerger, 73
Jardine, Charles, 86
Jassid, 60, 68
Johnston, Philip, 199
Kennet, River, 194
Killer Bug, 125
Kite, Oliver, 25, 32, 120, 126
Kite's Imperial, 93
Klinkhamer Special, 65-66, 94, 98,
Lambourne, River, 191-192, 193
Lapsley, Peter, 32
Large Green Dun, 33
Large dark olive, 42, 43
Last Hope, 34
Le Quesne, Tom, 187
Leaders, 85, 106-110, 124, 128
Leader rings, 85, 108
Lines, fly, x, 60, 84, 104-105,
Link, Leon, 69
Little Marryat, 31
Loop Mayfly, 86
Lunn, William, 25, 29, 34, 36, 46
Lunn's Houghton Ruby, 30
Lunn's Pheasant Tail, 30
Lunn's Yellow Boy, 31
March brown, 34
Marinaro, Vincent, 60 - 61
Marryat, George, 25, 56 - 57
Mayfly, 16, 26, 28-29, 42, 43, 45, 80-91,
Mayfly Nymph, 42, 86
Micro-patterns, 95,
Midges, 40, 42, 43, 92, 93, 94-95, 126
Mink, 176
Minnows, 170-171
Misbourne, River, 184
Mixed Fisheries, 75-76, 94
Mohican Mayfly, 86
Monofilament, leaders,
Mouter, Ian, 65, 68
Moustique, 66, 68
Moustique Devaux, 66, 68
Mrs Cox Mayfly, 86
Mucilin, 105
Nadder, river, xiv, 10, 11, 33, 100
Natural England, 9
National Ecosystem Assessment, 195
National Trout and Grayling Fisheries Strategy, 193
National Trust, the, 12
Needle fly, 39
Netheravon style, 123, 126
No-hackle Dun, 62, 68
Nylon, 60,
Nymphs, 42
Nymph fishing, xii-xiii, 100, 119 - 127
Ogden, James, 56
Olives, 20, 29-30, 42, 43, 50, 91, 92, 93, 97, 100, 179
Olive upright, 33
Orange Quill, 99
Orange Quill Variant, 34
Orographic rainfall, 2

Otters, 176 - 177
Pale evening dun, 32
Pale watery, 20, 30, 42, 43, 50, 51, 84
Palmers, 54
Paradun, 62, 68
Paraloop, 65, 68
Patterson, Neil, 63
Peeping Caddis, 125
Perch, 157 - 159
Petitjean, Marc, 69, 73
Pheasant Tail Nymph (PTN), 61, 74, 96, 98, 124-126, 130, 132, 134, 135, 136, 137
Pike, 153-156, 175 - 176
Pike flies, 156
Plazote, 91
Plunkett-Greene, Harry, 20
Poaching, 177
Poly May Dun, 29
Poly May Spinner, 29
Pond olive, 32, 42, 43
Power, E J, 56
Proctor, Paul, 86
Purist, dry fly school, xi
Quammen, David, 192, 194
Ransome, Arthur, 71
Red spinner, 29
Red Spot Nymph, 130, 136, 137
Reed smuts, 40
Reels, 84, 104
Reversed parachutes, 64, 68
Riparian rights, 180, 182
Riverfly Partnership, 45, 199
Rise forms, xii, 21, 70, 83, 86-88
Ritz, Charles, 108, 110
River bank, fringe & bank management, 174 - 175
Roach, 159 - 161
Rods, x, 60, 84, 103, 124, 128
Rules, for chalk stream fishing, xi-xiii, 18 , 22, 69, 181
Rununculus, 15, 97, 166, 173
Salisbury & District Angling Club, xvii, 52, 172, 184, 194
Salmon, xvi, 142
Salmon and Freshwater Fisheries Act (1975), 178
Sanctuary, Dr T, 56
Sand fly, 37, 42
Sawyer, Frank, 25, 61 -62, 74, 81, 83, 120, 123, 125, 194
Seal's fur, 59, 69
Sedge flies, 35-38, 42, 43, 97, 100
Shadow Mayfly, 85
Sherry Spinner, 21, 34, 98
Shrimps, 41, 100, 125
Sibbons, Bill, 138
Sinkant, 105
Skues, G E M, xii, 6, 39, 58- 59, 67, 85, 120
Smee, Alfred, 193, 194
Snails, 100
Sparkle Dun, 64
Spawning, trout, 99, 179 - 180
Spent gnat, 82
Spent spinner, 82
Spinner fall, 31, 98
Spurwing, large, 31, 43, 97
Spurwing, small, 31, 42, 43, 97
SRM Emerger, 78
Stoneflies, 38-39, 42, 43
Stocking, 7-8, 23, 178-180, 193
Stoddart, Thomas, 55
Strategic Restoration Framework, river Avon catchment, 10
Sub-imago, 26 - 27,
Swans, 174
Swisher & Richards, 62 - 63
Temperature, water, 15, 101
Tench, 169
Terrestrial flies, 97, 100, 102
Test, River, 33, 51, 81, 86, 143
Thorax (Thor-X) Dun, 60 - 61
Timmlet, Rose, 187
Tippets, 106-110, 128
Treatyse of Fishing with an Angle, 54
Triploid trout, 178
Turkey brown, 34, 42, 43
Uffe's Killer, 77
Ultra-purist dry fly school, xi, 102
Upstream dry fly only rule, x-xiii, 18 , 22, 69, 181
Usual, 64, 68
Van Klinken, Hans, 65 - 66
Venables, R, 54
Vesey-Fitzgerald, B, 11
WAEF, 138
Walker, Richard, 86
Wandle, River, 186, 193
Water meadows, 5-6,
Water Framework Directive (WFD), 191, 199
Weed beds, 93, 173
Weed cutting, 9, 97, 173 - 174
Weilenmann, Hans, 72
Welshman's button, 38, 43
Wey, river, 44, 45, 49, 51
Wiggle Nymph, 62, 68
Wild fish, xvi, 95,
Wild Trout Trust, 197
Willow fly, 39, 42, 43
Wissey, river, 91,

World Wildlife Fund (WWF), 186, 190
Wulff, Lee, 86
Wye, River, 49, 193
Wylye, river, 16, 17, 18, 184, 185, 193, 194
Wynkyn de Woorde, 54
Yellow May Dun, 32-33, 42, 43, 97
Yellow mayfly, 33, 42, 43
Yellow Sally, 39
Yellow water lily, 163
Zonation, of fish species, 143